P9-CSC-651

From the Shores of Hardship:
ITALIANS IN CANADA

From the Shores of Hardship:
ITALIANS IN CANADA

Essays by
Robert F. Harney

Edited by
Nicholas De Maria Harney

Preface by
Alberto Di Giovanni

éditions SOLEIL *publishing inc.*

© 1993 Centro canadese scuola e cultura italiana

No part of this publication may be stored in a retrieval system, translated or reproduced in any form by any means without the written permission of the Centro canadese scuola e cultura italiana.

Cover: Tim Harney
Layout: Deborah J. Vrbicek

ISBN: 0-921-831-34-X

Printed in Canada

éditions SOLEIL publishing inc.

In Canada:
P.O. Box 847
Welland, Ontario
L3B 5Y5

In USA:
P.O. Box 890
Lewiston, NY
14092-0890

Tel./Fax: (416) 788-2674

Table of Contents

Preface

In his unique and original writing, the poet and dramatist, Berthold Brecht foresaw more or less the architecture of thought of one of the most innovative historiographic theories of the contemporary world. Many have written about the king of Thebes and of the glorious achievements with which they guided the fate of that illustrious ancient Greek city. No one, on the other hand, ever wrote about the multitudes who, with their very own hands, built and defended the walls, the homes, the shops, the taverns, the streets, the squares, the theatres and the palaces of Thebes.

In Canada, the historian Robert F. Harney, was the first to dedicate his life and to labour daily in the field of micro-historical investigation applying what the ancient European universities knew quite well: namely, that in order to get a broad macro-historical picture, it is necessary to look at the specific events and contributions that common folk have made to the macro-historical scene. There is no doubt in my mind that Harney possessed this rare cultural intuition and methodological foresight. He denounced the "manipulation of the past to create a pedigree of the present" and urged us to "study the people, the humble people, the millions and not the few." It was the right approach to take.

As a result, Harney applied himself to studying and reconstructing the motivation, the patterns and the effects of communities which contributed to building a nation as well as its economic and social institutions.

Robert Harney firmly believed that the history of Canada could not have been written without looking at the role played by the numerous communities that have come from all corners of the world. His research and his writings bear witness to the moral courage and civic involvement of these communities which have converged to build a national character, while at the same time, maintaining their original characteristics. This is the essence of the Canadian mosaic, a model which, of course, may have some faults but which stands out as a monument to a better world.

In order to develop as a nation, Canada may draw upon the many strong and distinctive ethno-cultural communities co-existing within. Knowing one's own identity and sharing it with others contributes to our emergent identity as a whole.

In this scenario, it should come as no surprise to find that the peculiar fabric and identity of the Italian community caught Harney's keen eye and led him to conduct various important investigations on their contribution to the ethno-cultural mosaic of the Canadian nation.

Harney's work on the Italian community has become a veritable point of reference and of insight. Before Harney, very little had been written on the Italian community and the few works that did exist were rather incongruous. Harney knew not only how to overcome the previous methodological errors but also to develop the interpretation and analytical perspective. As Ezio Cappadocia pointed out in a recent issue of *Italian Canadiana* dedicated to Harney, Harney "ridiculed the Mayflowerian or those who paid more attention to Caboto, Verrazzano and Mazzei, etc. than to the uncomfortable reality of the immigrants in their midst."

At about the same time that Harney started his seminal work on the Italian community, this very same community started to advance culturally and began developing a collective consciousness.

The Italian community, as Harney showed, became aware of its contributions to this nation, its identity and its crucial role in the history of the Canadian character.

Robert Harney has left us many important studies. The Canadian Centre for Italian Culture and Education is proud to have published the volume in Italian, *Dalla frontiera alle Little Italies* (1985), and very pleased to publish, although posthumously, this present volume. By doing so, the Centre wishes to recognize the work of Robert Harney, his contribution to Canadian history, and the indelible mark he left as part of our heritage.

Alberto Di Giovanni
Director
Canadian Centre for Italian Culture and Education

Editor's Introduction

From the Shores of Hunger: Italians in Canada was to be the title of my father's volume on the Italian Canadian experience for the *Generations* series of the Multiculturalism Directorate of the Secretary of State of Canada; however, the family felt that a more appropriate publisher closer to the community would help us to remain true to the spirit of his work. The title of his volume was inspired by the Pasolini poem "Prophecy."[1] My father saw the sojourning and settling of millions of Italians in North America as a hunger, not a starvation born of *la miseria,* but as a flow of talent to opportunity by humble and resourceful people in search of a living. It was a hunger that saw immigrants as actors making choices and decisions about when, where, and how to migrate according to the opportunities available in such diverse targets as Sao Paolo, Sydney, Eritrea, Nanaimo and Toronto. Canada was part of that *Italia Oltremare* and for almost twenty-five years my father studied the Italian immigrant and ethnic experience in Canada. Without the benefit of my father's graceful and original writing style to explain the meanings he wished to draw from Pasolini's poetic verse, the title could be misinterpreted. At the risk of severing the poetic reference, I decided to alter the last word from "hunger" to "hardship" in order to avoid misunderstandings of a literal interpretation of the word "hunger."

In the fall of 1989 my father died as a result of complications from a heart transplant. In little less than a year following his death it was decided by his family to discover what of his *Italians in Canada* manuscript was finished and to publish those sections we felt were sufficiently completed to do service to his scholarship. The further we entered into his notes and files on the chapters he had declared important for an understanding of the Italian immigrant and ethnic experience, the more difficult and problematic the decisions about what to include and what to omit became. In the end an imperfect compromise was made between articles he had finished which were previously published and work in draft form that was unedited. My father also indicated in his notes a desire to edit further some of the previously published articles. Therefore, all essays in this volume should be seen as works that were in progress rather than completed. Readers interested in his work on several critical periods and topics of the Italian Canadian history such as the interwar years and the migrant labour experience before 1945 can turn to his previously published work.[2]

All of the essays in this volume were marked for inclusion in the Italians in Canada book. Several of the essays appearing in this volume have been published either in whole or in part in other places. The collection starts with an essay entitled "Caboto and Other Italian Canadian Parentela." This essay was published in a shorter version in R. Perin and F.Sturino. *Arrangiarsi. The Italian Immigration Experience in Canada*, (Montreal, 1988) p.37-62. The extended version in this volume was labelled in my father's notes as Chapter One and was not completely edited. The second essay, "Italophobia: An English-Speaking Malady " can be found in *Studi Emigrazione* XXII, no.77 (Rome: Centro Studi Emigrazione, 1985) pp. 6-44. The third essay, "If One Were to Write a History of Postwar Toronto Italia," is a revised work of a paper previously unpublished that was delivered in Philadelphia at the Balch Institute in 1985 for a session entitled "Societies in Transition: Italians and Italian Americans in the 1980s." The fourth essay, "Undoing the Risorgimento: Emigrants from Italy and the Politics of Regionalism," was prepared in 1987 for a volume on Molisani in North America but never published.[3] The fifth essay, "The Commerce of Migration," was first published in *Canadian Ethnic Studies* 9 (1977), pp. 42-53. The sixth essay, "Men Without Women: Italian Migrants in Canada, 1885-1930," appeared in *The Italian Immigrant in North America*, edited by Betty Boyd Caroli, Lydio Tomasi and Robert F. Harney (Toronto: MHSO, 1978). It was reprinted in *Canadian Ethnic Studies* XI, no. 1 (1979) pp. 29-47. Later it was reprinted in *Twentieth Century Canada: A Reader*, edited by Irving Abella (Toronto: McGraw-Hill, Ryerson, 1986). The seventh essay, "The Canadian Prairies and Peasant Lore," is an unpublished draft essay that was intended for the *Italians in Canada* volume.

In the last section of this volume are works that were incomplete and without footnotes, but I felt they would be of interest to the reader. "On Being Italian Canadian," an intended chapter in the volume, challenges historians to borrow anthropological method in order to gain a richer understanding of the *ambiente* of Italian Canadian life. "The Myth of the Americas: Migration and Village Discourse" was a densely written theoretical work which was incomplete, although I felt its central theme about the many discourses and texts read by a potential migrant was important. Finally, I have included my father's intended table of contents for this Italians in Canada volume. In searching through his files it became apparent that while he was working on this volume he was already thinking ahead towards a metahistory, titled *Italia Oltremare*, of worldwide Italian migration. While there were scattered notes in his papers for this second volume, I am including only the table of contents as a sign post to others.

In making my thanks and acknowledgements I must say first of all that it was an evening spent with Alberto and Caroline DiGiovanni that gave me the courage and encouragement to edit this volume. I would like to also thank Judy Young from the Ministry of Multiculturalism and Citizenship for her patience and dedication to my father's memory throughout this project and for funding to help with the initial organization of the work. Prof. Milton Israel's calming style encouraged me during the difficult task of approaching my father's work. Stephen Harney and Luigi Pennacchio offered helpful advice during the project. Finally I would like to thank my mother, Diana Harney, without whose love and support, my father could not have accomplished all he did and without whom I would have been helpless. I alone am responsible for the editorial decisions.

Nicholas De Maria Harney

Notes

1.   On boats launched in the Kingdom of Hunger.
      With them will be the children
      and the bread and cheese wrapped in the yellow
      foil of Easter Monday. With them will be the grandmothers
      and the donkeys, aboard the triremes stolen at
      the colonial ports.
      They will land at Crotone or at Palmi,
      by the millions, clad in Asian
      rags and American shirts.
      At once the Calabrians will speak
      as from one brigand to another:
      "Here are our ancient brothers,
      the children, the bread, the cheese!"

2.   For an overview of the Toronto Italian experience in the interwar years see
      "Toronto's Little Italy, 1885-1945. "In *Little Italies in North America*. Edited by
      Robert F. Harney and J. Vincenza Scarpaci (Toronto, 1981), pp. 41-62. Also for
      a collection of articles on early Italian immigration, ethnoculture and *ambiente*
      see Robert Harney's *Dalla Frontiera alle Little Italies: Gli Italiani in Canada 1800-
      1945* (Rome, 1984).

3.   "If One Were to Write a History of Postwar Toronto Italia" and "Undoing the
      Risorgimento: Emigrants from Italy and the Politics of Regionalism" have since
      been published in Pierre Anctil and Bruno Ramirez (eds.), *If One Were To Write
      A History... Selected Writings by Robert F. Harney.* (Toronto, 1991). The latter
      was also recently published in Matteo Sanfilippo (ed.) *Annali Accademici
      Canadesi* (Ottawa, 1991) Vol.2, pp. 49-74.

Introduction

*F*or me to write an Italians in Canada book is to decide that I am in my post modernist stance and say that the book can be seen either as a latter day version of those heuristic *pagine di storia* common in Italy or as an example of the kind of text Walter Benjamin had in mind when he spoke of a book that was solely quotations, or one that employed the art of interruption as the only way to freeze the dialectic in motion and to understand the complexity of the current moment.

What it cannot be is the smooth narrative history, analog to the bourgeois novel, by which Canadian and other national histories have been popularly represented. That would be doing a terrible travesty, doing violence to reality and to the marginal and episodic character of immigrant history which Gramsci talks about when he talks about history of *classi subalterni*. The mainstreaming structure – I have talked about this in my Finnish article on the Generations series[1] – imposes a false time and a false space upon the migrant experience, as well as false contacts and continuities.

The purpose of this volume then is not a canned national history of the Italians, a "book of Italian Canadians" like a whole earth catalog but an attempt to suggest appropriate frames and questions about the variety of Italian experience in Canada. We need a history using the newer modes and the newer sub-disciplines, talking about the sort of real places that Melville wrote about in *Moby Dick*, the places that do not appear on any map.

In fact, the title of the book, "Italians in Canada" has echoes of the dishonesty that distressed the wise old men – just plain village men inclined to only trust kin or *paesani*, or internationalist socialists, anarchists, haters of conscription – a dishonesty summed up in the politicians or orators false opening appeal to solidarity – *Noi connazionali or noi Italiani, figli di Caboto* – they knew that such lines meant that it was time to check to see if your wallet was intact. In the same way some sort of intellectual theft is announced by the title, some swindle denying the audience the right to the full truth, the full complication of the many and separate Italian encounters with Canada from Glace Bay to Nanaimo, and with the even more perplexingly rich global context in which those encounters occurred.

Piano, piano is the only way to go from the myriads of migration projects and targets, their results as local experience in Italy and Canada to the question of the success or failure of an ethnogenesis or ethnicization here creating something we can call an Italian Canadian (indeed studying the scoundrels and true believers who now provide the *noi connazionali* speeches becomes the historians task far more than accepting the simple census data and its blatant political uses). Concentrating on something like the Italian Canadian umbrella organizations does not bring one very close to the reality of Italian Canadian life and thought in the metropoles and the myriad smaller settlements. In the end, not census artifact but behaviour and belief about selves (as in my story about the Sikh Burns guard and the two *carabinieri*)[2] will be the only way to follow the Italian Canadian experience past the now-dominant generation of immigrants and children.

This book is written from a continentalist, global, sending town perspective (appropriate to the literature of Baily, Pozzetta and Mormino, and Sturino)[3] – not as an act of defiance against the mandate of the series – the making of assistant Canadian peoples – but for the purpose of creating a better Canadian national historiography which also is part of the mandate. An historiography that removes obscuring exceptionalism and filiopiety at the same time and puts the Italian migration to Canada in its truest context – that of the flow of labour from the peripheries to the advancing frontiers of industrializing Europe – a perspective in which the migrant is actor and not just victim, is carrier and processor of culture not just a given with inherited and immutable cultural baggage or a heathen to be converted to a new nationality, and one with whom species or stages of double consciousness and mental maps persist through generations affecting behaviour and identity. Immigrants must be seen as individuals in complex relationships to the subsocieties constructed for their subcultures which in turn exist as their ways to interpret and order their reality.

At the same time that this approach may seem to cheat Italians in Canada of their separate identity, it allows us to look at that identity without mythopoeics and assumptions in order to see how much of the identity is a construct in a Canadian discourse and what other identities, primordial or constructed, persist or have been superseded in the drive to establish a Canadian ethnic group as it comes from speakers in both the *ethnie* and the various host society hierarchies of discourse. It allows us to look at the unity (homogeneity) or pluralism of origin, target, project, and intent, and destination of those who migrate from the Italian peninsula. It allows us to see the degree to which Italian migrants are actors (*personaggi*) in search of an author, and the many authors, Italian government and intellectuals, Canadian gatekeepers and caretakers, community *notabili* and organic intelligentsia who present themselves as willing to turn collectivity into community, individual or familial or town migration into one or another nation state's essential drama of nationhood.

Notes

1. R. Harney, "Entwined Fortunes: Multiculturalism and Ethnic Studies in Canada," in *Siirtolaisuus - Migration 3* (1984), pp. 68-94. Special decennium issue of the quarterly of the Institute of Migration Studies.

2. For the story about the Indian Burns guard and the two *carabinieri*, see "If One Were To Write A History of Post war Toronto Italia" in this volume.

3. Samuel Baily, "The Adjustment of Italian Immigrants in Buenos Aires and New York", 1870-1914, *The American Historical Review* 88, no. 2, pp. 281-305. G. Marmino and G. Pozzetta, *The Immigrant World of Ybor City. Italians and Their Latin Neighbours in Tampa, 1885-1985.* (Urbana, 1987). F. Sturino, *Forging the Chain. Italian Migration to North America 1880-1930.* (Toronto, 1990).

Photo Roberto Lissia

1

Caboto and Other *Parentela*:
The Uses of the Italian Canadian Past

In the migration of Italians to North America, three phases are discernible. First, there was a pre-history, a time of intermittent contact between Italians and the New World, of random immigration by adventurous individuals often soldiers, clergy, mariners in the service of states other than those of the Italian peninsula. In an epoch when being Catholic, or being nobly born, counted toward identity more than what we now call nationality, it was easy enough for men from the Italian peninsula to emerge as important civil servants and soldiers of the Spanish, French and even the British crowns. Since Italy was also the religious centre of Catholic Europe and had long provided clergy for remote areas throughout the world, Italian-born missionaries joined more secular adventurers in the discovery and opening up of North America.

This kind of Italian contact, human and cultural, continued until the fall of Quebec when Canada became a British colony rather than an extension of the southern European cultural, political and religious imperium. For although Italian culture continued to have influence on French Canadian Catholicism, with the collapse of the French empire in North America, the first stage of Italian immigration was over.

A new phase of immigration began with the watershed period of the French Revolution and Napoleonic wars, and new types of immigrants from the Italian peninsula found their way to Montreal and Lower Canada. They were, for the most part, men without women, *demi-soldes* and demobilized soldiers whom the fortunes of an Anglo-French global struggle brought to Canada. In this category were the soldiers of the De Meuron and Watteville regiments disbanded after the American ratification of the Treaty of Ghent, as well as the first Italian resident of Toronto, a former officer in both the French and British service, Philip De Grassi. A short time later political emigres and exiles from the turbulent politics of Italy's *Risorgimento* began to arrive. Most characteristic of this second stage of Italian immigration to Canada, which took place between 1800 and 1870 and most appropriately seen as precursor to the mass migration after 1885, was the fashioning of small precise chains of immigrants from certain Italian towns and families, especially from the Lago Como region, north of Milan, to Montreal, and later of Ligurians to Toronto and elsewhere. Such family chains usually showed great occupational resilience and acumen, and the newcomers very quickly prospered and became civilizers, in the true urban meaning of the word, bringing to Montreal especially a refinement of accommodation, restaurant and cafe life, and music, which were stereotypically a post-Renaissance Italian attribute.

This stage of group settlement by artisans, entrepreneurs and by people carrying the varieties of European accomplishments from language skills and fencing to music and dancing to North American frontier cities such as New York and Montreal coincided in its latter stages with a flow of *girovaghi* – wandering street entertainers, hustlers and artisans – who were, in effect, the advance scouts for the mass migration which left Italy for all corners of the world after 1885. Such birds of passage are hard to track, but their numbers at any given time gave added visibility to an Italian presence in North American cities, and as we shall see in a later chapter, contributed to the emergence of unsympathetic stereotypes of the Italian among the rest of the populace.

The final stage of Italian migration to Canada came in two waves with the great waves of sojourning and settlement, which took place before and immediately after World War One, and then again in the two decades after World War Two. By the mid-twentieth century at least 7.5 million and possibly as many as 9 million Italians had settled permanently in the Americas. As many as 25 million had left Italy over the century as poly-seasonal migrants, sojourners and emigrants. Canada's place as a target in this massive diaspora was not, until after World War Two, a major one, but it is important to understand the stages of Italian immigration to Canada in relation to the larger patterns of Italian world emigration and to observe how myths and characteristics of each emigration wave affected both Canadian history and the attitudes of Italian Canadians toward their history. To do that we must go beyond antiquarianism and the quasi-genealogical search for the Italian presence in early Canadian history to an exercise in historiography and in the contemporary politics and psychology of ethnicism in Canada.

Before attempting such a reflective study of early Italian Canadian history, it is necessary to place the chronology of the delivering country, Italy, in the context of Canadian history.

Immigrants travel from one time and space frame to another. When they arrive in numbers, they usually create fossilized cultures of the country they leave behind and contribute to the one they enter commensurate with their energy, their skills and the stages of civility and modernity within which they have been bred.

Despite the cultural richness of her long urban past, Italy's career as a nation state did not antedate the political existence of Canada. The climax of the *Risorgimento*, the process which brought unity to the Italian peninsula in the 1860s and 1870s and the confederation of Canada took place in the same decade. Rome and Ottawa became national capitals within five years of each other, and in both new countries, large elements of the population were indifferent or hostile to subsequent efforts to forge a single national identity. Francesco Crispi, who began as a revolutionary nationalist during the early *Risorgimento* and ended as Prime Minister of Italy, pointed out a bitter-sweet truth in a speech to the Italian parliament in 1888: "Gentlemen," he said, "Italy arrived far too late in the family of Great Powers. She had the honour of discovering America but did not have the strength to impose her dominance there."[1] The point was well made, but it hinted at a confusion between immigration and imperialism in the Italian public mind of the turn of the century and prefigured an almost pathological concern with ethnic power prestige, which arose later among those in the Italian North American intelligentsia and in the Italian public service who found themselves victims of prejudice in North America and living in so-called *colonie* and Little Italies which were neither colonies nor legally little parts of Italy, but were in fact the ghettos, immigrant quarters and working-class neighbourhoods of other nations. The tendency arose then to read the history of early Italian North America in terms of the failure of Italian national sovereignty and power, on the one hand, and to assume, on the other, that Anglo-Saxon, or founding stock prejudice, abetted by the humble ways of masses of later peasant immigrants, has obscured or purposely obliterated the record of a major Italian role in the making of North America. It is that tendency, rather than the limited historical contact itself, which makes a true account of the early Italian presence in Canada important, gives it meaning not just as history but as contemporary politics.

Franz Fanon, observing the feverish use and abuse of history practised by both sides in the Algerian struggle for independence, came to understand the significance of the past as a legitimizer of status in the present. "While the politicians situate their action in actual present day events," he wrote, "men of culture take their stand in the field of history."[2] Ethnic history, as the story of each people's participation in the development of North America, has also become a weapon in the individual and group struggle to "make it" in the United States and Canada. The battle for status in North America has insidious impact on the writing of history, so we must look at some problems of how Italian North Americans perceive their history, especially their mass migration from Italy and their role in civilizing the Western Hemisphere.

The manipulation of the past to create a pedigree in the present is not unique to any one ethnic group. That it happens at all is the consequence of the rather understandable misunderstanding that North American ethnic group status – and thus, at least partly, the individual's own eth-class – derives from ideas about being "long in the land" and about respectability. In its American form, called "Mayflowerism," the uses of history have long been the device of the Old Stock (the term itself evolves from the attitude), of those from the British Isles and northwestern Europe, to justify their ethnocultural hegemony. In Canada the problem is made official in the concept of "the founding nations," which claims a special status on behalf of the French and Anglophone groups, even within the context of multiculturalism.

The response to the Old Stock's assertion of privilege based on historical contribution and longevity in the land has been a spate of counter-claims. Italian North Americans have participated in this unseemly race to establish respectability and roots in the land. One Italian American historian has written that, if he used the methods of computation used by German and Scottish-Irish historians, he could "prove" that there were many thousands of Italians in the American Revolutionary armies. As if to show his own susceptibility, that same historian remarks elsewhere, "The proportion of Italian officers and enlisted men who served during the Civil War was perhaps the highest of any ethnic group."[3]

The flyer announcing a 1981 conference in Washington sponsored by the National Italian American Foundation quotes a well-known Italian American educator thus:

> The Italians have been the most important ethnic group in their influence on the creation of America. This influence starts as early as the fifteenth century. It is only during the seventeenth and eighteenth centuries that other ethnic groups because of their larger numbers in America begin to influence the

mores and the habits of the white man as he populates our continent.

A short litany of the way men of culture have taken "their stand in history" is embarrassing. Was the giant foundling Peter Francesco, who saved George Washington's life, Italian or Portuguese? Were the glassblowers who carried out the first strike for labour justice at Jamestown in the 1600s Poles or Venetians? Did Columbus discover America or was he a johnny-come-lately after the Vikings, or St. Brendan in a leather boat?[4] And how would the resolution of these disputes enhance or diminish the status of the Italian ethnic group in North America? Can Italian Canada avoid such childish games, especially in the face of the official encouragement of filio-pietism which a misreading of multicultural policy in relation to ethnic studies seems to imply?

Speaking to this issue here prejudges neither the validity of the retrospective discovery of early Italian Canadian heroes nor the significance of those heroes' ethnicity in their own time. Fanon, as a trained psychiatrist, would have recognized the near hysteria in the use of history in the Italian American educator's claim. Fanon understood and sympathized with the need for this "passionate research and this anger" in the "sphere of psycho effective equilibrium"; but, as a good Marxist, he saw such nationalist and ethnocentric use of history as dangerous, as a form of false consciousness. "I am ready to concede," he wrote in *The Wretched of the Earth*, "that on the plane of factual being the past existence of an Aztec civilization does not change anything very much in the diet of the Mexican peasant of today. I admit that also proofs of a wonderful Songhai civilization will not change the fact that today the Songhais are underfed and illiterate, thrown between sky and water with empty heads and empty eyes."

There is a risk in using the claims of a "glorious past" as a tactic to combat bigotry. Such usage implies that contemporaneous unglossed reality somehow provides the bigoted with a legitimate case and assumes that when a people's "glorious past" is made known, bigotry withers away. Fanon observed that the native, and, we might add, that the ethnic intellectual has the secret hope of "discovering beyond the misery of today, beyond self contempt, resignation and abjuration some very beautiful and splendid era whose existence rehabilitates us both in regard to ourselves and regard to others."[5] For much of Italian America's ethnic intelligentsia, this means an era when the only Italian Americans were artists and sculptors; when a Tuscan named Mazzei was explaining democracy to Thomas Jefferson; when the "Italian" evoked images of Mozart's librettist, Lorenzo DaPonte,[6] in New York to create the opera; of Cesnola, who founded the Metropolitan Museum of Art; of Garibaldi and other *profughi* (political exiles), heirs to ancient democratic and republican traditions, finding refuge in the nation born of those antique dreams.

For the Italian Canadian intelligentsia, status comes from finding Italians a place as an auxiliary founding people. The need to achieve "psycho effective equilibrium," has led to what I call *culto degli scopritori* – a hunt for the *Italianità* of warriors, priests and explorers of Italian descent serving New France. Thus, names like General Bourlamaque and De Ligne become Burlamacchi and De Lino; Henri de Tonty must be recorded as Enrico Di Tonti and Father Bressan as Bressani or Bresciani.[7] No one tries to ascertain the sense of identity or the sentiments of those heroes, some of whom were Italian-born and Italian in culture, while others merely had ancestors from the Italian peninsula.

In the United States, and increasingly in Canada, the urge to own a respectable North American pedigree leads the various ethnic intelligentsia into the vapid and vacuous struggle to get the face of Filippo Mazzei or Giovanni Caboto on a postage stamp, reminiscent of the campaigns of Mussolini's consuls in the 1930s to *Italianizzare* the *colonie* by rallying the innocent population around the effort to have Cabot declared the official discoverer of Canada.

Another symptom of this need is the explosion of small conferences dedicated to pioneering Italians, most especially those that satisfy the need for respectability – sculptors, artists, musical *maestri*, scholars, *profughi* and nobleman. Such conferences often seem more intent on asserting how different these immigrants were from the later *poveri miserabili*, than on explaining the continuing causes and processes of immigration. Whatever the scholarly value of such gatherings, they have a complexly negative relationship to the history and perception of the post-1885 mass immigration of Italians to North America. Asked about the later "mean" and "bas-Italian" migration, organizers and participants become sullen; they are uncomfortable when one talks about more common folk, immigrants who were *suonatori ambulanti* (street musicians and hurdy-gurdy men), *figuristi* and *chincaglieri* (casters of cheap statuary and pedlars) and, worse yet, *contadini* (unskilled peasants turned ditch diggers in North America).

The discomfort with the "other" history, the "mean history of our people" as it was labelled at one conference, which seems to surround the simultaneous assertion of roots and respectability, suggests that Italian North Americans suffer from a condition which the ancient Greeks called *atimia*. Here we can translate *atimia* as ethnic self-disesteem, a phenomenon observed unsympathetically by a scholar writing in the *American Journal of Sociology* during the Second World War. He seems to have understood the way in which *atimia*, an ethnic inferiority complex, led to aggressive, ethnocentric assertions and to recitals of the ethnic group's past glories that in fact flirted with racism. He wrote:

> Italian ethnocentricism on the other hand is centered about the accomplishments of the inhabitants of Italy during the last two thousand years. On the assumption that any great man produced at any time during this period is proof enough that all individuals born within the group have all the biological potentialities of genius. *There is no nationality that produced more great people than the Italians. The Italians have contributed more to civilization than many other people. The greatest painters, sculptors, writers and composers have been Italian.'* This postulate should, however, be taken as defense against the helplessness in which Italians find themselves both in Europe and the United States.[8]

By invoking the greatness that was or is Italy, that was or is Italian culture, by parading the special skills of the early immigrant elites, the Italian North American intelligentsia is in danger of allowing the ethno-psychiatric uses of history – the skewing of perception that filio-pietism combined with *atimia* causes – to usurp serious study of the processes of Italian migration. Such celebrations provide a surrogate history, one that avoids coming to terms with the real history which requires accepting the humbler human dignity of Italians who came during the mass migration after 1885. That denial of history, that misdirection of research energy, of ethnic pride and, increasingly, of funding contributes to a failure to appreciate the heroism and human resourcefulness of the eight million Italian migrants who helped civilize the Americas.

The *atimia* which provokes this response is especially sad because at its source is a misconception born in the nineteenth century and fostered by the political intelligentsia in Italy, by the consular service and by Italian travellers to North America's Little Italies. Much of that Italian national intelligentsia had a psychological problem of its own: unity of the peninsula had not brought great power status, had not brought true imperial status, but rather humiliating defeat at the hands of Ethiopia. The result was a national inferiority complex among Italian intellectuals and officials which fostered irredentism, fascism and an image of emigration as haemorrhage.[9] Italian consular officials, usually recruited from the urban upper classes and often from the North, shared this sense of national embarrassment and so misunderstood Anglo-Saxon prejudice. The consuls believed that the first cause of prejudice was the Italian migrants themselves (*girovaghi*) and the large numbers of *suonatori ambulanti*, "che sono i peggiori e piu inutili delle specie" (who are the worst and most useless of the race).[10]

This view of the immigrants as *cafoni* from whom one had to distance oneself was shared by almost all those political intelligentsia, consuls, clergy and, then later, *fuorusciti* (political exiles), who made opinion and shaped the image by which immigrants measured their worth. That distance from the "mean history" of the Little Italy could be maintained by emphasizing blood ties to the glories that were Italian culture or by claiming to be from among the earlier immigrants, or well-born, or skilled, or simply northern. People who need to assert their superiority to the general migrant stream exist, of course, in every immigrant cohort and are best caricatured by the joke that emerged from the Hungarian Revolution of 1956. In that story two dachshunds are crossing the Hungarian border into Austria to escape the Soviet repression. As they cross the border, one turns to the other and says, "I don't know about you, but in the old country my parents were German shepherds." Studying those explorers, priests and soldiers of Italian descent who participated in early Canadian history then becomes more than an exercise in filio-pietist chronicling; it is a search for symbolic German shepherds. Since it goes on in the psychologically and competitively charged atmosphere of our "multicultural" times, it acquires political significance.

A pantheon of Italian Canadian heroes, rediscovered from the recesses of the earlier accounts, is being refurbished for contemporaneous needs. At the apex is the discoverer of Canada, Giovanni Caboto, a.k.a. John Cabot. Other figures are Father Francesco Bressani, the Jesuit missionary who wrote his *Breve Relazione* on Canada's Indians in Italian, though only a French translation was known in Canada for many years. The majority of the pantheon is made up of soldiers and adventurers serving the French regime such as Enrico Tonti, De la Salle's second in command, the Crisafi brothers, the Marini brothers and Francois-

Charles de Bourlamacque, (Bourlamacque's grandfather, Burlamacchi, had migrated from Italy to France), third in command to Montcalm.[11] About them we wish to know what role they played in Canadian history, who they were in terms of their loyalties and what we nowadays would call ethnic identity, and finally, how that identity has been perceived or manipulated in our historiography.

The career accomplishments of each of these Italian Canadian "founding figures" have generally been well described and, while forming part of fascinating biographies and the basis for their importance in history as a source of ethnic heritage pride, are not in their detail relevant to the story of Italians in Canada, so I have provided only the briefest narrative of their careers. In general one feels that the non-Italian accounts of these men are a bit niggardly and that the Italian accounts would have been served by recalling Charles Francis Adams' warning to a fellow historian writing about the Yankee heroes of early New England. "In the treatment of doubtful historical points there are fewer things which need to be more carefully guarded against than patriotism or filial piety."

So, if we approach the Italianity and accomplishments of the men in the Italian Canadian pantheon cautiously, it is to show the maturity of Italian Canadian historiography and that, at least in this semi-public volume, the unseemly and ill-founded *atimia* of some parts of the Italian North American intelligentsia and the tendency to play "king of the mountain" by aping the founding stock resting on a sense of priority in the land which affects so much official ethnic filio-piety is laid to rest.

In the 1930s Italians and French Canadians skirmished in the streets of Montreal over the question of whether Cartier or Cabot discovered Canada. I confess that I am not vexed over the question and cede the "high ground" to the following who may wish to be junior "founding peoples." The Portuguese volume in this series takes no sides in that issue, but points out that if Cabot did discover Canada, he was most likely acting on geographical information provided by the Portuguese, Joao Fernandes, who had already been in Labrador. Such johnny-come-latelys may fight out aimlessly in the pages of the series, for the Norwegian volume asserts that Paul Knutson and eight Goths and twenty-two Norsemen navigated Lake Winnipeg in the 1350s. That happened only two and a half centuries after two Scots, according to the Scottish volume, joined the crew of Thorfinn Karlsevni's expedition to Nova Scotia. Compared to such antiquity in the land, the Greek volume's reminder that Juan de

Fuca, who explored Puget Sound in the sixteenth century was really a Greek seaman named Yannis Phokas, has the ring of modernity and authenticity.[12]

Since the Italian peninsula was not unified under a single strong government between the mid-fifteenth and the mid-nineteenth centuries, her petty monarchies played no military or colonial role in North American history. Adventurous and ambitious young men, especially after the decline of Venetian and Genovese imperialism in the eastern Mediterranean and Black Seas, had to look beyond the peninsula's frontiers for careers or for a chance to apply the technology or humanism of the Renaissance's new learning. So, in a sense, all of early Italian history in North America is the history of individual migrants. All of Italian immigration from the earliest stage of adventurers to our own times is one of a flow of suppressed or underemployed talent to opportunity. So, for example, for much the same reasons that mariners or soldiers emigrated from the peninsula, Italian-born clergy served as carriers in the American southwest and Father Bressani, even if they wrote parts of their correspondence and reports in Italian, they lived and worked in the idiom of the Spanish and French religious orders they served.

North America's historical myths and political paradigms about the founding of nations took little notice of those who did not belong to the dominant political or ethnic groups and so the role of these individuals has been generally discounted or subsumed into the myths of the regnant culture. Perhaps the best Canadian instance of this was the tendency to portray Caboto, one of the earliest explorers of Canada, indeed its discoverer, as a Bristol English gentleman named Cabot, or even to pronounce his name in Canadian high school classrooms with the *t* muted in the French manner, rather than mention and explain his Venetian and Genovese family heritage. Of course, Italian Canadian responses to that slight – the insistence that Cabot be seen as Giovanni Caboto, an Italian – has, on occasion, been equally manipulative of history. Between the hegemonic filio-pietists of the "Old Stock" and those who challenge them, there is little difference of view about the right to mould historical evidence for the needs of the political culture.

Caboto's family history was typical of that shaped by the chaotic petty state system of the Italian peninsula. Italian seafarers, merchants and soldiers took foreign service and were at the vanguard of Spanish, Portuguese, English and French exploration of the Western Hemisphere. In no instance could they carry on their trade or their explorations for an Italian state. The career and sentiments of Caboto's father reflected his times. He is said to have given up his Genovese citizenship for the Venetian one because of the "prospettiva d'un migliore avvenire" – the prospect of a better future – for himself and his children. Remarkably that very phrase "prospettiva d'un migliore avvenire" often appears more than four centuries later in the reports of prefects from throughout Italy which try to explain why, beyond *la miseria* and seductive steamship recruiting *agenti* the common people emigrated in vast numbers.

Caboto's motive probably differed little from those of the millions of labourers and peasants who came to North America in the nineteenth and twentieth centuries, men whose philosophy of survival, like Caboto's, was summed up in the Latin proverb, *Ubi panis, ibi patria*. Despite his symbolic importance to the Italian search for a place in the history of the founding peoples of Canada, serious study of Giovanni Caboto has not advanced or been very central in Canadian scholarship. There are occasional Italian works of filio-piety, but certainly we know more of Cabot from American and British maritime historians like Morrison and Williamson than from any equivalent Canadian source.[13] The grievance expressed by elements of the Italian Canadian intelligentsia that Cabot is little studied and little understood in Canada then deserves a hearing, although the omission is less glaring when placed in the context of scholarly neglect of fifteenth and sixteenth century Canada generally.

Most of the facts of Cabot's public life and career are not subject to much dispute. However, ascribing to him in some simple form sentiments of either "Englishness" or "Italianness" is not very useful. Like many men of his time, Caboto possessed multiple and shifting loyalties. His ethnocultural sense of self, if a man of that century can be said to have had one, may have been in continuum, or various loyalties may have superseded and conflicted with one another over time. Indeed, he may have seen all ethnic or national loyalties simply as flags of convenience. In other words, he may have, in the modern phrase, "negotiated his ethnicity" continuously, according to circumstance and encounter. In a continuum of possible loyalties where did John Cabot, the Italian Giovanni Caboto, and the naturalized Venetian Zuan Cabot stand? Was his first loyalty to his Genovese birthplace, his Venetian family and business connections, his Italian culture, his Catholic cosmopolitanism, the Bristol business community, or the English king who employed him?

Giovanni Caboto, when he landed in Cape Breton in 1497, planted a cross and two flags – the Royal Standard of England and the banner of St. Mark, the patron of the Venetian city state that had been his second home. There was, of course, no Italian *tricolore* yet created for him to plant. Would he have planted the *tricolore* if it had existed? The bare facts of Caboto's career cannot tell the reader with any certainty about the explorer's Italianity or lack of it.

It would be wise to pause and make a general comment on the anachronism of applying concepts of ethnicity to the early modern period. I do so not to dim the colours of the emerging Italian oriflammes in the pantheon of Canada's founding peoples, but to remind us of what our thought processes are when we try to assess the numerical importance of an ethnic group in the North American past. The question of the meaning of what we call, in modern terms, ethnic identity is vexed. And we are unlikely to capture the true sense of self-identity, or of hierarchies of sentiments and loyalties, which a man harboured two centuries ago simply by equating his surname with membership in some modern nationality or his ethnic sentiment with his place of origin on a map. Such exercises in ethnic labelling are best left to the Canadian census-takers. Some weighing of the problem would seem to be a requirement for a book of this kind. It may help to stem the flood of filio-pieties, official and otherwise, now unleashed by multiculturalism as policy and by ethnicism as newly respectable modern North American sentiment. Because of the nationalist inculcation we have received in Canadian or Italian schools, it is difficult to grasp the cosmopolitanism and easy multilingualism which prevailed among the Italian upper classes until after the French Revolution. This way of being and its style may be epitomized by the great Habsburg soldier of the eighteenth century who signed himself Eugenio von Savoie, that is trilingually. Was he an Austrian, a Piedmontese, a Frenchman? Did he feel himself Italian or German? Of course, he was none of those things, yet all of them. Caboto himself signed his name differently in different phases of his life. Would these questions about identity make sense to him, and, if not, is it sensible for the modern historian to ask him?

In a case almost as relevant to Italian Canadian history as that of Cabot, we can look at one of the great explorers of the Canadian coast, Verrazzano. The explorer was probably born in Florence in the 1480s though no records of his birth exist. He often referred to himself as Verrazane, the Latinized version of his name, and was known to his contemporaries by a number of names, most of them French, such as Verracen. He sailed from the French port on board the *Pensee* in the early 1500s and was assumed by most contemporaries to be a Norman sailor, named Jehan Verassen. Verrazzano referred to himself as a Florentine, never an Italian, but the latter-day presence of the Italian version of his name on bridges, straits, headlands and social or cultural halls has Italianized his identity.

However damaging to historical truth and fraught with structural prejudice is the Canadian habit of Anglicizing or Gallicizing the names and, by extension, the realities of men like Caboto, Tonti and Bressani, the practice of applying high levels of Italianity to them leads to further pitfalls. It tends to underestimate their cosmopolitan fealty to their social class and European Christendom, or simply Catholicism. It assumes that loyalty to city and family were in continuum with the post-Napoleonic sense of nationality and feelings of patriotism for the nation-state. Mazzini, of course, knew better and recognized that the "insurrection" which was the Risorgimento, would have to be followed by the "revolution," which in his mind would be the establishment of a national school system educating Italians to their shared culture and destiny. Gramsci has commented precisely and acidly on this need of the Italian "hegemonic liberal bourgeoisie" to encourage the common people in a cult of past national accomplishments in the fields of exploration and warfare in order to draw attention away from the contemporaneous squalor and powerlessness of post-Risorgimento Italy. I do not claim here that North American ethnic leadership is so clever, evil, or successfully hegemonic.[14]

It is incumbent on scholarship, especially that imbued with a humane passion for telling the story correctly, to prove the *italianità* of those Italian Canadians emerging in the pantheon of Canada's founding greats. If scholars can do so in a thoughtful and researched way, then learning will be served and the governing narratives, or what Foucault calls "regimes of truth," of the two founding peoples at least will be brought into question in a manner which might be beneficial for contemporaneous intergroup relations. This work cannot therefore be done as filio-pietistically as that of the earlier anglophone and French historians: all immigrants know they must be better to be as good as the "Old Stock." The upbringing, language-use, mores, folkways and environmental experience, the "ethnoversion" of Caboto and Bressani, need to be subjects of scholarship not speculation. Otherwise we come dangerously close to suggesting that what is significant, what links the Cabotos and Bressanis to modern Italian Canadians, is some concept of shared Italian "blood." Indeed, Father Vangelisti made such a link by describing early Italian Canadian heroes as people of whom Italians could be proud and who reflected "una limpida e tersa luce sul nostro sangue... " (a limpid and clear light on our blood).[15]

That noun, blood, despite its allegorical charm, refers to a generic pool. Its unsophisticated use in the search for the "Adams" of each ethnic group in Canada is not harmless; it accustoms us to think in biological, somitic and racial terms about ethnic history and contemporary ethnicity. Italian Canadian heritage-boosters should not flirt with such imagery, even if Anglo-Canadian historians only very recently, if at all, have given up the apparently allegorical uses of the word "race" to explain historical behaviour. Donald Creighton praised the stoicism "so characteristic of (Prime Minister Wilfrid) Laurier's race," and John Dafoe could describe Laurier's mind as "typically French with something else Italianate about it, an inheritance from the long-dead Savoyard ancestors who brought the name to this continent."[16] The hunt for Italianity of blood in New France becomes more comprehensible in this context of the use of such racialist language in mainstream Canadian historical writing. But it is no less reprehensible, if only because such abuses have brought exclusion or discrimination in North America upon the parents and grandparents of those who now play historical bloodhounds.

In the late 1920s, shortly before the 400th anniversary of Jacques Cartier's reconnaissance of the Canadian coast (1934) and in the face of some virulently hostile French Canadian public opinion, the Montreal newspaper *Il Cittadino* began to agitate for the official recognition of Cabot as discoverer of Canada (*scopritore del Canada*). This campaign was encouraged by the Italian fascist consul in Montreal and taken up by *notabili* in various Canadian cities: Toronto, North Bay and Hamilton, among others. Since 1897 a plaque had been in place in the Nova Scotia legislature to commemorate the 400th anniversary of Cabot's landing. Now, in the wake of the *Cittadino's* agitation, funds were raised for a Caboto memorial in Montreal. But in order to salve French-Canadian sensibilities about Cartier, the community thought it wise to put off the planned ceremonies to honour the *scopritore*.[17] Eventually, a statue of Caboto was presented to Mayor Camillien Houde by the so-called doyen of the community, Onorato (Honore) Catelli, and it was duly put in place opposite the Forum. Subsequently, the name Caboto was increasingly used by Italian Canadians for their clubs and halls. Even though the *Cittadino's* campaign took place under suspect auspices and was a device by the fascist consular service to rally Italian Canadians behind Mussolini's nationalism in the world, it was supported energetically by most Italian Canadians.

Mussolini, of course, encouraged them from the start. In a letter responding to an invitation from the Montreal committee to honour Caboto, he struck an insightful note about the ties that bound Caboto and the modern Italian immigrants of Montreal together:

> Giovanni Caboto, whose name you wish to honour as that of the man who discovered the land where today you live as welcome and hardworking *ospiti* (guests) is a symbol of the *genialità* and of the daring with which our great Fathers then and now our tenacious brothers have brought their labour and vibrancy to new lands.

But the *Duce* also stated that his Italy joined in honouring Caboto, not least because it was "seeking to reaffirm her ancient greatness upon the seas."

Mackenzie King, for his part, also touched on the proper themes of integration into Canadian life and praise of those talents of virtuosity which he presumably assumed all Italians shared:

> It is a great honour for the Italians to be associated in such a direct manner with events which signal the beginning of the new age and it is typical since men of their race have always stood at the forefront in all spheres of human activity, in that of the intellect, of the imagination, of science and of art. The names of Galileo, Dante, Michelangelo, to mention only a few, prove that assertion.[18]

Many organizers of Caboto committees found themselves, like the Sons of Italy, compromised by their ties, innocent or purposeful, with *consolar-fascismo* when World War II broke out. Still the annual Caboto celebration in Montreal on June 24 survived, and in 1955 the Montreal square containing the statue was renamed Caboto Square. Mr. Pickersgill, the Minister of Citizenship and Immigration was present and the ceremony represented a political echo of the new Italian mass migration to Canada then underway. But until the emergence of multicultural policy in the 1970s and the renewed ethnic steeplechase to be "assistant Canadians," public interest in Caboto as *scopritore* declined. In fact, efforts to use Columbus as an emblematic figure eclipsed the Caboto lobby between 1945 and 1975.

In the 1970s new Italian Canadian spokesmen showed concern for what they believed to be the lack of just recognition both of Caboto's role as discoverer of Canada and Caboto's essential Italianness. They saw the use of the English surname, Cabot, as both cause and effect of this neglect. The two issues, while apparently separate, tended to come together. One Toronto Italian magazine, *Comunità Viva*, has dedicated much space in various issues over the decade to the drive for the *riconosimento dello scopritore del Canada*. Senator Peter Bosa recommended in a December 6, 1979 to the Senate that the government remedy the improper Anglicization of Caboto's name in Canadian toponymy so that, for example, the Cabot Trail would become the Caboto Trail.

It is worth trying to understand Senator Bosa's reasoning.[19] First, he believed that there was no evidence that Caboto ever wished to be known by any name other than Giovanni Caboto. Then he explained his understanding of the civic uses of history to the chamber:

> The fact of knowing that our predecessors have had a significant role in the discovery of this nation inculcates in us a sense of pride. There are many other personages among us who have made their contribution in diverse ways and in diverse times in the history of Canada. Some of these are: the navigator and explorer Giovanni Da Verranzano in 1524, the assistant to De La Salle, Enrico Tonti in 1678, the governor of Trois Rivières, Captain Crisafi in 1703, Brigadier-General Carlo Burlamacchi, third in command to General Montcalm, Joseph Marini, a senior officer who was killed in the Battle of the Plains of Abraham in 1759.

Senator Bosa's efforts to give Caboto back his Italianity irked some Anglo-Canadians. The narrow-mindedness of some of the public responses to this gave him an opportunity to expand on his reasons for emphasizing the Italian role in early Canadian history. Those reasons are worth repeating at length since the Senator's views reflect an era in which the official policy of multiculturalism encourages concepts such as ethnic heritage, "contribution" and group longevity on the Canadian scene.

First, the Senator considered it important to celebrate pluralism of origin as a way of enforcing an egalitarian, open-minded sense of a shared Canadian history:

> However the most valid reason for recognizing people of various ethnic backgrounds who have played a part in the history of Canada is that it instills

in the people from those ethnic groups a sense of pride, a feeling of belonging and more important still a feeling of being part of this country.

These feelings and emotions are the very essence that gives Canadians a common denominator which binds them to one another. History shows that loyalty to a country and national unity are more prevalent in a nation where its citizens have something in common with their past and share a common goal for the present and the future.

I endeavour to promote this concept which is a concept that is not always understood and I hope that other Canadians who realize how important it is to strengthen national unity in this area will take the lead in encouraging recognition of legitimate contribution made to Canada's history by anyone, regardless of his or her ethnic background.[20]

For much the same reasons, the Senator, along with people like the editor of *Comunità Viva*, favour the use of Caboto as an emblematic for Italian Canadian organizations, buildings and projects. The use of Columbus (as in Columbus Centre and Villa Colombo) has acquired an insidiously continentalist resonance from an American tradition in which the explorer became a symbol to unite Italian Americans. The Columbian tradition is seen as less relevant to Italian Canadians or as positively subversive of some potential Canadian civic identity.[21]

More problematic is the other declared reason for emphasizing the early Italian contribution to Canada, a reason which seems to reflect both *atimia* and a tendency to see history as a therapeutic tool for contemporary inter-ethnic relations and, thus, something that is adjusted for a civic good. Responding to criticism of his desire to reassert Cabot's Italianity by changing place names, the Senator wrote:

Most of the news relating to people with Italian names are invariably negative to the point that Canadians have a distorted image of Canadians of Italian origin. In support of this view I am enclosing a survey on public opinion, as well as a press release dated July 13, 1979. I believe that as a parliamentarian, it is my duty to correct the false image that Canadian society has of a large segment of Canadian citizens. My view is shared by my parliamentary colleagues, the Human Rights Commissioner, as well as prominent members of the law enforcement agencies. I am sure that every Canadian who is free from racial prejudice will see the English fair play in this objective. What possible injurious consequences could be derived from restoring a name to its original spelling?[22]

What injury indeed, although one can understand that changing the name of a trail from Cabot to Caboto undoes for many people a century of local history and usage. Nor does a campaign to identify heroes of an Italian Canadian past seem a very effective weapon against defamation of Italians by the North American media. It is unlikely that a documentary on Caboto would appeal to the CBC as much as the market possibilities of a series, such as "Connections," which trades cheaply on the "mafia mystique." However, the reader by this point can hardly deny that the study of the Italian Canadian pantheon of explorers, priests and soldiers is an aspect of contemporary multicultural politics. The attempt to have a Caboto Day declared a Canadian holiday would bring both current rhetoric and the malleability of the past to its highest pitch. But a glance at the history of the struggle to make Columbus Day a national rather than a state option holiday in the United States should daunt organizers.

The imminence of Caboto's meaning for Canadian history and for Italian Canadians; the ambiguities about race, sovereignty and identity, ethnicity today involved in invoking his name today, can be glimpsed in the words of Guglielmo Vangelisti, a Servite priest in Montreal, who ranks as the best amateur historian of the Italians in Canada to date. In 1958, he wrote, in terms reminiscent of Crispi's 1880 speech, that in Caboto we remember "the great Italian who *gave* England her right on the continent, a right which the colonizing spirit of his sons profits from much later on."[23]

Thus Father Vangelisti, as early as the 1950s, seemed to be claiming first place for Italy among contributors to the making of Canada. Part of the vehemence which surrounds this discussion may have to do with the fact that in the filio-pietist steeplechase for first place, Cabot served as the British entry against Cartier many years before the Italians seized his colours. Vangelisti seems to have shared this simple faith that the "old stock would stop resting on their priority in the land" and recognize their non-British, non-French neighbours as peers in Canadian history and society.[24]

"The roles of the French and British communities have dominated the written history of Canada. Contributions by Canadians of other cultural origins have received little attention. As a result most history books present an incomplete record of Canada's past." These words in a government hand-out called *Multicultural Update* (October 1978) seem to promise, or threaten, instant redress and a reworking of the textbooks. They remind us too that as the justification or basis of hegemony changes, the "caretakers" of the nation see the rewriting of history as a tool for fashioning contemporary society. No doubt, for those uneasy with the concept of "contribution" and unhappy with the apparent attempt to push aside the charter groups to make room for others, such assertions by the Multiculturalism Directorate of the Secretary of State might be reminiscent of the efforts made in the 1920s by the Chicago School Board. Under the influence of German and Irish-American politicians, the Board tried to create a new history of the American Revolution for schoolchildren which "must not be pro-British statistically or psychologically." As one wag wrote:

> Every people and race
> In Chicago will trace
> Its hand in the ousting of Britain
> We shall learn 'twas our town
> That pulled George the III down
> When the real revolution is written[25]

It is within such an atmosphere where the record of the past is malleable and is made to serve the civic good, or the therapeutic needs of those uneasy about their status in the land, that most of the writing about Canada's ethnic past goes on. Ethnic studies within multicultural policy should not be reduced to that same sort of ancestor-worship, to that same sort of confusion of individual psychological well-being with that of the Canadian nation-state as now lurks in the Canadian historiographical mainstream. Even if we are on the edge of a post-nationalist age and a global village, however, it is not likely that many immigrant groups will have the courage and dignity to reject such manufactured national traditions, especially if these are slightly amended to include them. The consequence will be:

- an emphasis on a history of warriors, priests, notables and artists at the expense of the heritage, which is of immigrant families and the more immediate history of their peasant, artisan and labourer parents and grandparents;
- a search for instances of what Redfield has called the "great tradition" at the expense of the "little tradition" of common people; and
- an avoidance of the study of issues of capitalist exploitation, segmented work-forces and the accompanying justificatory super-structure of prejudice toward migrants and ethnics.

Like his father and those who came later from Italy, Caboto

lived within a pattern of the flow of labour to capital, talent to opportunity, a pattern in which national boundaries counted for little. Perhaps he and they would understand the dangers inherent in the retrospective distortion which turns immigrant history into the history of nation-states and notables.

Notes

1. Francesco Crispi. *Discorsi parlamentari*, III, 75-76. In Shepard B. Clough and Salvatore Saladino. *A History of Modern Italy. Documents, Readings & Commentary* (New York, 1968) p.219.

2. Frantz Fanon, *The Wretched of the Earth* (New York,1968),p. 209.

3. G. Schiavo, *The Italians in America before the Civil War* (New York,1934),pp. 266,279.

4. P. Sammartino cited on jacket of Andre Rolle. *The Italian Americans: Troubled Roots* (New York,1980). For a critique of the Canadian situation see R.F. Harney, "Entwined Fortunes: Multiculturalism and Ethnic Studies in Canada," in *Siirtolaisuus-Migration 3* (Turku, Finland, 1984).

5. Fanon, *Wretched of the Earth*, pp.209-211.

6. G. Schiavo's writings in the 1920s and 1930s, especially *The Italians in America Before the Civil War* began this filio-pietist tradition. The work of Sister Margherita Marchione, *Philip Mazzei: Jefferson's Zealous Whig* (1976), the studies of early Italian artists by Prof. Regina Soria of Baltimore's Notre Dame College and of Dr. Sammartino, past president of Farleigh Dickinson University, continue the tradition.

7. Guglielmo Vangelisti. *Gli Italiani in Canada*, 2nd ed. (Montreal,1958), remains the most thorough genealogical and historical study of early Italians in Canada. Recently the Library of Parliament, Research Branch, has prepared historical reports on a number of early Canadians of Italian descent for Senator Peter Bosa. The latter has kindly made these available to me. The reports carry the curious caveat that such projects "are designed in accordance with the requirements and instructions of the Member making the request. The views expressed should not therefore be regarded as those of the Research Branch..."

8. D. Rodnick, "Group Frustration in Connecticut," *American Journal of Sociology* XLVI, 2 (Sept. 1941), 159-160. Such a view of "blood" in history is obviously not an ethnic malady alone. Behind much local history and genealogical study, the same urge to use "longevity in the land" or illustrious ancestors to bolster newfound respectability operates. One might even see its traces in the determinedly national frame of postcolonial historiography.

9. See, for examples of *atimia* among Italian diplomats, the various consular responses in L. Carpi, *Delle Colonie e dell'emigrazione italiana all'estero sotto l'aspetto dell'industria, commercio e agricoltura e con trattazioni d'importanti questioni sociali* (Milano, 1874) II, 80-145. See also, L. Villari, "L'Opinione pubblica americana e i nostri emigrati," *Nuova Antologia* CCXXXII (1910), 503. For a general discussion of the issue, see A. Aquarone, "The Impact of Emigration on Italian Public Opinion and Politics," in *The United States and Italy: the First Two Hundred Years, Acts of the American Italian Historical Association*, H. Nelli, ed. (Washington, 1976). The campaign to create a Marconi museum in Cape Breton, led by a recent Italian ambassador, displayed some of the same tendency to ignore the "mean" history for the "glorious." Glace Bay and Dominion, where Marconi lived for a few years, have been home of Trevisan coalminers since before the turn of the century; Calabrians and others helped build Whitney Pier in Sydney shortly after 1900. None of their story, apparently, seemed important to the museum's organizers.

10. R. Paulucci de Calboli, *Girovaghi italiani in Inghilterra ed i suonatori ambulanti* (Citta di Castello, 1898), 5.

11. Vangelisti, *Gli Italiani* used in conjunction with L. Jeune's *Dictionnaire général de biographie, histoire, littérature, agriculture, commerce industrie et des arts, sciences, moeurs, institutions politiques et religieuses du Canada* (Ottawa, n.d.) remains the quickest way to discover something about these early Italians, more specifically whether they were Italian-born or from families long removed from the peninsula. Some confusion results from the fact that the Vangelisti volume, published in Italian, presents Italian forms for most surnames; Le Jeune naturally presents French spellings. The first filio-pietist use of these Italians, it is important to note, seems to have come, not from within the group, but from J.M. Gibbon whose proto-multicultural patriotic volume of 1937, *The Canadian Mosaic: the making of a Northern Nation*, actually suggested that General Bourlamacque, Montcalm's aide, was born in Italy. Le Jeune and Vangelisti describe Bourlamacque as a Parisian noble with an Italian grandfather. C.P. Stacey, in the *Dictionary of Canadian Biography*, remarked that "Bourlamacque is said to have been of Italian descent." In the 1970s the Research Branch of the Library of Parliament, undoubtedly sensing the multicultural temper of the times, wrote, "It is often forgotten that an Italian

F.C. Burlamacchi, called Bourlamacque in French, served as Montcalm's third in command." Obviously, one's ethnicity in North America continues to be a matter of negotiation even beyond the grave.

12. Grace M. Anderson and David Higgs. *A Future to Inherit. The Portuguese Communities of Canada*, (Toronto, 1976), p.6. Gulbrand Loken. *From Fjord to Frontier. A History of the Norwegians in Canada*, (Toronto, 1980), p.11. W. Stanford Reid (ed.). *The Scottish Tradition in Canada*, (Toronto, 1976), p.ix. Peter D. Chimbos. *The Canadian Odyssey. The Greek Experience in Canada* (Toronto, 1980), p.22.

13. I have depended on the following for details about Caboto: J.A. Williamson, *The Cabot Voyage and Bristol Discovery under Henry VII* (Cambridge, 1972); S.E. Morrison, *The European Discovery of America. The Northern Voyages* (Oxford, 1971); S.E. Dawson, *The Voyages of the Cabots. Transactions of the Royal Society of Canada* III, 2 (1897).

14. A. Gramsci, *Gli Intelletuali e l'organizzazione della cultura* (Rome, 1971), p. 78-80.

15. Vangelisti, *Gli Italiani*, p. 70.

16. J. Levitt, "Race and Nation in Canadian Anglophone Historiography," *Canadian Review of Studies in Nationalism* VIII, 1 (Spring 1981), 1-16.

17. Roberto Perin, "Conflits d'identité et d'allégeance. La propagande du consulat italien a Montréal dans les années 1930," *Questions de Culture No 2: Migrations et Communautés Culturelles* (Ottawa, 1982), 81-102. See for example, *Il Cittadino of Montreal* editorial of 26 September 1934, which observes "...the French Canadian press dauntlessly carries on its campaign to the detriment of the glory appertaining to one of our race."

18. Mussolini's and Mackenzie King's letters appear in "In onore di Giovanni Caboto," *Bollettino dell'Emigrazione*, no. 7 (Rome, 1927), 1007-09.

19. I would like to thank Senator Bosa for providing me with copies of his speeches about Caboto, of letters received in response to those speeches and research work done for him by the Library of Parliament. If this paper seems critical of his views of history and skeptical about his belief that improved knowledge of an Italian-Canadian past can combat Italophobia now, I wish to record here my respect for his energy, commitment and ceaseless work on behalf of the Italian-Canadian community.

20. Senator Peter Bosa, Speech to the Senate, 6 December 1979.

21. "Occasioni perdute," in *Comunità Viva* IX, 6-7 (June 1980),p. 34. Other issues of *Comunità Viva* with extensive sections on the issue of Caboto as *scopritore* appeared in September 1972, April 1975, May 1978. In a letter to the editor in 1972, a reader expressed the relationship among Canadianism, multiculturalism and *italianità* well, "I see that our neighbours honour Colombo, even though they call him Columbus, why shouldn't we honor Giovanni Caboto who had the merit of discovering Canada, this marvellous land that has also given us Multiculturalism in order to *sentire affratellati e sullo stesso piano civico.*"

22. Letter of Senator Bosa to former constituent, 22 January 1980.

23. Vangelisti, *Gli Italiani*, 20: "il grande italiano, che diede all'Inghilterra un diritto sul continente, che lo spirito colonizzatore dei suoi figli mise a profitto piu tardi." Crispi, *Discorsi parlamentari* pp. 75-76: "Gentlemen, Italy arrived far too late in the family of great powers. She had the honour of discovering America but did not have the strength to impose her dominion there..."

24. R.F. Harney, "*E Pluribus Unim*: Louis Adamic and the Meaning of Ethnic History," *Journal of Ethnic Studies* 14, 1 (Spring 1986).

25. E.R. Lewis, *America. Nation or Confusion: a Study of Our Immigration Problems* (New York, 1928), 342.

Photo Multicultural History Society of Ontario

2

Italophobia:
An English-speaking Malady?

*T*here are a number of reasons why the study of anti-immigrant bigotry, in this case Italophobia, threatens to skew understanding of ethnic group life in North America. Even if we believe that how something is perceived is invariably an aspect of what it is, conflating the career of an ethnic group with the history of attitudes toward it, if done thoughtlessly, can constitute a final extension of ethnocentrism, an opportunity for North American scholars to treat immigrants as significant historical actors only in the context of the receiving country's national myth, the making of a new people. For those who choose to see the immigrant experience in terms of ethnic boundaries, inter-ethnic hostility, and abatement of friction through acculturation, prejudice and responses to it, once granted explanatory power, become a vortex swallowing up analysis of every aspect of group behaviour and turning ethnic studies into a vehicle for claims of victimization or conversely the triumphal asertion of easy assimilation.

It is clear nonetheless that the encounter with bigotry does shape aspects of Italian North American history. Italian immigrants to Toronto changed their names and religion to gain work opportunities in large protestant-owned department stores; Mayor LaGuardia banned street musicians from New York City because as a little boy he had been called a "wop" after his playmates heard his father, a U.S. Army bandmaster, chatting in Neapolitan dialect with an itinerant hurdy-gurdy man. The Sicilian-American writer Jerre Mangione relates how his father distrusted the Boy Scout movement and thought it unwise for a young Italian American to carry a jack knife, one of the movement's paraphernalia. All immigrants retain or alter cultural patterns in response to the reception they encounter in the new land. It is natural enough that as they "negotiated their ethnicity" in North America, Italians did so with an awareness of hostile or derisive stereotypes from mendacity to knife-wielding which existed about them. The extent to which they did so is sadly obvious when issues surrounding a warm encounter between two musicians or a boy's camping knife can leave scars or affect behaviour. If immigrants respond to prejudice thus, the reaction to the discovery of bigotry about their countrymen by consular and diplomatic officials or Italian intellectuals stationed or travelling abroad, especially in English-speaking countries, is even more unsettling. Betraying those class and regional prejudices which exist in Italy itself, much of the Italian elite abroad took easily to blaming the victim. Rather than looking to the nature of English-speaking Italophobia, they saw it as justified by the sort of migrant or settler who had gone abroad from Italy, in effect they imposed a double disapprobation on the immigrant abroad by providing precise regional, class, and cultural reasons to justify to themselves the hostile stereotypes held about their countrymen. In one of the first questionnaires circulated about emigrants in 1871, Italian consuls were asked to comment on the *condizione morale della colonia*. It is significant that many answered this question about the well-being and civility of Italian settlements abroad by commenting exclusively on how the Italians were perceived in the given host country or city.[1]

For such officials and intellectuals, the phrase Little Italy, coined by the English-speaking hosts, carried a secondary meaning, best expressed by Adolfo Rossi who, in 1904, described New York City's *colonia* for his peers in the Commissariat of Emigration by dismissing it as composed of *elementi inferiori del nostro popolo*, with a substrata made up of *basso proletariato* and that from such a *rozza base*, upon which *è venuto incrostandosi* a species of *petit-bourgeoisie*, little that was progressive or culturally correct could be expected.[2] From denunciations of street musicians, wandering artisans, and peddlers as *vagabondi* in the 19th century through assertions that large numbers of *camorristi* and other thugs had migrated to New York City by 1910 to efforts to ignore the migration of honest working class masses in order to emphasize the accomplishment of *notabili* or the role of Italians in the founding of North American society (*culto degli scopritori*), many Italian officials and intellectuals have through their class and regional prejudices abetted Italophobia and confirmed patterns of *atimia* among immigrants.[3] Excusing North American anti-Italian manifestations by asserting them to be a natural reaction to the predominantly rural, unskilled, undereducated and southern, and swarthy characteristics of Italian mass migration has been a case of believing that things cause what they merely reflect.

In 1942, reporting on the wartime morale of Canadians of Italian descent, Tracey Phillips, an English official seconded to the Canadian Government as an expert on ethnic minorities chided Britons and

Anglo-Americans alike. "It is significant," he wrote, "that it is only in English-speaking countries that the *Anglo-Saxon Master Race* seemed to try to fix upon Italians the insulting or condescending names of *wop* and *dago*."[4] Phillips added that one could see the impact of this prejudice on Italian populations outside of Italy. "It has been to feel that Mussolini whose methods they generally deplored, had at least restored their prestige and status from *wopdom* to that of Roman Italians however much more they might be disliked." The historic English anti-Italian prejudice he described, did not have the virulence of English, and later American, hatred for the Spanish. No image of Italians as cruel, treacherous and intolerant was used to justify Anglo-Saxon hatred for the Italian as it was for the Spaniard nor of course did Italy ever launch an Armada against England. Italophobia was usually not even as sharp-edged as the traditional English anti-French feeling that cropped up everything from fear of Bonaparte to fear of syphilis as the *French disease*. But hostility or derision toward Italians, perhaps since it served no immediate political purpose until the first half of the 20th century, had more insidious staying power than either the so-called black legend of Spanish cruelty or rivalries with France. Though Italians have not been the national foes of England,except briefly and haltingly during World War II, Italians when they have not been the object of hatred and fear, have been persistently and more hurtfully the object of disdain and derisive stereotypes.

This paper looks at the roots of anti-Italian feeling, Italophobia, its various guises and the different themes invoked to show the Italian to be different from Englishmen and northern Europeans generally, and less desirable as a colonist both for the United States and Canada. Only by including such a survey of sentiment, no matter how unpleasant, can we comprehend the meaning of *Italianita* or, of being first Italian then Italian-Canadian.

Large scale encounter between Italians and Englishman, when it came in North America, triggered responses of Italophobia drawn from traditions present in the recesses of the culture of English-speaking peoples.[5] If we were to study this problem using a sociological or psychological concept such as *nativism* which John Higham used in his *Strangers in the Land* to explain American attitudes towards immigrants, we might contribute to Canadian intellectual history, but this study is not seeking general rules which explain why, in a too rapidly changing society, natives turn on outsiders.[6] Rather it tries to describe in historical, not psychological,

terms the presence of anti-Italian sentiment before and after the
arrival of large numbers of Italians in Canada. Italophobia as a
phenomenon has an English-speaking history of its own, a
morphogenesis, from at least Renaissance or Elizabethan times to
today. It should be added that vehicle of the attitude is not
Englishman but English-speaking culture and thus acculturated
North Americans of any ethnic origin can suffer from Italophobia.

Anti-Italian feeling was not merely an aspect of the late
nineteenth century mass encounter between immigrants and English
speakers or of the vogue of scientific racialism accompanying it
which placed Mediterranean peoples well down in hierarchy of races
and nations. To assert that would be like claiming that there was no
anti-Jewish feeling before modern racial antisemitism. Pseudo-
scientific racism merely intensified older antagonisms, couching them
in a new and in its time more convincing language. Lurking
Italophobia encouraged stereotyping about race, about fecundity,
religious zeal, levels of trustworthiness, proclivity to crime; and
while prejudice was certainly triggered by large scale migration of
Italians to Canada, the anatomy of the tradition of anti-Italian feeling
needs to be studied diachronically and in its contemporary forms.
English-speaking Italophobia may have begun in the Middle Ages,
but the potential for antipathy upon cultural contact between North
Americans and Italians remains an issue today. A poll of Canadians
carried out by the Canadian Institute of Public Opinion on October
30, 1946 showed that 25 per cent of those polled would have wished
to keep Italians out of Canada. If this seems merely to reflect the
shadow of wartime hostilities, it should be pointed out that a similar
poll in February of 1955 showed that only 4.4 per cent of those
interviewed welcomed immigration from Mediterranean area while
30 per cent welcomed north-western Europeans.[7]

J.S. Woodsworth, one of Canada's most famous expounders of
the *Social Gospel* and a founder of the CCF, wrote and spoke
ambivalently about Italian immigration. In his 1909 book, *Strangers
Within Our Gates*, he had the sense to see some of the problems and
confusions in Anglo-Canadian anti-Italian thought. He noted that
chief among the paradoxes in Italophobia was the presence of a
strong counter-tradition of sympathy for the Risorgimento. Modern
Italians, it was assumed, might be, if one rubbed off mildewed
centuries of counter Reformation and Catholicism, of oppression by
corrupt governments and irresponsible nobility, made of the same
human stock as the men of classical Rome and the Renaissance.

Woodsworth remarked on the problems of the stereotypes,

> Soft Italians airs, Italian landscapes, not for a moment do we connect such
> ideas with Italians, Garibaldi and Mazzini, what have they to do with *dirty
> dagos*? *Of few people have we so many unreconciled detached ideas.* Rome, Naples,
> Venice, Milan these cities we know but their citizens are strangers and yet
> there is no people whom we should know better. More Italians are coming to
> the United States than any other class immigrants. In Canada, of all our non-
> English immigrants the Italians stand second. Surely we cannot afford to
> remain ignorant concerning them.[8]

Despite ambivalence about his Italy of his time, Woodsworth
was quite certain he knew what Italians were like, and most other
Anglo-Canadians were also certain. They derived their view of
Italians from deeply embedded English-speaking cultural traditions,
bits of information about Italians passed on like folklore and in
complex relation to English literature itself.

There is no single volume that traces the history of anti-Italian
feeling in the English-speaking world. Salvatore Lagumina's *Wop: a
Documentary History of Anti-Italian Feeling in the United States*,[9] a
compendium of newspaper and other sources of stereotyping of
Italians, is useful but does not involve itself with the deeper question
of cultural disparity between the English-speaking and the Italian
world. The most useful books to draw upon for a method seems to
me to be Perry Curtis's *Anglosaxon and Celt* or Philip Wayne Powell's
*Tree of Hate: Propaganda and Prejudices Affecting U.S. Relations with the
Hispanic World* (New York, 1971) or Winthorp Jordan's classic study
of attitudes towards Blacks, *White Over Black American Attitudes
toward the Negro, 1550-1812*. The latter's definition of Attitudes is
especially appropriate for studying Italophobia.

> I have taken attitudes to be discrete entities susceptible of historical analysis.
> This term seems to me, to possess a desirable combination of precision and
> embrasiveness. It suggests thoughts and feelings (as opposed to generalized
> faiths and beliefs). At the same time it suggests a wide range in consciousness,
> intensity and saliency in the response to the object.[10]

The writer and philosopher Jorge Luis Borges, in an article
entitled *The Argentine Writer and Tradition*, noted that great artists
endow their countrymen with attitudes. The example he used,
almost offhandedly, was "in the same way that the treatment of
Italian themes belongs to the tradition of England through efforts of
Chaucer and Shakespeare."[11]   Undoubtedly, Borges is right, "an

Italian" character and a cast of stock dramatic types appear first in
Chaucer and then in Shakespeare. When Shakespeare has his hero,
Petruchio, remark in *Taming of the Shrew*, "Who doth not know
where hides the wasp his sting in his tail, nay on his tongue," the
poet could have been describing himself, for much of the English
and thus the North American image of Italians as fractious, fickle,
preoccupied with intrigue, foppish, occasionally treacherous and
always quick with the *arma bianca* – a reference to the use of swords
and knives as opposed to firearms – moved from the Elizabethan
stage to the English consciousness. In the settings and dramatist
personae of *Taming of the Shrew, Romeo and Juliet, Othello, Merchant of
Venice* and *The Two Gentlemen of Verona,* Shakespeare created a world
of stock Italians for the English mind. Few of them had the ethnic
precision or impact of his portrayal of a Jew, Shylock, or a black
Othello, but they did affect future English encounters with real
Italians. It is worth noting that Shylock and Othello have been
addressed as sources of bigotry by Jews and Blacks respectively, but
the impact of Iago, a far more villainous figure, does not seem to
bother anyone.

This image of the Italian as different from the reliable, stolid
English peasant or yeoman, or even the faithful English nobility, as
we have suggested, never became as universal or bitter in England
as the "black legend" of the Spaniard but it nonetheless lurked in
English-speaking culture when the most extensive encounter
between myths about the Italian and his reality finally took place in
English-speaking North America. The original overtones of England
good and pure, of Protestant and feudal honour versus
Mediterranean treachery, cruelty, Catholicism and cravenness had
begun to turn into hard racialist definitions by the time of the actual
mass immigration of Italians at the end of the nineteenth century.
But it would be well to remember that the roots of the English usage
"swarthy" lie in blackness,[12] and that even before pseudo-scientific
racism, "English men," in the words of Winthrop Jordan,
"distinguished themselves from other people, they also distinguished
among those different peoples who failed to be English. It seems
almost as if Englishmen possessed a view of other people which
placed the English nation at the center of widening concentric circles
each of which contained people more alien than the one inside of
it."[13] Proto-racism and the cultural tradition provided a distorted
glass through which all those heir to an English-speaking tradition,
whether aware of Shakespeare or not, British in origin or not, could

conjure up a cluster of traits, a little troupe of stereotypes so powerfully drawn that the Italian *artisti, vagabondi*, political exiles, and then the honest peasant immigrants, who came later in the nineteenth century, appeared not simply as real characters in an encounter but as fulfillments or contradictions of some English presentiments about Italians.

For the 25,000 or so Italians who reached North America before the American Civil War or Confederation of Canada, the reception was usually bemused but favourable – the welcoming of a certain sort of civilizing or entertaining asset by a society aware of its own rudeness. Truth to tell though, the stereotypology for that earliest migration of urban civilizers – artists, restaurateurs, music teachers, tenors, fencing masters, language tutors – did nothing to undo some of the imagery derived from Shakespeare's scenes of dandies, seducers, fops and intriguers. Social distance from such frivolous and alien ways was maintained unless the Italian in question succeeded in raising his stock by aristocratic or professional status, much money or learning, protestantism, or recognizably noble birth. Mark Twain had the good folks of Dawson's Landing (an isolated Mississippi valley town) in his *Pudd'nhead Wilson* react to Italian newcomers thus, "Italians. How romantic! Just think, ma – there's never been one in this town and everybody will be dying to see them and they are all ours! Think of that." The Italians in this case were reputedly young noblemen. A New York newspaper expressed the contemporaneous North American image of Italians perfectly when it wrote of every good American having "a soul for Italian music and a heart for Italian freedom."[14]

Two changing circumstances among the immigrants were to end this sort of innocent welcoming of the Italian as a potentially interesting or entertaining *rara avis*. The first was the spilling over of the polemics and violence of the Risorgimento to North America. Garibaldi had been received in North America as a hero after he fled the Habsburg counter-revolution in 1849, however, by the 1850s, when a defrocked Barnabite monk and a Garibaldian – and his enemy Mgr. Bedini, a papal apologist, made their respective tours of New York and Montreal, the political bickering that followed in those cities seems to have troubled the host society more than the question of which cause was the just one. The *New York Herald* did not believe that America should have been made the "theatre of noisy brawls between foreigners" and in Montreal, the loss of life in the Gavazzi Riots, though it involved French Canadians and Irish rather than Italians, discredited neither radicals nor ultramontanes as much as it identified Italian politics with violence.[15]

The stirring events of the Risorgimento that brought Italy and Italians to centre stage also confirmed divisions among North Americans along religious and ideological lines. This was truest in Canada where French Canadians generally were hostile to the Risorgimento and English Canadians, except for a Catholic minority among them, romanticized and identified with the effort to free Italy from native tyrants, the Papacy, and Austrian domination. In the confusion of polemics for and against the Risorgimento. Italophobia fuelled both sides, so that two Canadian systems of hostility to Italians emerged. On the one side, the good Italy for liberal and protestant Canadians was the potential one of Garibaldi, the anti-clerical and democrat; of Mazzini, who told Englishwomen on more than one occasion that Italy might very well convert to Protestantism after unification; of Cavour who broke the powers of the Catholic clergy and copied British and parliamentary traditions. In the view of Anglo-Canadian protestants, the real Italy of Catholicism had become reactionary, ineffectual and unmanly. The Bourbon South, the Papal States and the Austrian territory in the northeast were "inhabited by a race of people who became degenerated by superstition and popish slavery." These were the very people, Abruzzesi, Neapolitans, Calabresi, Sicilians and Furlans who formed the majority of the migrants to Canada several generations later.[16]

While the colonial English Canadian and English view of the Risorgimento tended to coincide, only one of the two competing attitudes towards Italian unity then current in France informed French Canadian opinion. In France itself, strong Jacobin and Bonapartist traditions of sympathy with the Italian people's struggle against oppression dominated public opinion. Pro-Papal and pro-Bourbon elements existed but had no chance of carrying the day. Not so in Quebec, there a devout peasantry and a clergy unencumbered by an alliance of throne and altar believed that the Temporal Power was a *clef voute* of civilization and that Catholicism was a natural ally of Canadian (Quebecois) national identity rather than its enemy. Quebec's Catholic youth organizations were named after Louis Veuillot, author of *Le Parfum de Rome* and *Les Odeurs de Paris*, considered in France an extremist enemy of the Italian cause. Quebeckers learned from the ultramontane press that Italy was full of antichristical revolutionaries, atheist Piedmontese monarchists, and saw Garibaldi's Red Shirts described as "Garibanditti"[17] and "veritables brigands."

An ultramontane penumbra of hostility toward all things Italian national persisted into the 20th century until, not logically, sympathy for the Lateran Pact, Mussolini and Fascism was manifested by some elements. Pierre Savard has pointed out that even the toponymy of the province of Quebec reflects the commitment to the defense of Papal Rome, and that one has to travel west to British Columbia to find anything named after Garibaldi. As late as 1909, the hierarchy of Quebec was able to turn out large crowds to protest the visit of Rome's mayor, Ernesto Nathan, to Canada.[18]

Admittedly, the mayor as English born, a Jew, and a grandmaster of Italian freemasonry provided a fairly large target for ultramontane agitators. It is only fair to add that Italophobia in Latin Quebec never took on a cutting edge of racism as it did in English Canada and the United States. It is equally true that hostility to Italians as disloyal subjects of the Pope and carriers of the virus of *incroyance* was not confined to the French Canadian clergy. In response to a request for help from a Toronto archbishop in 1908, the Redemptorist Provincial, a German American, wrote that "we know that the spiritual betterment of these southern Italians is an almost impossible task... partly on account *of the inborn indifference of this people...* [19].

Whether it was Egerton Ryerson in 1845 reporting from atop Mt. Vesuvius to protestant Upper Canada in the pages of the *Christian Guardian* about the Neapolitan monarchy and the backwardness of its people, or Gustave Drolet, describing French-Canadians who had volunteered as Papal Zouaves as the only trustworthy men in a sea of Italian treachery and paganism, the people of Italy came off badly. One is tempted to believe that a traditional attitude such as Italophobia can draw the confirmations of its reasons for hostility from any historical circumstance.

Even when Garibaldi was perceived as a hero, his virtue was juxtaposed to the assumed vices of the Italian people generally. In such a view Garibaldi was a unique hero who might lead the Italians from their servile ways. Later in Toronto, a city where library copies of G.A. Henry's adulatory *Out With Garibaldi* were as dog-eared as copies of the same author's *With Wolfe to Quebec*, the "hero of two worlds" reputation did not seem to improve the reception for his humbler countrymen. Lithographs of Garibaldi made him frailer, taller, blue-eyed, possessor of a profile worthy of classical Greek sculpture. Toronto Italians – "The bare-armed, bare-necked, sturdy brown fellows" who accompanied each swing of the pick with some

"utterance, an unintelligible muttering or a snatch of song"[20] –
could not fulfil the image of the General's loyal troops, though they
themselves organized Red shirt bands and raised subscriptions for
further Garibaldian adventures. In fact, it seemed easier for people
on either side of the polemic on Italian unification to absorb into
their imagery an Italian backdrop of savagery, fratricide and
fanaticism than to comprehend the real issues.

The more generous view of the awakening of a newly brave,
"almost English," people resisting of tyranny and Austrian
occupation, struggling against superstition and oppressive
Catholicism collided with the reality of Italian immigrants in the
British Isles and North America – itinerant street musicians, *padroni*
of indentured and exploited children, waiters, day labourers, barbers
and a variety of importuning pedlars. A Canadian poem of 1895
hovering between derision, doggerel and respect for the
Risorgimento political tradition was typical. Its contradictory moods
side by side reflect the effort of Canadians to reconcile the baffling
differences between the Italians of the pro-Risorgimento literature
and the menial and apparently frivolous occupations of the *girovaghi*.

> Ice 'a cream – sex banana 'vive cent
> pea nut drhee cent sze glass
> Ah Lady! sez 'Talyman's cheap
> You no tink he will sell, and he vass.
> ...
> Thus night after night as I stroll down the street
> At his cart on the corner the same man I meet,
> At the southwestern corner of Ad'laide and Yonge,
> Where the Saxon falls sweet with the soft Latin tongue.
> ...
> But hard 'tis the trumpet fierce calling afar,
> Its summons is rousing the valleys to war.
> The banners are floating o'er mountain and sea,
> With golden words gleaming and crest of the free
> And brave Garibaldi rides forth in his might
> And Victor Emmanuel leads far in the fight... [21]

In each of the phases of modern Italian migration to North
America, beginning with that of the *girovaghi*, street musicians,
artisans and *profughi*, themes of derision emerged along with those
of outright hostility. This may appear at first to be solely the result
of that disjuncture between the romantic myths Englishmen held
about the Risorgimento and the reality of that early migration. For
it is true enough that the elements of that Italian immigration

provided fuel for cultural misunderstanding and for a dismissal of Italians as morally lax and unmanly by English standards. Moreover the *girovaghi's* transience, apparent insouciance, like that of the gypsies with whom they were sometimes confused, aroused suspicion and led to a tendency to see them as childlike at best, shiftless at worst. If they were not all *vagabondi* who embarrassed Italian officials, many of the migrants were, in terms of their skills and their ways, the *populo minuto* from the peninsula accompanied by a generous sprinkling of the desperate and the unscrupulous.

Henry Mayhew's three volumes on *London Labour and the London Poor* in those years offered ample evidence of a reality in which Italians lived on the line between legitimate street entertaining and importuning mendicancy.[22] Among the Italian entertainers in London whom Mayhew described, were hurdy-gurdy men, Punch and Judy puppeteers, a group of pipers, trainers of dancing dogs, etc., and an ex-soldier who went through the entire Piedmontese arms drill in return for small coins. It is not surprising that public images of these Italian migrants served Italophobia better than those of migrants such as Panizzi who was at about the same time organizing the modern British Museum or Cesnola then founding the Metropolitan Museum of Fine Arts in New York. (Of course there is little remedial value in accounts by filiopietists which emphasize only the notabili, artists, maestri, and ignore the meaner immigration. Ironically such atimic efforts only add to the Italophobe's arsenal). Suffice to say that the virtues of Italians or Italian culture rarely stood recognized without some derisive or hostile implication of their otherness as a function of those concentric circles of distancing from the English norm which Jordan described. French-speaking Quebec, more gently perhaps, shared the same tendency to see things Italian with ambiguity.

> L'italien est aujourd'hui la langue des salons, des arts, du bon ton... La possession de ce magnifique idiome est le complement des etudes, et tout homme et toute femme qui vient passer pour lettre, doit connaître l'italien – but why, because – "c'est la langue des diminutifs, carissants or railleurs, des augmentatifs burlesques... "[23]

We need to understand the use of derision to belittle or undermine the "seriousness" of Italians and Italian culture for what it is. To treat derision lightly, to contrast favourably with harsher traditions of racism, exclusion, imputations of criminality is to miss the functional meaning of belittling and its place in English-speaking

Italophobia. The uses of derision to control both fear and those one fears has been described amply by those who study racism or the psychology of the colonial relationship between masters and slaves. The arrival of unskilled foreigners creates situations analogous to the colonial confrontation. Laughing at "Little Tony" the peanut vendor, endowing him with a simple and sunny soul, little ambition, and childlike ways, describing him in diminutives is simply the Italophobes way of rendering him impotent, reducing him the way the term "boy" reduced slaves and colonials. It is also of course the obverse of "Big Tony", the padrone, the strikebreaker or anarchist, the womanizer, the impassioned knife-wielder – the habitual lawbreaker. Both Tonys are projections made by the English-speaking host society upon the powerless, yet threatening because less inhibited, Italian migrant, projections very much of the sort Prospero made on Ariel and Caliban in Shakespeare's *Tempest*.[24] The Italian immigrant male is at once the good primitive Ariel, laughing, happy, childlike, submissive, and the bad one, Caliban, rebellious and lecherous. Both projections upon the Italian see him as inferior to the English in his comprehension and because of his tendency to act instinctually.

Throughout the remainder of this essay, the reader will see the two Prospero-like responses of the North American host society for controlling the "stranger in their midst," the Italian migrant. The responses arise in a series of parallel readings of encounters. It seems almost as if the derisive mode, that which treats the Italian as frivolous but harmless, is used when the host society feels little fear and only a moderate need for distance; the more openly hostile mode of Italophobia which sees the migrant as instinctual, of a lower order, and dangerous emerges when the perceived threat of "inundation," economic competition, alien social and cultural impact is greatest. In such a schema then a form of belittling and a form of open hostility/fear exists among English-speakers at each stage of Italian immigration. The response to the early wave of migration of artisans, *artisti*, fruit peddlers, and street people was generally of the derisive sort. The Italians at best brought civilities and urban refinements to North American life, at worst they were simply pesky and perhaps lacking moral standards, a problem more for social gospel preachers and city officials than for immigration, criminal justice, or labour legislation. The Italians, according to a Toronto turn of the century account,... "always will remain a contented pleasure seeker, with more thought for his Chianti and snatch of song than for all the sanitation sermons of the universe."[25] The undermining of the Italian immigrant's consequence as a person, his manhood, in English-speaking conventional wisdom, folklore, print and even graphic arts may not seem a significant aspect of Italophobia but once sensitive to this variety of inter-ethnic hostility, few readers will fail to begin to notice its systematic and pervasive character.

The harmless primitive, Ariel, was represented best by "Little Tony" selling fruit or popcorn, or digging ditches. In the popular graphics of the time – sheet music covers, trade cards, book and magazine illustrations – a diminutive man with black fedora, black mustaches, bright kerchief is shown arranging fruit, selling peanuts or ice cream, or playing a street organ. Usually there is a monkey nearby. Invariably whether through T.A. Daly's popular dialect poetry, song titles such as "Guiseppe Da Barber", "My Mariutch, She Come Back to Me", or "Mr. Pagliatch" – none written by Italians – Ariel typically cannot achieve a serious use of his own culture or that of his new masters. This use of pseudo-dialect "to poke fun," actually to reduce to proper status, by the English-speaking host had been used as extensively with Irish maids, Black slaves, and Jewish peddlers in North American popular culture. J.M. Gibbon, writing sympathetically of Italian immigrants in his *Canadian Mosaic. The Making of a Northern Nation* could not resist.

> We work little bit, then we take the leisure. We love very much the music, art, poetry. We love the poetical life – poetry today, and tomorrow we take what's coming with the good patience... Verdi, we adore him... He speak the voice of the people, in the big romantic utterance, he speak fearless like a man, he express our emotions by the great genius.[26]

The condescension of the mandatory broken English demonstrates that themes of a propensity for frivolity for fondness for grandiloquence and inconsequence which formed part of the traditional Italophobia still were belittling when used apparently sympathetically.

Alfred Fitzpatrick's Handbook for New Canadians,[27] a publication of the populist Frontier College, which tried to bring literacy to immigrant and isolated labour throughout Canada, used Italian motifs in several of its language lessons. The two, one entitled the "Fruit Peddler" and the second "At The Market," left little doubt where Italians as "assistant Canadians" were expected to be niched in the national life. The illustration of Mr. Conti, the peddler, included the usual stereotypical clothing and hat. Such a publication seems to represent the English-speaking "caretakers" and teachers urge to include a species of Italophobia in the very processes of acculturation for other immigrants.

Harmless primitives such as Mr. Conti were represented by several recurrent stereotypes about the Italian psyche, each of which implied their childlike processes of thought and values. The immigrants were most often described as
- of sunny and easy-going disposition,
- of having a special affinity for music, like Blacks having natural rhythm one assumes, and
- of having innately high aesthetic standards, albeit in this discourse more often evidenced in piling up fruit artistically in shop windows than in painting masterpieces or building palazzi.

A few examples for the portrayal of these innate "Italian" qualities, it was assumed these Ariels brought to Canada will suffice. The first is drawn from an advertising card for coffee; appropriate illustration accompanied the text, and the cards had wide distribution, especially among children.

> They are poor but happy, careless, lighthearted, impulsive, impetuous, affectionate, sanguine, emotional, languorous and generous. Pomp and circumstance dazzle them. Ribbons gewgaws and bright colours enslave their fancy.

> Music is to the Italians as the breath of their nostril's even their children evoke from the violin, the harp and the flute melody to thrill the most unsentimental, and their voices in song are pathetic and sweet. Who could believe that owing to this wonderful susceptibility to music by Italian children, a society was formed, known as the Padrone for the purpose of teaching children music and then making mendicant of them.[28]

As late as 1927, the United Church Record of Toronto referred to the Italians "sunniness of nature and love of art and music"[29] as if these were inevitable traits, and the only significant ones, of everyone in the ethnic group. Of course, love of music and art, and sunny dispositions suggested insouciance and perhaps even laziness and social irresponsibility to the English-speaking host society. The Italians of Toronto were described in a 1910 newspaper editorial in which derision masqueraded as sympathy.

> The multitude of little fruit stores in Toronto suggests that may Italians have here attained the summit of their hopes. Only to look into the cheery faces of

some of the vendors of popcorn and peanuts who perambulate our streets...
confirms this pleasing suspicion.[30]

Ontario's authorized public school geography in the late 19th
century included these nuggets of information. "Many of the people
of Italy are skilful in painting and sculpture; and are fond of music."
"Nearly all of our street *organ grinders* are the music-loving Italians... "[31]
Even when Canadian observers tried to express appreciation of
the Italian's skills, a patronizing tone not unlike that of a master
well-pleased with his servant's talent crept in. For example,

The artistically decorated windows of our fruit stores bear witness to his
innate love of colour and orderly adornment.[32]

They... work in fruit or small grocery stores. The majority are illiterate, but
very bright and ambitious. They have artistic temperaments, are naturally very
religious.[33]

Edmund Bradwin whose classic study of railway navvies in the
1920s, *The Bunkhouse Man*, contained no conscious anti-Italianism,
was among the few Canadians in his appreciation of Italian workers
to avoid the usual tone of condescension.

One needs only a superficial acquaintance with men of the frontier work to
note at times the love of the aesthetic that lingers with many Italian labourers.
Even while mucking, or employed at the heavy tasks that seemingly
woulddemean culture, there are not wanting to the observer evidence of
genuine refinement among these men. It is the Italian worker rather that the
Greek today who is prone to blend the grace of Athens with the stern mind
of Sparta.[34]

If the tradition of derision had as its purpose the reaffirmation
of Italian males in Canada as Ariels, innocent, good natured, and
unthreatening as strangers, the picture of their mates, like that of
negresses and native women of their time, were also pictured as
rather fickle, if harmless, children of nature, especially by those in
settlement houses and missions who saw them as targets for
civilizing much like their primitive sisters in Asia or the British
Empire. "Much has been accomplished in the years in the way of
creating and fostering a spirit of responsibility towards the House,"
observed a Toronto social worker who nonetheless found Italian
women still to be "volatile and carefree... inclined to take where she
can without the reciprocal giving."[35] An account of one
Neighbourhood House has the unmistakable rhythms of racialism as

in Vachel Lindsay's the Congo: "Fat black bucks in a wine barrel room. Barrel house kings with feet unstable, sagged and reeled and pounded on the table."

> One of the Neighbourhood workers enters and places an Italian record on the gramophone. The golden needle is lowered, the disc spins around. It is the famous tarantella, Italy's beloved dance. At once, the enchanted song stirs the pulse of the listeners and the rise. Joyously they interpret the naive spirit of the dance as they move to the throb of the rhythm. Each dancer holds a tiny tambourine between thumb and finger and with exhilarating abandon snaps off the lilting measures as they pass "Forgotten are life's handicaps."[36]

Obviously the English-speaking host society had little to fear from the good-natured and childlike little people, but then there was Caliban with naivete turned to deception and instinctual violence. The Presbyterian Record saw both the good and the bad primitive in the Italian immigrants, when it wrote that they "are physically... strong but low in mentality; they are warm-hearted, kind and grateful, but also hot-blooded and given to fighting and violent crimes... They present problems of overcrowding, ill health intemperance, Sabbath desecration, political impurity..."[37] From the middle to the end of the Nineteenth Century, Italophobia fed on both derision of the migrant Italians outside of Italy and an especially filtered view of the political, religious, and social violence convulsing Italy during the Risorgimento and the civil war called Il Brigantaggio which followed it.

During the Risorgimento and the contemporaneous migration, English-speakers absorbed a number of Italian words into their language. They borrowed the words in order to help bear the freight of their stereotypes of Italians, but such words, as they passed into general usage, contributed on their own to an underlying identification of things objectionable with things Italian. One of the early borrowings, *ruffiano*, reflected initially English protestant and liberal disapproval of royalism and religious extremism in southern Italy. Ruffian carried both its Neapolitan dialect meaning of pimp and was a convenient homophone for the English word "rough" as well as a designation for the men of the Army of the Holy Faith which Cardinal Ruffo, primate of the Kingdom of the Two Sicilies, had organized to drive the native Jacobins and their French allies from the land during the Napoleonic Wars. The ruffian, has, by the 20th century, lost its specific ally, Italian flavour in English but, a century ago, it, like the words brigand and bandit, did as much as

the modern use and abuse of the term *mafia* to identify southern
Italians with violence, blood feud, civil disorder, and obscurantism.
(It is unclear to me whether it strengthens or weakens a case for the
existence of a subterranean stream of Italophobia that the Oxford
English Dictionary continues to include *banditi*, the Italian form, as
an acceptable English plural for bandit).

Lurid tales of *banditi* existed in most English travel accounts of
Italy, and the imagery was powerful enough that English writers
found it an effective device to apply the term to the other ethnic
types that they found repugnant. The Reverand Joseph Wolff
described his Muslim captivity thus "in the garden of the infamous
nayeb, Abdul Samut Khan, surrounded by his *banditti*..." It seems
a gratuitous anti-Italianism, surely there is a more apt term to
describe Muslim fanatics or Bokhara cutthroats. James Fenimore
Cooper described Mohawk warriors as "dark and stealthy banditti."
One begins to understand those Italian Americans who flinch on
hearing or reading about Chinese mafias, Jewish mafias, political
mafias, literary mafias. Their plaint may be a bit tiresome, but they
have glimpsed and live with a special problem, the symptom of an
underlying malaise. Italian catchwords for the criminal or antisocial
capture the English-speaking imagination, and it is very troubling
that even when the bigotry is directed at another group, the
epitomizing term is borrowed from the lexicon of Italophobia. The
apparent ability of such words to carry prejudice, to sell movies and
pulp fiction parallels the power of blackness as imagery in fiction.

One reformist observer of the padrone system in New York
evoked the image of a white slave trade and described young
children "as carrying ponderous harps for old ruffians late at night."
Describing a padrone as a ruffian is a case of the English language's
ability to practice anti-Italian overkill. In a sense then every Italian
migrant to English-speaking lands faced not just Italophobia, not just
nasty nicknames, but also this undercurrent of hostility evoked by
a series of words which titillate the English-speakers that are its
symptoms. At one time or other, each of the following words has
served those, who either consciously or because they inherited
without much reflection an English-speaking tradition of hostility to
Italians, link the ethnic group with asocial behaviour and criminality.
*Padrone, ruffiano, bordello, banditi, brigante, vendetta, stiletto, omertà,
mano nera, Camorra, Mafia* and *Cosa Nostra* are merely the most
obvious.

In the Canadian Immigration Act of 1919 only one foreign word (italicized) appears: "No immigrant shall bring into Canada, any pistol, sheath knife, dagger, *stiletto*, or other offensive weapon that can be concealed upon the person."

The presence of the word stiletto, even though knife or dagger would seem to be acceptable English synonyms, may be as innocent as the discussion which broke out over illegal permit entries in a Canadian parliamentary committee on Immigrations, the tone of which is reflected in an honourable member's question "How do you protect yourself or the department. Suppose somebody makes an application for say, Mr. Spaghetti to come into Canada; how do you know whether it is Mr. Spaghetti that came in or Mr. Vermicelli... "[38] The latter example is surely harmless, if yet symptomatic, but behind the words associated with crime and violence is their obvious power to move the imagination and in that lies something deeper and pernicious. Long before Kefauver mispronounced Mafia to rapt audiences, other American officials had found the magic in Italian words for describing deviance and crime. For example in the 1880s, the image of the padrone, exploiters of immigrant children as beggars, shills, street musicians, and bootblacks proved so powerful that officials used the word to describe leaders of Italian migrant labour gangs, immigrant bankers and travel agents in Little Italies. For the Senate's Industrial Commission of 1900 and the Dillingham Commission of Immigration in 1911, padrone came to include the Greek and Lebanese system of serial family sponsorship in migration and even the Japanese foremen who headed Asian work camps in the West. The word Padrone did for immigration restrictionists what Mafia does for those who cannot conceive of members of the Italian ethnic group succeeding in America without clannish and conspiratorial criminal help.

So far we have been describing attitudes of that diffuse yet continually effective type that Winthrop Jordan sees as the basis of the study of intercultural prejudice. From the 1880s to the 1920s two important things happened to give a cutting edge to the cultural hostilities. First there was a change in the kind of migrant who arrived in North America after 1885. There were far fewer street entertainers and far more labourers, far fewer children and women and more bachelor men, more southerners than northerners. This new immigrant profile triggered new forms of Italophobia which drew sustenance from job competition, sexual fantasy and male jealousies, and increased awareness of somatic distinction between the migrants and the old stock in North America. It is difficult to know how these changes in the type of Italian newcomers after 1885 would have affected the view held of Italians as newcomers to North America if it had not coincided with the embracing in much of western Europe and North America of the concept of race as an explanation of human behaviour and of the history of nations. Italian mass migration also coincided with the stagnation or decline of the old Latin Catholic Spanish and Portuguese commercial empires, the Italian defeat at Adua, and the rise of the so-called Teutonic nations – Germany, England, and the United States and "Frankish" or "Norman" France to hegemony in the world. In some sense, the fact that Italians had to come to other people's empires to find livelihood and the way they were treated there provided many English-speaking observers with a confirmation of the belief in a hierarchy of racial talent in the world. Corradini's assertion, which at first appears only to be nationalist rhetoric that Italian mass migration and failed colonialism amounted to "un antimperialismo della servitu" has the value of reminding us of the international racialist context which confirmed Italophobia or at least a view of the Italians as inferior among North Americans.

By the 1890s sojourning southern Italian male labourers were often viewed as brutish lumpen-proletariat, not just because of the way in which North American capital inserted them into its economy but also because that conformed to the view of Mediterranean men held by some among the host society. In the United States South, this racialism took the extreme form of treating Italian immigrants as part of the black underclass. A candidate for Governor of Mississippi, the Hon. Jeff Truly, harangued an election crowd with the words "I am opposed to an inferior race. The Italian immigration scheme does not settle the labour question; Italians are a threat and a danger to our racial, industrial, and commercial supremacy."[39] Efforts were made to keep Italian children out of white schools in parts of the South and the fact that more Sicilians than any other group of Euro-ethnic immigrants were lynched in America suggests that something akin to colour racism was at work. Later with all the certainty of a pseudo-scientific report, the 1911 Dillingham Commission of the United States Senate asserted the importance of Negroid admixtures in the Neapolitan and Sicilian populations, not just as an explanation of appearance but also of behaviour and proclivities.[40] Racism in North America, especially in Canada, was a much more involved phenomena than simply measuring peoples' humanity by their distance from blackness. In fact, Canada and the industrial northeastern United States formed part of an Atlantic intellectual community whose members more and more after 1870 subscribed to a belief in an elaborately constructed hierarchy of peoples, a hierarchy in which Italians, especially south Italians, did not fare well.

Racial attitudes crossed English-speaking borders, and J.S. Woodsworth was right when he wrote that the problems of immigration were "essentially the same for the United States and Canada." As if to prove it, *Strangers Within Our Gate* sported an almost entirely American bibliography. When the medical profession threw its weight behind racial exclusion it repeated Woodsworths point, "Change the word American to Canadian and it applies to this side of the line as well as the other."[41]

With the use of the shibboleth assimilable, Canadian writers had by the turn of the century clearly defined the desirable immigrants to Canada. Most Italians were not among them and those few who were Piedmontese, Lombards and Venetians achieved desirability by a sleight of hand of racial pseudo-science which described them as teutonic. The Canada that these writers had in mind would in the words of the Foreward of the First volume to use the now common multicultural imagery of the mosaic, Kate Foster's *Our Canadian Mosaic* (1926) did not encourage Italian immigration.

> "The nation defends itself against armed invasion. Is there a possible national peril from peaceful invasion by immigrants with lower standards and ideals? How then shall we guard the frontiers? In the present aspect of the question there seems to be a pretty general consensus of opinion, that only the readily assimilable races should be admitted. This would practically limit admission to the Anglo-Saxon, Teutonic, Scandinavian and more northern Celtic races."[42]

The hierarchy of racial acceptability (assimilability) is easy enough to discern as writer after writer lamented the decline of British immigrants, of "Teutonic people" men from the northern part of Europe." In the Canadian Annual Review of 1902, Castell Hopkins put the matter with utmost clarity – Many Canadians he said wished to prevent aliens from settling in Canada.

> By this term I do not intend to include people from the United States or the northern countries of Europe, more or less allied to our own race by common descent and by characteristics similar to our own; but to the large class of immigrants included among Chinese, Japanese, Hindus, the people of the southern races of Europe, and those which are openly classified as

"undesirables" of whatever nationality then our own and those of Teutonic stock.[43]

Even those Canadians confident enough in the power of environment and the Anglo-Canadian way to receive and assimilate and who preached a Canadian melting pot were loathe to include Italians.

Out of breeds diverse in traditions, in ideals, in speech in manner of life, Saxon and Slav, Teuton, Celt and Gaul, one people is being made. The blood strains of the great races will mingle in the blood of a race greater than the greatest of them all.[44]

Although none of the guardians of the gate acknowledged the possibility of Italians per se as good immigrants for Canada, there was a tradition of distinguishing between immigrants from the north and the south which predated the pseudo-scientific attribution of "teutonism" to North Italians. When Dr. Bryce, Canada's chief Medical Inspector of Immigration wrote to Smart, the Superintendent of Immigration, to explain that he had found the Tuscans in Toronto "to be more of the German race than any other,"[45] he was continuing a distinction established when Canada first sought immigrants abroad. Dr. Bryce found it necessary to base his distinction on the racialist scientific categories of his time but the Canadian preference for north Italians as immigrants has persisted until our time.

The correspondence of the Commissioner of Immigration to the Acting Commissioner of Immigration Overseas Service in October 1949 is even more telling for what it says both of the attitude and the pedigree of the attitude among Canadian officials – in this case, Colonel Laval Fortier –

My tour of Italy confirms a view I have heard expressed in Ottawa when discussing Italian immigration. Generally speaking, the Italian from the south is not the type of migrant we are looking for in Canada. His standard of living, his way of working, even his civilization seems so different that I doubt if Italians from the south could ever become an asset to our country.[46]

The Colonel went on, that from among the people of northern Italy, one could select, "a much better type of migrant and migrants who could fit into our way of living, our way of thinking, our way of working." Rumours persisted throughout the 1950s that Canadian authorities for much the same reasons were loathed to extend consular services south of Rome or bring regular airline service to anywhere but Milan. So "good" Italians were good because they were Teutonic and less welcome dark Mediterranean, southern Italians were not good because, following the United States restrictionists, who borrowed from Italian ethnology, they were inferior stock infected with African blood. As race became the explanation of all things, environment, assimilability, and individual attitudes became irrevelant.

Theories about race provided blanket explanations about assimilability and scientific justifications for exclusion of "certain classes" of people. Such people, if they succeeded in settling in Canada, often carried with them the rage or self-doubt of those who have been treated as unfit or unwelcome. The definition of the latter had gone far beyond physical type. The study of race and its meaning for peopling the United States and Canada hovered between a new moral science and the social engineering as public policy of later years. Quoting the Italian sociologist Niceforo, the U.S. Immigration Commission's 1911 Dictionary of Races claimed that the two ethnic groups – North and South Italians – "differ as radically in psychic characters as they do in physical."[47] The report suggested that the genetic tendency of the South Italian was to be "excitable, impulsive, highly imaginative, unpracticable; as an individualist having little adaptability to high organized society. The North Italian, on the other hand, is pictured as cool, deliberate, patient, practical and capable of great progress in the political and social organization of modern civilization." In a phrase, the latter was a perfect proto-Upper Canadian.

Both Italian authorities and North American restrictionists observed the remarkable difference between the Italian experience in South America and in English-speaking North America, but rather than suggest that real conditions such as less Italophobia, the tendency of immigrants to settle rather than sojourn, Latin affinities between host country and immigrants, etc., might explain the remarkable higher level of economic success and acculturation of Italians in Brazil and Argentina, the Dictionary's experts explained all difference by emphasizing the superiority of the Italian stock that went there as opposed to those going in the United States.

> The North Italian is an educated, skilled artisan, coming from a manufacturing section and largely from the cities. He is teutonic in blood and appearance. The South Italian is an illiterate peasant from the great landed estates, with wages less than one-third his northern compatriot. He descends with less mixture from the ancient inhabitants of Italy. Unhappily for us, the North Italians do not come to the United States in considerable numbers, but they

betake themselves to Argentina, Uruguay, and Brazil in about the same numbers as the South Italians come to us. It is estimated that in those three countries there are 3,000,000 Italians in a total population of 23,000,000 and they are mainly derived from the north of Italy. Surrounded by the unenterprising Spanish and Portuguese, they have shown themselves to be the industrial leaders of the country. Some of the chief buildings, banks, flour mills, textile mills, and a majority of the wheat farms of Argentina belong to Italians. They are one-third of the population of Buenos Aires and own one-half of the commercial capital of that city. They become lawyers, engineers, members of parliament, and an Italian by descent has been president of the Republic of Argentina, while other Italians, have been ministers of war and education. While these North Italians, with their enterprise, intelligence, and varied capacities, go to South America, we receive the South Italians, who are nearly the most illiterate of all immigrants at the present time, the most subservient to superiors, the lowest in their standards of living, and at the same time the most industrious and thrifty of all common labourers.

Ironically American, and by direct borrowing Canadian, hostile views on the Italians in their midst, although shaped partly by encounter and early traditions of Italophobia, derived much of their precision and force from Italian intellectuals.

In Italy after unification, victorious positivism in the universities encouraged attempts to make sociology, anthropology and criminology into exact sciences. One result was much measurement and theorizing about the new nation-state's population. Some southern critics of both Piedmontese hegemony and positivism rather aptly compared the vogue with the pseudo-sciences of the white man's burden as it emerged as justificatory colonialist theories for European overseas imperialism. The nasty North Italian jest that "Africa begins twenty miles south of Rome" seemed to inform the thought of the Italian academy discourse even when the scholars were themselves of southern origin. It was in the writings of the father of the new "scuola antropologica criminale" that American restrictionists found the most telling arguments against Italian immigration. Ironically as the new criminology, especially the work of Lombroso, found international acceptance, the image of Italian criminality spread abroad. From the outset, racial hostility to Italians went hand and hand with theories of their being regions of endemic criminality of genetically determined criminal human stock. When Niceforo wrote about crime in the South Sardinia actually – *La Delinquenza in Sardegna* (Palermo, 1897) – he described "zone delinquenti" criminal zones and attributed their nature to racial strains including, for example, such non-scientific nonsense as the presence of "molto sangue vanitoso spagnuolo."

Military conscription in the new Italy gave the urban and northern ruling class a chance to have its scientists study and explain the ways of the masses of southern rural people who had been incorporated in Italy after 1860. Military recruits were weighed, measured, judged, and usually found wanting. For some of the positivist scientists and Sabaudian officer corps, fear and revolution of southern rural masses transmogrified into elaborate theories about the relationship between cranial index, criminality, and *paese*. Blaming *delinquenza* on poverty, illiteracy, or social and political oppression was simply not as convenient or absolute as falling back on race and heredity for explanations. Such explanations obviated the need for social reform in Italy just as they papered over the need for urban and labour reform in North America.

The scientism, specious argument, and supporting detail available for those in North America who wished to reinforce their Italophobia with racialist proofs was massive. Rodolfo Livi's *Anthropometria militare* (Roma 1891) was typical of the genre. The work offered statistics on every physical detail about Italy's conscripts down to "piccolezza e grandezza della bocca"; such statistical analysis was always broken down by region and *paese* and became ammunition in the slurring of rural southerners. Niceforo's *zone delinquenti*, Lombrosos's regions where the criminal type did not differ physically from the general populace, cephalic indices (rapporti tra indice cefalico e civiltà) which predicted the homicidal tendencies of the dolichocephalic type were all to be found, to no one's surprise on the backward island of Sardinia or in the recently conquered areas of the South of Italy, especially Calabria, the Neapolitan Campagna, and Sicily. It seemed the new criminology and sociology in Italy were remarkably pliable exact sciences. What began as literature of class and regional prejudice in Italy became a vehicle of ethnic prejudice and attempts to define and exclude undesirables in North America. The presence of such themes in Italy neither fully explains nor justifies bigotry in the New World, and if this "mismeasuring of man" as Stephen Gould has called it reinforced the view of Canadian Italophobes at the turn of the century, the encounter itself led to emphasis on other themes – of inundation, of unfair labour competition and of crime.[48]

For the many who saw the purported tendencies to crime and inferiority of intelligence as immutable racial facts, what we might today call static ethnic essence rather than negotiable ethnoculture, then the problem of controlling immigrant numbers became paramount.

The problem as J.S. Woodsworth in the early 1900s saw it was one of both quality and potential quantity. It was that masses of South Italians were arriving annually in North America – the second largest group of immigrants per year in Canada – and their social, cultural economic – and genetic – impact could not be calculated or predicted. And thus the problem of quantity and of racial quality merged in the speech. "Surely if we look to the importance of our gain, our stock, our cows and horses, it is high time we look after our human stock – and the men and women who are to be the citizens of tomorrow." The Italian government knew that Woodsworth's view had impact. One of the *Bollettini* of the Commissariat of Emigration in Rome had devoted space to a long review of *Strangers Within Our Gates*.[49] In that volume, Woodsworth had written. "In Canada, of all our non-English immigrants the Italians stand second. Surely we cannot afford to remain ignorant concerning them."

Annual large scale South Italian migration to Canada – to settle or to sojourn – was but the shadow of the nemesis for those who held racialist views. The real problem with South Italians was that they, like Chinese and Japanese immigrants and unlike most of the other European undesirable peoples, were so numerous in their homeland. By 1900 there were more Irish in America (about 5,000,000) than in Ireland but even though Italians annually led the list of non-English speaking immigrants there were more than 35,000,000 with apparently undiminished fecundity back in Italy. "The immense capacity of the Italian race to populate other parts of the earth is shown by the fact that they outnumber the Spanish race in Spanish Argentina and the Portuguese race in Brazil, a "Portuguese country." The lesson or omen for English-speaking countries was obvious. The Italians could continue to colonize North American cities long after the other "new" or "undesirable" races, "then contributing largely to the immigrant tide receded. For after all there were in the world only 8,000,000 Jews, 2,250,000 Slovaks, and 3,500,000 in the Croatian-Slovenian group... "

Once Asian immigrants were excluded by law or prohibitive head taxes from entering North America, only Italians had the numbers to pose a threat to Anglo-saxon cultural and genetic domination of Canada. Borrowing upon a post-Darwinian eugenic fear which suggested that the fittest for survival might not be Canada's old stock, social evangelists warned that immigrants "being inferior and having no appearances to keep up, propagate like fish of the sea," and that "just as the human body cannot with safety accept food any faster than it can assimilate nourishment, so a nation cannot without great peril receive a mass of foreign population that over-taxes its powers of assimilation."[50] Such hostile observers saw Canada's cities as growing too rapidly and the alien presence in them, mainly Italians, Jews and Slavs, as constituting a pathology. "Every large city on the continent has its four-fold problem of the slum, the saloons, the foreign colonies, and the districts of vice...".[51] Among such pathological "foreign colonies," Little Italies followed only Jewish ghettoes in their ubiquity and visibility in Canada, by World War I. Even though the avowed policy of Canada's Ministry of the Interior after 1901 was "to promote the immigration of farmers and farm labourers" and even though the Minister had informed his Deputy that "no steps are to be taken to assist or encourage Italian immigration to Canada,"[52] congested Italian neighbourhoods sprang up, not just in Toronto and Montreal, but at railheads, mining camps and little industrial towns across the country. It was in fact the presence of sojourning Italian workers, usually organized in mobile labour force gangs answerable to a subcontractor or labour boss (padrone) which provided Italophobia and the fuel it needed until related themes of criminality caught public attention.

There was no reason to expect that a native labour force would look at with equanimity on efforts by capitalist employers to import cheaper, more supine, and manipulable workers. What is distressing is the way in which themes borrowed from the new racism and Italophobia seemed to usurp those of class consciousness and the search for solidarity in the encounter with the Italian migrants who came to Canada at the turn of the century. At the same time, Canadian officials, not quite comfortably reflecting the hegemonic power of the railways, lumbering and mining interests, condemned the importation of Italian labour on ethnic grounds but condoned it as an economic necessity. Describing Italian labourers passing through Winnipeg in 1901 as "quite worthless as settlers, and having ruined to a large extent the prosperity of Boston, Mass.," the Immigration commissioner there added that it was unfortunate that they were brought in "by the railway company for any kind of work at all except it be work in the coal mines."[53]

A leit-motif of the times, among both labour and management – and a painful memory for all Italian sojourners who worked in Canada – asserted the existence of two kinds of work opportunity in Canada, not accidentally given the racism which pervaded North

American life, described as work for "white" labour and work which required "black" labour. Italians, Macedonians, Greeks, and Asians who did "black labour" – that is work so dangerous, dirty, underpaid, unregulated, or noxious that no northwest European immigrant or old stock Canadian would take it, or be directed to it – were seen as confirming their racial inferiority and low standards for doing so. They were of course also seen as tools of capitalism, used to undermine labour's position. In a sense this was a new stage of Italophobia, one more salient in Canada because of the lack of large Black and Hispanic underclasses than in the Unites States. Virulence toward Italians, even when it arose from real concern or abuses in the work place, carried a freight of ethnocentrism and outright Italophobia which has not vanished completely, even from the writing of labour history in our time. Italophobia fed on the fact that the established work force in Canada was mainly of northwest European origin and infected with the new racialist thought. (Although friction arose between Italian migrants and French Canadian workers, as well as with immigrant Jews, that inter-ethnic tension remained focused on economic issues and not those of race).

> Italians, Slovaks, Poles and other immigrants of eastern Europe, together with the Russian Jews, have struck hard blows since 1880 at the standard of comfort of the American workmen. They have made New York City a great reservoir for the pipelines that run to the misery pools of Europe,[54]

wrote the American historian, Frederick Jackson Turner in the Chicago Record-Herald in 1901. Several years before that, Canadian artisans had denounced Italians as unfair competitors before the Royal Commission on Capital and Labour. The tone of the denunciations suggested a substructure of ethnic rather than class hostility.

A.   Tailors are, however, beginning to dispense with workshops and are allowing tailors to take work home.
Q.   Then the work is being done outside?
A.   Yes.
Q.   Are there any Italians doing labouring work?
A.   They take the work home, and they run what are known as sweating shops. They are making quite a pile of money and have a few slaves under them in the shape of women.
Q.   Do they work cheaper than *regular men*?
A.   They do the work cheaper, and they get women to do the work cheaper still.[55]

The refrain of Italians as enslaved by bosses, as unfair competition for native labourers and artisans, as a device of capitalism to keep the larger workforce in thrall was heard as early as the United States Ford Commission hearings on indenture, peonage, and padrone systems in 1880s, but that theme became an especially acute adjunct to Italophobia in Canada in the 1900s. Irish labourers had acted violently against new Italian workers on the Welland canal system in the 1870s. Although much of the Italophobic idiom was borrowed from American nativism and the English-speaking tradition, the intensity and extent of the image of the Italian as scab, blackleg strikebreaker (and always ironically as anarchist) in Canada's isolated mining, lumbering, smeltering, and railroad towns suggests that some true typologies greatly reinforced the prevalent stereotype.

Writing about Chinese exclusion in the 1920s, R.D. MacKenzie observed that "as a region passes from a pioneer to a settled condition, the human material that was once of value becomes a source of annoyance and trouble."[56] Italians had been drawn to Canada by a species of guest worker systems which meshed neatly with their own sojourning tactics. They were never welcome except to the large employers who saw them as a good and malleable working class.

When they spoke of their imported Ariels, the employers' joy at finding pliant assistant Canadians spilled over.

> The Italian is a good navvy. He obeys the orders of the boss, he is not anxious to go on strike, as he counts that any increase in wages would in the short period he intends to remain in the country not more than reimburse him for the wages lost while the strike is on.[57]

A Canadian railways representative told the Royal Commission on Fraudulent Labour Practices in 1904 that Italians were the best workers for the remote track sites. They were, he said, as hard working as the Scandinavians but while the latter usually bought land and settled after a season of track work, Italians remained a mobile work force of men who "came out here for gain and do not assimilate with the country." They were also, he said, the only "class of labour we can employ in Canada who can live for a year on the wages they earn in six months." Thinking about that testimony, the significance of MacKenzie's point for the study of prejudice emerges. Heedlessly wrapped in the security of their sojourning mentality and *padroni* or *paesani*-based networks, Italians offered

Canadian capitalism the transient and supine work gangs they wanted. They were cheerful and vociferous among themselves but taciturn and oblique with outsiders, including non-Italian labour organizers. They were capable of such prodigious hard work and displays of stamina that they inadvertently helped to subvert efforts at worker control of the job site. All those things which made them attractive to big business made their neighbours, especially in the work force, distrust them. As the monarchs of Europe had once used Jews as bankers and businessmen to achieve their state and capitalist aims, so Canadian big business used foreign navvy, especially the Italian, to accomplish their objectives, free of hinderance from the native population. As with those earlier "symbolic strangers," the Italian migrant labour served as scapegoats. Like the Jews, the sojourning Italians had the classic qualities of aliens, of intruding outsiders. Their garb, language, physiognomies, apparently transient ways, the true pathology of communities made up mainly of young males without women of their own kind, made them fearsome and reinvigorated Italophobia. For, if big business saw them as countless obliging Ariels, the common people and caretakers of the circumambient Canadian society increasingly glimpsed Caliban in their behaviour.

The Italian migrant Calibans were endowed in the press and in popular mythology with all the qualities of the bad native in the colonial world. They were portrayed as dirty and shiftless, as closer to man's raw animal nature, and finally they were described as unpredictably dangerous. They might strike out violently or be swayed by leader of the moment in ways which northwest European man would not. These views of the migrants led with logic of Italophobia to the increasing identification of Italians with criminality in the public mind. In Toronto, social evangelists, muckraking newspaper editors, and the city health inspectors agreed that the Italian section of the city was an infectious running sore that could spread. Although much of the plaint was couched in the languages of urban social pathologies, the underlying assumption of ethnocultural inferiority was there. They were put baldly enough by the anti-alien labour newspaper, *Jack Canuck*.

> The Anglosaxon comes here to make a home for himself and family. His ambition is to have a home of his own and when he gets it, however humble, his spare time is largely devoted to improving the same. Not so the Italian. He is content to PIG IN with a crowd of others and live under conditions which an Anglosaxon would be ashamed of. The Anglosaxon spends his money

where he earns it. The Italian spends hardly enough for the necessities of life and saves all he can so that he will be able to return to Italy and retire. The Italians are taking money out of the country all the time and giving little in return for it.[58]

It should be clear from reading *Jack Canuck* that the qualities of one man's Ariel were those of another man's Caliban. Italians were condemned because they came, and further condemned for not behaving as if they intended to stay. The editor of *Jack Canuck*, for all his pro-labour stance, was not sufficiently rigorous in his critique of capitalism, and so he attacked the victims of the guest worker system rather than its creators.

Clear out the Italians and introduce a manlier spirit into the work, and you will get hundreds of manly Britishers who will spend their wages in the city, live in decent homes and generally promote cleanliness and health... it is the hardy grit of the Anglosaxon race that has made this country what it is and all that the Italians have done or are doing is retard its development.[59]

It was a short step from complaints about crowding, dirtiness, and lack of work force solidarity, to viewing those traits as innate marks of a racial inferiority. No matter how much the temptation of anachronistic moralizing should be resisted by the historian, no human should fail to be shocked by the tone of comment on Italians at the turn of the century. An editorial in *Popular Science Monthly* (Dec. 1890) entitled "What Shall We Do with the Dagoes?", appearing next to one on "The Identity of Light and Electricity" by Henry Hertz and presumably carrying the same scientific weight as the latter, reduced its analysis to that of an ethology or zoology. Reading it should have given even Italophobes pause.

What shall we do with the "dago"? This "dago", it seems, not only herds, but fights. The knife with which he cuts his bread he also uses to lop off another "dago's" finger or ear, or to slash another's cheek. He quarrels over his meals; and his game, whatever it is, which he plays with pennies after his meal is over, is carried on knife at hand. More even than this, he sleeps in herds; and if a "dago" in his sleep rolls up against another "dago" the two whip out their knives and settle it there and then; and except a grunt at being disturbed, perhaps, no notice is taken by the twenty or fifty other "dagoes" in the apartment. He is quite as familiar with the sight of human blood as with the sight of the food he eats. His women follow him like dogs, expect no better treatment than dogs, and would not have the slightest idea how to conduct themselves without a succession of blows and kicks. Blows and kicks, indeed, are too common an experience with them for notice among "dagoes." When a woman is seriously hurt, she simply keeps out of sight somewhere till she is well enough for the kicking and striking to begin over again, and no notice whatever is taken of her absence meanwhile. The disappearance is perfectly well understood, and no questions are asked. The male "dago" when sober, instinctively retreats before his employer or boss, or any other man, and has no idea of assaulting him, or indeed of addressing him, or having any relations with him except to draw his pay. But, when infuriated with liquor, he will upon any fancied occasion use the only argument which he possesses – his knife.[60]

The point to be made is not that such reductive pictures of other peoples had not been drawn before or since. Irish immigrants, Blacks, and Chinese coolie labour had all been similarly described, and, in all cases, a tradition of derision as well as a more openly hostile racist one existed. It is obvious that it was the Italians "turn" to pay the price of entry into North America's ethnocentric society. It is less obvious but more morphologically important to see such biological racism as a phase of a continuing tradition of Italophobia. Although that Italophobia battened on the themes of pseudo-scientific racism, it began to emphasize specific themes of Italian inferiority in the first decades of the century, one of which a purported Italian propensity to criminal behaviour soon eclipsed derision, racism, and accusations of scab labour as the central theme of Italophobia in twentieth century Canada.

The increasing identification of Italians with crime grew integrally from the other forms of Italophobia. In its earlier derisive modes, Italophobias had included both implications of lightfingeredness and of flaunting of convention, along with the darker image of the *padrone's* "Fagin-like" [sic] control of street urchins. The use of the new *scuola antropologica criminale* to fortify racism has been discussed. The Italian's role in the Canadian work force also provided transitional material for the emerging emphasis on "criminal tendencies."   As we have seen, Italian workers in Canada were often drawn into situations where they served as strikebreakers or scabs, even more often they were believed to play such a role. If this exposed them to the anger of other workers, it was not less than the employers expected of their Ariels. On those occasions when Italians struck out against exploitation or unfair labour practices, when they showed solidarity, at least with one another, they were rarely treated as heroes of the labour movement. Rather through the counterpane of Italophobia, they were seen as male violent primitives, Calibans, striking out not just against employers but against public order and the Canadian way. Such

Calibans, the organized English-speaking working class, seemed to
have believed, were too impulsive and childish to demonstrate the
organization, will, "attention span" to resist the bosses. A description
of a Hamilton strike in 1910 reflects English-speaking hostility and
also the shadow of conspiracy and crime.

> Fearing violence, the company called in the police, but a number of old trade
> unionists laughed at the prospect of a struggle. To them, the foreign element
> lacked the "nerve" and staying power to stand up to authority. Led by
> agitators and unscrupulous "interpreters" the ethnic workers were likened to
> sheep, an unthinking "mob" following blindly the utterances of demagogues.
> The skilled would have nodded knowingly when the strikers returned to work
> in defeat four days later.[61]

The inclusion of words such as unscrupulous "interpreters,"
agitators, and demagogues reflects the popular press' emphasis on
the role of bosses, *padroni*, and later godfathers among Italian
immigrants. The description, whether the contemporaneous one of
English-speaking workers or that of their historian, unconsciously
reflects the view of Stanford professor E.B. Ross who in his 1904
"Value Rank of the American People" wrote the higher types of men
are prompted to act together because they believe in the same
principles or love the same ideals. The inferior pull together from
clannishness or allegiance to a leader.[62]

As themes of anarchism and labour violence spread, so did
those of urban criminality. Little Italies and the growing Italian
proletariat in Canada could no longer be psychologically niched by
derision alone. Italophobes more and more saw themselves
confronted by "Big Tony," knife in hand, rather than smiling "Little
Tony" selling peanuts or ice cream. Ariel had given way completely
to Caliban, and it would be very difficult to comprehend the degree
to which the real situation, the mass flow of south Italian labourers,
interacted with stereotypes to produce the Italophobic urgency which
led to the embracing of myths about violence and criminaltiy and
renewed efforts to restrict an immigration which had never been
welcome in the first place. Emphasis on purported Italian crime
and/or a violent ethnic or racial quality of being more instinctual,
less reasonable, closer to the animal, than English-speaking man,
provided the Italophobe with a twentieth century flag of convenience
which has yet to fail him.

Social gospellers, Anglo labour leaders, and a variety of North
American "caretakers" could, without resort to outright racism,

concur with C.A. Magrath who wrote in Canada's "Growth and Some Problems Affecting It in 1910."

> There are many sections in southern and eastern Europe very many years behind in the march of civilization, occupied by people ground down by centuries of oppression, many of whom cannot understand the meaning of liberty, which to them is license, and who evidently have an intense hatred for the majesty of law.[63]

If anyone had doubts about the Italian proclivity to crime and its transfer to North America, the Dillingham Commission's volume on Emigration Conditions in Europe offered itself as a vademecum for the Italophobe. Remarking on the fact that decreases in criminality in Italy coincided with mass migration to North America, the Report stated.

> An alarming feature of the Italian immigration movement to the United States is the fact that it admittedly includes many individuals belonging to the criminal classes, particularly of southern Italy and Sicily. Moreover, the prevailing alarm in this respect is not occasioned entirely by the fact that a good many actual criminals come to the United States from Italy. But also by the not unfounded belief that certain kinds of criminality are inherent in the Italian race.

> In the popular mind, crimes of personal violence, robbery blackmail, and extortion are peculiar to the people of Italy and cannot be denied that the number of such offences committed among Italians in this country warrants the prevalence of such a belief.[64]

It can of course be denied and historians since Oscar Handlin have remarked on the unfairness of the statistical base and racial bias of the Dillingham Commission. However, since Italophobia feeds on its own attitudes, not realities,[65] the truth of the charges made against Italian immigrants is almost irrelevant. What is clear is that everywhere in official sources and the popular press, Italian immigrants from the 1880s to at least the execution of Sacco and Vanzetti were identified in North America with crime. At first, accounts of individual violence included a knife and an issue of passion, increasingly in the form of urban banditry in the form of extortion, armed robbery, etc., and finally in its modern guise, the existence of large scale criminal conspiracy in the form of Mano Nera organizations, the Camorra of Naples and the Mafia of Sicily transplanted to North America and finally to Cosa Nostra, the North American Stepchild of Italian crime.

The origins of the English-Speaking sense of the Italian as knife-wielding, fond of the *arma bianca*, the sneakiest and least British of weapons began at least with Shakespeare, and a remarkable concordance of the use of the imagery of the dagger or stiletto reverberates through Canadian and American newspapers and literary descriptions of the Italian immigrant. Some observers who were not Italophobes, such as the Jewish American immigrant writer Mary Antin, understood how the image of the knife made good copy and became the stock in trade of anti-Italianism. "Half a dozen Italians," she wrote, "draw knives in a brawl on a given evening, and the morning newspapers are full of the story. On the same evening hundreds of Italians were studying civics in the nightschools... "[66] Headlines about stilettos and the Italians who use them abound in Canadian newspapers, especially between 1900 and 1910. A sampler of Canadian comment will show the English-speaking attitude.

> They would have us think well of them. A propos of their hot southern blood and the too ready knives of some immigrants, they suggest added stringency in the regulations barring out any with criminal record.[67]

> The Swede prefers his fists, the Italian a knife, the Pole and Russian a revolver, and the Hungarian uses anything from a rock to his teeth.[68]

> There are scatterings of other races, the last arrived being the Italian with his grinding organ and we hope without his knife.[69]

> Giuseppe Mardone was given eight years for shooting and killing Mike Pappu in a quarrel. Are Italian murderers becoming more respectable? This is the second Canadian in a short time to use a revolver instead of a knife.[70]

> Too often he prefers to settle his disputes directly rather than wait for the slow process of the law, and in doing this inclines to prefer the knife to the fist, the natural first weapon of the Britisher.[71]

> Quick as a flash, Rugia whipped out a keen-edged stiletto and buried it in Young's abdomen. Then the murderous Italian darted eastward, leaving his victim weltering in blood.[72]

A series of occurrences less than a decade apart, and covered in lurid detail by the North American press began to redraw the imagery of Italophobia away from crime caused by passion, instinct, and individual violence and toward the concept of conspiracy and organized criminality. First Sicilian gangsters murdered the New

Orleans chief of police and were themselves lynched. Those events in 1890-91 made the words, mafia and mafiosi common coin in North American Italophobia. In 1900 an Italian from New Jersey assassinated Umberto I of Italy and confirmed an existent identification of Italians with political anarchism which survived through the trial of Sacco and Vanzetti. Between 1905 and 1910, a series of sensational Mano Nera trials in New York and rumours that large numbers of Camorristi had fled arrest in Naples by migrating to New York added to Italophobe hysteria about an invasion of Italian professional criminal classes. Then in 1909, the head of New York's Italian squad, Lt. Petrosino, was killed in Palermo. Not only were these events followed closely in the Canadian press, they were almost invariably accompanied by articles on the same theme in its local manifestations. The Toronto Daily Star in September of 1905 called for an end to light sentences for those who used knives as weapons.[73] The Courrier de Montreal quoted the chief of police of that city as saying Camorristi elements existed there.[74] The Toronto News in May 1906 carried a headline: "Is a Black Hand Gang working in this city?"[75] and the Hamilton Spectator in March 1908 had sensationalist front page accounts of the Mano Nera in Hamilton.[76]

The emphasis on organized crime and the conflation of political violence (anarchism) with criminal violence (Black Hand extortion) gave Italophobia a convenient consistency and universality. Later Italophobes would add Fascism to the frame of extra-legal criminal violence with almost no adjustment necessary. "The Fascist Society is only a Camorra on a large scale," wrote the British president of the League of Nations. In Hamilton, the city's skilled workers, according to their best historian, in response to newspaper accounts of immigrant violence and the presence of a Black Hand Society in the city "increasingly viewed the ethnic community with disdain." In the labour intensive Lakehead ports, Fort William and Port Arthur, the press described the city's Little Italies as "effective refuges for criminals and places where vice would breed best." The Port Arthur Daily News carried the headline in 1909, "Black Hand has appeared in Forth William and Port Arthur – Several Residents of Foreign Quarter receive Letters from Dreaded Order."[77] A good example of the sort of literature, read throughout North America, which fuelled Italophobia at the time, is "The Terror of the Camorra" which appeared in Cosmopolitan in August 1911.[78] The cover picture to the article shows a cloaked brigante, knives and skulls at hand, standing astride the Atlantic with one booted foot crushing Naples, the other New York City. Although he is described as a member of the Camorra, the urban Neapolitan malavita, his costume and weapons are suggestive of the romanticized brigands of an earlier period. The article continues with other pictures including those of urban Camorristi in chains awaiting trial in Naples, and juxtaposition of moods in the text and of the pictures perfectly represents North American Italophobia's transition from emphasis on the individual violence of bandits, brigands, and those who committed crimes of passion to elaboration of the presence of secret criminal conspiracies such as the Camorra and the Mafia. At the turn of the century such organizations were neither a figment of the nativist press's imagination nor the pervasive force in Italian life that the headlines suggested.

A glance at the newspaper press of a remote Canadian metropolitan area such as the Lakehead in northern Ontario gives some indication of how pervasive Italophobia had become and of how hostility battened on a stereotypology, rich in assumptions of racial inferiority and proclivity to political or individual violence. We have already mentioned headlines about the Mano Nera operating in Little Italies of the Lakehead. South Italians were continuously depicted as scabs or violent proto-anarchist crowds and referred to as "Black Italians." A headline in the Port Arthur Daily News in April of 1910 read "Black Italians implicated in rioting."[79] The Ft. William Daily Times-Journal on the same day reported that the Canadian Pacific Railway had promised a citizen's committee that they would not hire "Black Italians" for the rail and yard work in the coming year. It was dutifully reported as well that "White Italians," mainly Trevisans and Friulans, had not engaged in violent strike action. The Port Arthur Daily News had a few years earlier revealed the full fear and anger of Italophobes in the region.

> The major concern is the circumstances that among the strikers are a majority of foreigners, chiefly Italians who are reported to have prepared to meet opposition to their demands at the point of the knife, the national weapon of the dago...

> A community of British citizens should not have to submit to the obloquy of insult and armed defiance from a disorganized horde of ignorant and low-down mongrel swashbucklers and peanut vendors... [80]

The relationship between Italian immigrants and the English-speaking host society, although obviously eased by acculturation, did not improve greatly between the wars. Italians who had never been welcome immigrants were among those classified as undesirable when clearer, and clearly racially inspired, definitions of desirable immigrants became a matter of quotas and restrictions in the 1920s. An Italian Canadian veteran of the Great War wrote with a bitterness that reflected much of the group's frame of mind in 1928. Lieutenant Francesco Gualtieri in his *We Canadians* regretted

> that memories begin to fade in the cloudy river of our daily life while we close the door of the home to friends. During the months of January to November 1928, there came to Canada 10,600 Germans (during the war they were called barbarians) and 501 Italians (during the war they were called Allies in the cause of civilization).[81]

The recognition that the wartime alliance between the Kings of Italy and of England had not made them any more welcome or mitigated underlying Italophobia, and that conversely Germans remained preferred immigrants in Canadian public opinion polls after both wars, certainly prepared many Italian Canadians to believe they could achieve respect in the land by accepting the "tutela energica" coming from Fascist Rome through the consulates.

This is not the place to discuss consolarfascismo in Canada between 1928 and 1940, or the easy target it afforded Italophobes. Preliminary analysis indicates that the response of the Canadian authorities and public to the outbreak of war between Italy and Canada – the street violence, ostracism, police harassment, and numerous internments – varied considerably from city to city and bore a direct relationship to the local ecology of Italian settlement and inter-ethnic relations (especially to the intensity of attitudes about Italian propensity to crime in a given locale). Contrasting public reaction when war broke out with Germany is instructive. In Kitchener, Ontario, the Mayor assured the populace through the press that "older Germans here are out of touch with Hitler and the younger ones are even father away from Germany."[82] (He did this despite an incident involving local Nazis a week before). Less than ten miles away in Guelph, everyone of Italian descent, regardless of citizenship, had to report to the chief of police when war broke out in 1940, a number of those active in the Figli d'Italia were interned.

In a way, Canadian government efforts to exclude Italian immigrants by their indirection and their ineffectual nastiness were a perfect mirror of Italophobia. The Italian faced no prohibitive head tax as potential Asian immigrants did. Internments during World War II were based, at least officially, on political considerations rather than ethnic or racial ones. Italophobia was neither as pervasive, or later considered as morally reprehensible, as antisemitism. Yet in many small regulations and asides, Italians were made to know their coming to Canada permanently had not been in the authorities' plans. From the Minister of the Interior's "non-encouragement" of Italian immigrant to the effort to avoid distributing immigration promotional pamphlets, except around Milan, to the reforms sought by CPR in its agreement with the government to simplify the means by which good immigrant stock got to Canada and the unwelcome were excluded without telltale legislation. An example of the political pressure to exclude Italians and other undesirables follows.

> Fort William, Ont. 22, 1925
> The Honourable the Prime Minister of Canada, Ottawa, Ont.
> Modified and simplifies immigration instructions issued by CPR to their agents as follows: The blank is now given a free hand to select and grant permits to all bona fide agriculturists, domestics wives and children joining husband and father, bona fide matrimonial cases and any other applicants that appear to our representative as qualified and capable of becoming a worthy addition to Canada. This arrangement refers to Poland, Latvia, Rumania, Estonia, Russia, Lithuania, Jugoslavia, Germany, Hungary, Austria and Czechoslovakia, *but it does not cover passengers from Turkey, Bulgaria, Greece, Italy, and Syria in which cases it will be necessary to secure* permission from the immigration authorities as before, as well as those not able to qualify with the passport, continuous journey or literacy tests of the Immigration Act. It is of course unnecessary to secure papers for passengers from British Isles, Switzerland, Luxembourg, Ireland, Denmark, Sweden, France, Finland, Belgium and Norway.
> Fort William Liberal Campaign Committee.

Post war Canada is not free of this issue: rumours spread in the 1950s and 1960s 0f efforts by immigration officials to define "close relatives" who could serve as sponsors more narrowly for the Italian and Chinese groups than for northwest Europeans. Italian Canadians, except during the war years, have not suffered under civil disabilities and prejudice has rarely led to clear cases of official discrimination. The situation has fallen just short of that. In employment, in schooling, in access to civic life, anti-Italian prejudice has been evident.

Since Italophobia, like anti-semitism, feeds on that which it derides or dreads, the new postwar Italian community of Canada has faced revived hostility. Anti-Italian feeling, Italophobia, remains a respectable sentiment in North America. The political scientist Michael Parenti notes that "every Italian American knows persons who would never utter a racist or sexist remark who seem to think themselves clever when making a joking reference about the Mafioso in our presence. It is one of those forms of bigotry that remain quite respectable." Toronto and Montreal have had their share of sensational headlines about Italians and organized crime in the last two decades. After the Canadian Broadcasting System broadcast a series of shows on organized crime full of innuendo about Canadian Italians role in it, there was considerable protest and mobilized response from the community. Few other Canadians apparently found the show Italophobic.[83] A Gallup Poll taken shortly after the films were shown in April 1979 reported that 40% of Canadians associated Italian Canadians with organized crime. Significantly, even more, 47% of those who had seen the Connections series made the association of Italians with crime. Studies such as Francois Ribordy's *Culture, Conflict and Crime among Italian Immigrants* (Montreal 1975) which conclusively show the low incidence of crime among Italian Canadians are irrelevant. Italophobia has never needed much negative reality as grist to turn into hostile or derisive myth. What a Jewish American rabbi wrote in the 1840s about antisemitism seems to hold for Italophobia. The rabbi told his American audience that antisemitism would disappear when Jews did. Italophobia will renew itself, feeding on old themes and stereotypes, drawing strength from new inter-cultural encounters, as long as Italians migrate throughout the English-speaking world.

Notes

1. L. Carpi, *Delle Colonie e dell'emigrazione d'italiani all'estero sotto l'aspetto dell'industria, commercio, agricoltura,* etc. (Milan, 1874) 4 volumes see Rapporti consolari e privati sullo stato delle colonie, 1969-71, Vol. II, chap. VIII.

2. A. Rossi, "Per la tutela degli italiani negli Stati Uniti," in *Bollettino dell'Emigrazione,* n. 16 (1904), p. 20.

3. See above consular reports in Carpi and R. Paolucci di Calboli, *I girovaghi italiani in Inghiliterra ed i suonatori ambulanti* (Citta di Castello, 1893), p. 5. On *scopritorismo* and *atimia,* see R.F. Harney, *Dalla Frontiera alle Little Italies,* (Rome, 1984), pp. 39-54.

4.   T. Phillips, "Canadians of Italian Descent," report presented to the Committee
     on Co-operation in Canadian Citizenship of the Dept. of National War Service
     PAC RG25 G-2 File 773 J40 External Affairs. Of course, anti-Italian feeling was
     not as uniquely an English-speaking problem as Phillips and the focus of this
     paper suggest. See R. Forester, *The Italian Emigration of Our Times* (Cambridge,
     1919), p.504. "No one can follow the fortunes of the Italians abroad without
     being struck by a sort of contempt in which they are often held. Dago, gringo,
     carcamano, badola, cincali, macaroni – how long the list of epithets might be!"
     It might be well to point out here that a discussion of Italophobia does not
     claim in any way to dismiss Italian bigotries – between regions, against *i neri*
     and the *"airisci"* in the United States, or in contemporary Canada toward
     "mangia-cakes" (acculturated Italians) and *"pesci"* (their Portuguese immigrant
     neighbours with fishy diets). It is simply another subject.

5.   "The disturbance of any relationship between individuals and groups
     necessarily has a prehistory which is as old as the relationship itself. Thus
     estrangement has its roots, in the final analysis, in the same situation which
     determines... the specific character of the relationship." A. Leschintzer, *The
     Magic Background of Modern Antisemitism. An Analysis of the German Jewish
     Relationship* (N.Y., 1956), p. 107.

6.   J. Higham, *Strangers in the Land. Patterns of American Nativism, 1860-1925.* (N.Y.,
     1963).

7.   N. Tienhaara, *Canadian Views on Immigration and Population. An analysis of
     Postwar Gallup Polls.* (Ottawa, 1974), p. 59.

8.   J.S. Woodsworth, *Strangers Within Our Gates.* (new ed. Toronto, 1972), p. 132.

9.   S. La Gumina (ed.), *Wop. A Documentary History of Anti-Italian Discrimination
     in the United States.* (N.Y., 1973).

10. L.P. Curtis, *Anglosaxons and Celts. A Study of Anti-Irish Prejudice in Victorian
     England* (Bridgeport, Ct, 1968). W. Powell, *Tree of Hate: Propaganda and
     Prejudices Affecting United States Relations with the Hispanic World.* (N.Y., 1971).
     W. Jordan, *White Over Black. American Attitudes toward the Negro, 1550-1812.*
     (Chapel Hill, 1968). In accepting Jordan's definition of attitudes and applying
     it to Italophobia, I am sidestepping a debate in ethnic and immigration studies
     best exemplified by two views of anti-Chinese feeling in North America. One
     view propounded by S.C. Miller in his *The Unwelcome Immigrants. The
     American Image of the Chinese, 1785-1882.* (Berkeley, 1969), see hostility to the
     Chinese as rooted in negative missionary accounts of Chinese ways and
     culture; the other view, in Gunther Barth's *Bitter Strength.* (Cambridge, 1964),

blames anti-Asian virulence on the encounter and competition between white and yellow labour in the western part of North America.

11. Jorge Luis Borges, "The Argentine Writer and Tradition" in *Labyrinths* (N.Y., 1964).

12. See Lynn Thorndike, "De Complexionibus" in *Isis*, 49 (1958), pp. 398-498 for mediaeval views on the significance of skin colouring.

13. Jordan, *White Over Black*, p. 86.

14. H. Marraro, "Italians in New York during the First Half of the 19th Century" in *New York History* 26 (1945), pp. 278-306, p. 23.

15. A. Principe, "Il Risorgimento visto dai protestanti dell'Alto Canada, 1846-60" in *Rassegna storica del Risorgimento* LXV: II (April, 1979), pp. 151-163. R. Sylvain, *Clerc Garibaldien Predicant des Deux Mondes. Alessandro Gavazzi (1809-89)* Vol. II (Quebec, 1962), pp. 387-423.

16. J. Willerts, *An Easy Grammar of Geography.* (London, 1815), p. 12.

17. The term for Garibaldi's troops was "Garibaldini." Transforming the proper term "Garibaldini" by substituting the ending with the word "banditti" therefore is meant to critique and belittle Garibaldi, his men and the Risorgimento, (editor's note).

18. P. Savard, "L'Italia nella cultura franco-canadese dell'Ottocento" in L. Codignola (ed.), *Canadiana. Problemi di Storia Canadese* (Venice, 1983), p. 104.

19. Rev. W.G. Licking to Archbishop McEvay (12 Aug. 1908) in McEvay Papers, Toronto Diocesan Archives. One other source of hostility or, at least of invidious views of Italians came from travellers accounts of encounters with "tourist" Italy. See P. Savard, "Voyageurs canadiens-francais en Italie au 19eme siècle" in *Vie francaise* XVII, 1-2 (Sept. 1961) and H. Marraro, "Viaggiatori Americani in Italia durante il Risorgimento" in *Rassegna storica del Risorgimento* LIV:IV (Oct. 1967), pp. 525-547.

20. Margaret Bell, "Toronto's Melting Pot," in *The Canadian Magazine* (July 1913) 41:3, p. 234.

21. W.A. Sherwood, "The Italian Fruit Vendor," in *The Canadian Magazine* (Nov. 1895) 6:1, p. 60.

22. H. Mayhew, *London Labour and the London Poor* (London, 1851) 3 volumes; London's Underworld (London, 1862).

23. *La Ruche Litteraire et Politique* (1854), quoted in E. Goggio, "Italian Influences on the Cultural Life of Old Montreal" in *Canadian Modern Languages Review* IX (Fall, 1952), pp. 5-7.

24. O. Mannoni, *Prospero and Caliban. The Psychology of Colonization* (N.Y., 1964).

25. Margaret Bell, "Toronto's Melting Pot," p. 242.

26. J.M. Gibbon, *Canadian Mosaic. The Making of a Northern Nation* (Toronto, 1938), p. 387.

27. A. Fitzpatrick, *Handbook for New Canadian* (Toronto, 1919), p. 21.

28. Arbuckle Coffee Advertising Card c. 1870. This is one of a series of 50 Cards giving a pictorial history of the Sports and Pastimes of all Nations. I wish to thank John and Selma Appel for bringing the card to my attention.

29. *United Church Record* (Toronto, 1927), p. 28.

30. E. Weaver, "The Italians in Toronto," in *The Globe Saturday Magazine* (16 July 1910), p. 10.

31. *The Public School Geography* (Authorized for USA in the Public Schools, High Schools and Collegiate Institutes of Ontario), Toronto, n.d.

32. G.A. Kuhring, "The Church and the Newcomer," Joint Committee on Education of the United Church of England in Canada (Toronto, 1925).

33. "Methodist Missions Among Italians in Canada," in *The Missionary Outlook* XXXVII:1 (Jan. 1917), p. 6.

34. Edmund Bradwin, *The Bunkhouse Man* (N.Y.,1928).

35. Central Neighbourhood House Pamphlet (1930), City of Toronto Archives, p. 13-14.

36. Central Neighbourhood House. Newspaper Clipping Collection (1921), City of Toronto Archives.

37. *Presbyterian Record* (July 1910) p. 307.

38. *Report of the Select Committee on Agriculture and Colonization* (1928), p. 69.

39. Quoted in R. S. Baker, *Following the Colour Line. American Negro Citizenship in the Progressive Era* (N.Y., 1964), p. 268.

40. *Dictionary of Races of People. Reports of the Immigration Commission*, 61st Congress, V.S. Senate, Washington 1911, Vol. V, pp. 81-85 (Dillingham Commission).

41. J.S. Woodsworth, *Strangers Within Our Gates* (Toronto, 1909), p. 181. *The Lance*, Oct 1, 1909, p. 1.

42. Kate Foster, *Our Canadian Mosaic* (Toronto, 1926), p. 14.

43. Castell Hopkins, *Canadian Annual Review of Public Affairs* (Toronto, 1902), p. 328.

44. Ralph Connor, *The Foreigner* (Toronto, 1909), Prefact.

45. Dr. Bryce to James Smart, *Immigration Superintendent* (30 April 1904), I.B. File 28885 Memorandum RG M6 PAC.

46. R.G. 76 Vol. 151 file 28883, n. 11, (4 Oct. 1949), PAC.

47. *Dictionary of Races of People* (Dillingham Commission), p. 84.

48. *Emigration Conditions in Europe*. Vol. IV of the Dillingham Commission depends heavily on Italian Anthropometria, especially pp. 200 on. For modern judgment on Lombroso, etc., see S.J. Gould, "The ape in some of us: criminal anthropology" in *The Mismeasure of Man* (N.Y., 1981), pp. 122-145.

49. "Gli stranieri nel Canada giudicati da un Canadese" in *Bollettino dell'Emigrazione* n. 19 (1909), pp. 56-75.

50. J. Cameron, *Canadian or Foreigner?* Toronto, Baptist Mission, 1913, p. 7.

51. *Missionary Outlook* (Toronto) XXX:12 (Dec. 1910), p. 267.

52. *Clifford Sifton Papers*, PAC File 89315 quoted in D. Avery, "Canadian Immigration Policy and the Foreign Navy 1874-1914" in *The Canadian Historical Association*. Historical Papers (1972), pp. 135-156.

53. Commission of Immigration (Winnipeg) to J.A. Smart, Dep. Minister of the Interior, 27 Aug. 1901, I.B. Papers RG M6 Vol. 129, file 28885 part I PAC.

54. Frederick Jackson Turner, quoted in E. Saveth, *American Historians and European Immigrants, 1875-1925* (N.Y., 1948).

55. Testimony of Allenby in *Royal Commission of Capital and Labour*, Vol. V. *Ontario Evidence* (Toronto, 1889), p. 828.

56. R.D. McKenzie, *Oriental Exclusion* (1928) Univ. of Chicago Reprint 1979, p. 12.

57. W.D.Scott, Commissioner of Immigration in J.M. Gibbon, "The Foreign Born" in *Queen's Quarterly* (April 1920), n. 4, p. 332.

58. *Jack Canuck* (Toronto).

59. *Jack Canuck* (Toronto).

60. Editorial entitled "What Shall We Do With the Dago", in *Popular Science Monthly* (Dec. 1890).

61. Bryan Palmer, *A Culture in Conflict, Skilled Workers and Industrial Capitalism in Hamilton, 1860-1914.* (McGill-Queens 1979), p. 231.

62. E.B. Ross, "The Value Rank of the American People" in *Independent* (10 Nov. 1904), p. 1057. For descriptions of Toronto Italian leaders which contained the same implications of padronism or undue influence see *Saturday Night* (17 Sept. 1904), p. 1 and *The Globe* (21 March 1891), p. 2.

63. C.A. Magrath, *Canada's Growth and Some Problems Afflicting It* (Ottawa, 1910), p. 54.

64. Dillinghamn Commission, Vol. V *Emigration Condition in Europe*, pp. 205-209.

65. For an analysis of the misdirection in Dillingham Commission statistics, see O. Handlin, "Old Immigrants and New" in *Race and Nationality in American Life* (N.Y., 1957).

66. Mary Antin quoted in J.M. Gibbon, "The Foreign Born", *Queens Quarterly* XXVII:4 (April 1920), p. 331.

67. E. Weaver, "The Italians in Toronto" in *Globe Saturday Magazine* (16 July 1910), p. 10.

68. W. Lacy Amy, "The Life of the Bohunk", *The Canadian Magazine* (Jan. 1913), p. 219.

69. Goldwin Smith, *Canada and the Canadian Question* (1891), republished (Toronto, 1971).

70. *Jack Canuck* Vol. I:4 (16 Sept. 1911), p. 2.

71. G.A. Kuhring "The Church and the Newcomer", Joint Committee on Education of the Church of England in Canada (Toronto 1925).

72. "A Keen-Edged Stiletto" in *The Empire* (Toronto 3 Dec. 1888), p. 6.

73. "Disarm the Knifeman" in *Toronto Daily Star* (5 Sept. 1905), p.1.

74. *Courrier de Montreal* (31 March 1911).

75. *Toronto News* (5 May 1906), p. 1.

76. *Hamilton Spectator* (28 March 1908) and 28 Dec. 1909).

77. *Ft. William Daily Times Journal* (16 Jan. 1909) in G. Pucci, *The Italian Community in Fort William's East End in the Early Twentieth Century.* (M.A. Lakehead Univerity 1977), p. 257.

78. George B. McClellan, "Terror of the Camorra" in *Cosmopolitan* 61:3 (Aug. 1911).

79. *Port Arthur Daily News* (13 Ap. 1910).

80. *Port Arthur Daily News* (1 Oct. 1906), p. 1.

81. F. Gualtieri, *We Canadians* (Toronto, 1931), p. 71.

82. "Bund Closes Headquarters in Kitchener", *Toronto Globe and Mail* (Sept 2, 1939), p. 17.

83.   The Gallup Poll was conducted in May of 1979, one month after the airing of
       the Connections series. Sen. Peter Bosa carried the issue to the floor of the
       Canadian parliament. See *Senate Debates* (17 Oct. 1979).

3

If One Were to Write a History of Postwar Toronto Italia

*M*etropolitan Toronto ranks with Sao Paolo, New York, Chicago and Buenos Aires as one of the largest Italian settlement areas outside Italy. Estimates of the number of those of Italian descent among Toronto's two and half million inhabitants vary from a quarter of a million to half a million; that is, up to one-quarter of the city's population.[1]

The remarkable feature of Toronto Italia is not its size but the immediacy of its ties with Italy, an immediacy born of the fact that the vast majority of Italians in the city are post-World War Two immigrants or their children. Toronto Italia then is an immigrant collectivity, and that fact, more than the serendipity of residing in a country which professes, through its multicultural policies, a belief in pluralism and the right of immigrants to maintain their language and ways, accounts for the vivacity and the kaleidoscopic permutations of ethnic identity and ethnoculture which characterize the city's Italian neighbourhoods.

When the noted English Risorgimentalist, Denis Mack Smith, was asked why he had confined most of his scholarship to the nineteenth century and had never tried to write about post-World War Two Italy, he responded by observing that the postwar period was too much of a muddle for the kind of history he liked to write. He found contemporary Italy "immensely complicated and lacking in form and shape."[2] His reaction may mirror that of all historians asked to deal with a looming recent past in which trends seem inchoate and random facts defiant of encodation in an interpretative narrative.

It is time for the postwar Toronto Italia experience to be organized in more than demographic and sociological frames. The tendency of historians of the earlier mass migration to accept unquestioningly a synchronic view of the postwar era as if the forty-year history of the *ethnie* were a single anthropological or sociological moment, a long present tense, should end. We have followed too readily the historicist American scholarship which tends to study immigrant settlement and ethnocultures from a third-generation perspective lying beyond assimilation or ethnicism (the "new ethnicity" of the 1960s). This approach is preoccupied with the study of the ethnic group in terms of boundaries – measuring social, economic and geographical data for those tell-tale signs of acculturation, success, "startling" ethnic persistence, prejudice or "ethnically blocked mobility." Its practitioners seem to assume that no interior political, cultural, social history of the *ethnie* itself, worthy of study, exists. Their approach has the advantage of making study of the group diachronic rather than simply synchronic, but it remains about boundaries rather than content and seems inadequate to the Canadian situation.

I have found myself then in search of what Hayden White has called an emplotment,[3] a particular and appropriate story form, in which to fit the facts of postwar Toronto Italia so that they offer more than merely a chronicle and transform themselves into "a comprehensible drama of development," which I shall refer to as a narrative. The reader will recognize the allusion to Italo Calvino's *If on a Winter's Night a Traveller* (Se una notte d'inverno un viaggiatore) in the style of the title for this essay. From the title, he or she should gather either that I believe that I have failed to find an emplotment that works, or that I am content to suggest some of the many narratives that seem possible, or that I have found for myself a deeper narrative in my encounter with the chaotic mass of source material, memory culture and folk wisdom which exists.

Preliminary work of an archival and monographic kind will be necessary before a full-fledged history of Toronto Italia, 1945-85 is possible. Despite the existence since 1953 of an Italian newspaper and, fitfully, of competitors to it,[4] no analysis has been done of editorial policies, publishers' attitudes, advertising, or readership. No effort to trace changing immigrant concern about *paese*, Italy, their *paesani* in diaspora, Toronto, or Canada, by sampling and measuring press coverage over an extended period, has been undertaken. Although much analysis of census material goes on, it is rarely made congruent with data arising from the community such as parish records and association membership lists, data which could be used to correlate immigrant cohort (year of arrival), age, occupation, region of origin, residential history and what I will call degree of ethnoversion – intensity and frequency of involvement with Italian networks, institutions and emblems.

For this last measure, of course, the adjective Italian is inadequate. Distinctions must be made among *paese*, regional, Italian and Italian Canadian – the latter the hybrid result of a Toronto ethnogenesis in the late 1960s and the 1970s. Over forty years, one can, for example, observe the decline or loss of meaning of *paese* and regional emblematics in commerce. Gran Sasso plumbing, Sila trucking, La Ciociara food slowly, perhaps generationally, give way to Italian this or Italian Canadian that. This process of ethnicization takes its own path, which is neither in the service of acculturation nor of the maintenance of primordial ethnicity. For example, neither a regional sports hero such as Primo Carnera once was for the city's Friulani,[5] nor Italian Canadian sports heroes of prewar stock such as the NHL's Esposito brothers appear able to compete for a share of the adulation that the World Cup winning Squadra Azzurra, Italian Soccer team, receives. In the heart of the *ethnie*, soccer, not hockey or other "North American" games, has been reasserted as the sport seen most appropriate for the immigrants' children.

A sensitive study of such variations in emblems of identity over time, as well as one which would deal with the continuum of identification and association from *paese* to region, from Italian to Italian Canadian, or new Canadian, that could distinguish between immigrant family ethnoculture and the North American ethnicization process, also would seem to be a prerequisite for giving form to a history of Toronto Italia.

Despite the lack of "interior history orientation" I have referred to in statistical studies,[6] I would like to stop here and offer a brief demographic profile of the postwar Italian Torontonians – who they are in terms of time of arrival, education, occupations, regions of origin, ethnoculture and their position in the life of the city. Between 1951 and 1981, the population of Toronto has doubled from a little over a million people to its present two and a half million people. The source of that growth is made obvious by the fact that in the 1981 Census, 43 per cent of the city's population was listed as born outside the country and that after immigrants from the United Kingdom, the largest group of newcomers came from Italy. While the city's population had doubled in those thirty years, the Italian descent group had grown eight to tenfold, from under 30,000 to upwards of 300,000. This new concentration of Italians, generally in one broad corridor of settlement throughout the west end of the city – there is an outrigger community made up heavily of Sicilians and Foggians in the east end as well – plays a central role in public perceptions of change and development in Metropolitan Toronto. Despite large new urban concentrations of Chinese, Portuguese, Greeks and east Europeans, it is the Italians who are seen as the immigrants whose arrival coincided with the rapid growth and economic development of the city and its hinterland.

If the Italians of Toronto play a central role in the city, they also dominate – increasingly at the expense of Montreal's beleaguered "Little Italy" – *Italianità* in Canada. As many as six out of every ten Canadians of Italian descent live in southern Ontario, four out of ten in Metropolitan Toronto. During the period of mass Italian migration in the late 1950s and 1960s, almost 40 per cent of the Italians entering Canada gave Toronto as their destination.

The Italians of Toronto, according to the 1971 Census, were 54 per cent immigrant and 28 per cent the children of immigrants. Only 17 per cent of the group were the children of the Canadian-born. In an earlier study of the census, the impact of immigrants on the collectivity was even more apparent. Anthony Richmond showed that only 3 per cent of the ethnic group were prewar immigrants, and that over 50 per cent had come to Toronto between 1951 and 1961. In 1971 only 6 per cent of the group had both parents in North America; and in the latest census, the Italian-born continue to make up more than half of the population of the *ethnie*. That figure, however, includes a very large number of young adults, born in Italy but educated in Toronto. (They are the Italian children who made up 45 per cent of the non-English-speaking students in the school system in the 1961 Census.)

Beyond the boon they provided for the separate (parochial) school system, these young adults, in their behaviour now, quintessentially represent the choice between living an ethnoverted existence in the *ethnie* or acculturation. From their ranks come the bureaucrats and "organic intelligentsia" of Italian-Canadian institutions, the small businessmen and heritage language teachers as well as the *ethnie*'s increasing number of young professionals, but I have found no reliable way of measuring how many from those same ranks simply move on into the larger English-speaking city.

Almost 10 per cent of Toronto's people list Italian as their mother tongue. It is difficult though to determine what that means in terms of tendencies toward language retention or loss since the mother-tongue group and the Italian-born group are roughly the same size. (A figure which shows only 4 per cent mother tongue retention in the third generation in the 1971 Census is skewed since the vast majority of third-generation Italian Canadians in 1971 were descendants of those prewar immigrants who underwent rapid assimilation in the 1930s and 1940s to escape from the *braccia gigantesca* of *consolarfascismo* and the subsequent Canadian Italophobia.)[7] The rate of endogamy – marriage within the group – in 1971 was 74 per cent for males and 84 per cent for females in contrast to a pre-World War Two rate of only 55 per cent for Italian-Canadian males.[8] The increased percentage suggests the large pool of potential mates within the new *ethnie*, the thousands of hopeful young immigrant couples who arrived in the period, as well as some of the tribalizing thoughts that may accompany both official multiculturalism and efforts by immigrant or ethnocultural leadership to hold the collectivity together.

Typically none of the important statistics on marriage between immigrants from different regions of Italy, or marriage between descendants of pre- and postwar immigrants are readily arrived at. Those last figures would be quite useful for, despite the nasty habit of referring to prewar immigrants and their children as mangia-cakes -presumably because of their high levels of acculturation or fossilized Umbertine peasant ways – the postwar immigrants initially depended a great deal on these Italian Canadians (for a while it was voguish for the immigrant intelligentsia to refer to themselves as Canadian Italians and the mangia-cakes as Italian Canadians).

Statistics on schooling and occupational skills do not lend credence to the view of those Canadian Italians that they came with more sophistication rather than just more *Italianità* than their predecessors. Of the 28,000 Italian immigrants listed as entering Canada with skilled trades between 1945 and 1965 – presumably the remainder were peasants and labourers with a sprinkling of urban white-collar workers and professionals – 20,000 practised the following traditional trades in rank order: stonemasons/bricklayers, carpenters, tailors, seamstresses, barbers, mechanics and shoemakers. (Of course, these Canadian government categories do not reflect real skills or artisan pride. The census for the same period shows that roughly 65 per cent of Italian household heads in the city had less than eight grades of elementary education, and there are indications that female formal education levels were even lower. As with the earlier Italian mass immigration, it is difficult to chart the rise of, or arrival of, *prominenti* – middle-class leaders and intelligentsia – among the newcomers. Perhaps it takes fewer "*trombetti*" than one thinks to make a loud noise.

Much is made of regionalism among Italian immigrants to Toronto. In popular narrative, regionalism, or more narrow paesanism, is accorded explanatory power in shaping alliances which inform socio-economic and political activity in the *ethnie*. In terms of reliable facts and numbers, or of a means for measuring their profundity of significance, regionalism and paesanism remain among the most illusive subjects in the search for a way to encode and interpret behaviour in the *ethnie*. While I was preparing this paper, a call came to me from the office of CIBPA (Canadian Italian Business and Professional Association) where a heated argument had broken out over which regional group, Calabrese or Abruzzese and Molisani, was a majority in Toronto. I called them back for the answer, but we could only agree on the fact that it didn't matter really because the Friulani and Sicilani, though fewer in number, were just as important in the collectivity. I should add that there was a humour to the exchange which implied that some of the sharper edges of *campanilismo* (parochialism) have been blunted, perhaps by the general success of the immigrants, or the fact that no statistics which might show the rate of success to be invidious by region of origin are available.

Although no separate figures on regions of origin for Toronto Italians exist, statistics from 1957, a typical year of high Italian migration to Canada, seem to correspond to current folk wisdom about origins. In that year, 5,000 each of Abruzzesi-Molisani and of Calabresi came to Canada. Two thousand each arrived from Friuli, from other parts of the Veneto and from Lazio, and a little over a thousand each from Sicilia, Puglia and the Campania.[9] The fact of regional origin is not the same as regionalism.[10] The narrative will have to look more closely at the power of regionalism, at its relationship to factionalism and to the image of factionalism.

The complicated relationship between regional pride and inter-regional suspicion and rivalry is one of the many reasons I have chosen to use the word *ethnie* to describe the collectivity of Italians in Toronto since the war. I have chosen it also in order to avoid a misleading use of community, which carries with it concepts claiming too much in this instance. "Little Italy" seems a demeaning and ultimately meaningless archaism, and *colonia* has always been less a description than an organizing slogan for rascals *truffatori* from Italy or from within the *ethnie*. The adjective or ethnonym Italian also, upon closer examination, has little power of valid description. It is a census artifact which becomes a tool for enabling the bigoted or aspirant to deny the variety of views, identities and conditions which exist in the *ethnie*. One of the results of a well-wrought history of the *ethnie* might be discovering a valid usage for Italian, or Italian

Canadian, and a subtlety in the use of *ethnie* which could distinguish sub-communities in the collectivity, as well as occasions such as the World Cup victory, or responses to earthquakes in Friuli or Calabria when the collectivity acted also as a community.

Two final points about material life and attitudes before I turn to the emplotment of the narrative. The first deals with the issue of intensity of participation and ethnoversion. In 1977 the new National Congress of Italian Canadians carried out a survey which proved embarrassing (not least because it was so unscientifically done).[11] The survey showed that 68 per cent of the respondents had never heard of the NCIC, that – if one ignored parishes – 69 per cent belonged to no Italian-Canadian organization. Of the ethnic clubs or associations, in which 30 per cent did participate, less than half carried on their business in Italian. The rest used either English or a mix of English and Italian. The findings were based on nation-wide statistics and certainly both participation and Italian language use in Toronto would be higher, but it should also be noted that the survey was done in the mid-1970s, at the height of both "ethnicizing" campaigns led by the National Congress of Italian Canadians and government attempts to encourage ethnocultural maintenance through official multiculturalism. The figures simply reinforce the point that the census category Italian is not a measure of sentiment or commitment.

Study of occupational, social, geographical and economic mobility, as it exists in Toronto now, seems unable to penetrate to the reality of socio-economic status and the sensibilities of the immigrants and their children about class, paesanism and camaraderies. In the memory culture,[12] there is a very common tendency among older postwar immigrants to recall lost days of the 1950s and 1960s when all were *paesani* or *fratelli*, when there were few class differences within the group, or within regional sub-groups, when men helped one another, giving of their trades and skills freely, and all were exploited by a variety of *stranieri* – Irish union bosses, Anglo-Saxon officialdom, Jewish developers and mangia-cake contractors. It would be ungracious or ignoble to deny them this "founding myth," but it, like the obtuse nature of mobility analyses of the collectivity, obstructs the effort at a true history which must deal with efforts to organize the Italian labour force, the rise of a class of successful contractors and the emergence of some truly rich developers and land speculators.

In the most recent Statistics Canada extrapolations on the *ethnie* by Kalbach and Richmond,[13] some of the limits of the method emerge to perplex the practitioners. For although the immigrant generation shows almost "ethnically blocked mobility" in terms of listing the same occupations, neighbourhoods and taxable incomes in 1981 as in 1961, any observer can see that the development of the city, which has largely depended on Italian construction workers since the 1950s, produced, along with a surfeit of injured workmen and *ritornati*, miles of Italian family-owned housing (according to the 1971 Census, 77 per cent of the ethnic group owned their own home. One should include in the analysis all the homes paid for or built with the immigrants' money in the sending *paesi*), well-off contractors, a "brokering" commercial middle-class (*borghesia mediatrice e commerciale*) and an elite of developers and industrialists. More to the point, the analysis of the latest census demonstrates that the children of these "immobile" immigrants are statistically over-represented in the city's universities, professional schools and, by age cohort, in the professions. Moreover, this second generation of postwar Toronto Italia already has achieved the average income of the British and French charter groups.

The answer to this paradox suggested by Franc Sturino and others lies in the lack of subtlety of the census, or those who use it, and the *furbizzia*, or wisdom, of the immigrants.[14] Public university education in Canada is relatively cheap; much work goes on in residential construction as part of an untraceable and untaxable sub-economy, immigrants of mainly rural origin know how to maximize their family well-being by seasonal food processing, and extended family and *paesani* cooperation make Italians prosper materially beyond the ken of their non-Italian neighbours and enumerators.

A heuristic device much favoured by post-Risorgimento historians was that of writing *pagine della storia* as telling examples. For now all the various possible narratives for the years 1945-85 can only be such "pages." Narratives could exist, given the proper research base, for the following:

- changes in the geographical enclave and its *ambiente;*
- the internal politics and institutional development of the *ethnie;*
- the labour history of the Italian immigrants, men and women;
- the rise of a business and professional middle class;
- the ecclesiastical and folk religious history of the group; and
- an intellectual history of changing perceptions of identity

and destination, e.g., attenuated ethnicity, full assimilation, return to the *madrepatria*. Study of prejudice which the group encountered from the circumambient society, as well as the prejudice of some Italians towards the *pesci*, their Portuguese neighbours, the Jews, their competitors in business, the *neri*, the West Indians and East Indians moving into the neighbourhood, the Irish with whom they compete for control of the separate school board and *sistemazione* as teachers, would also be necessary for a complete picture of the *ethnie* to emerge.

For the founding years, 1945-60, it seems possible to combine the many narratives into one story. That story centres on attempts to regain control of the so-called Casa d'Italia[15], the downtown mansion that had been bought in the mid-1930s by community subscription and given as a consulate to the fascist government. The attempt to regain the Casa was to have been one of the first concerted efforts to overcome the fear, shame and *atimia* which fascism and the war years had produced in the community. From a period of intense fascist tutelage and official ethno-nationalism, a period when most community-based institutions had been undermined or subjected to fascistization in the guise of Italianization, the Italians of Toronto had passed to a time of recrimination, "lying low", internments, suspicion and hostility from the non-Italians around them - a period of discredited leadership.

A few organizations had not been compromised; they had kept their headquarters (*sede*) outside the Casa, and that fact alone gave them an anti-fascist image. Two benevolent societies, the Fratellanza and the Società Italo-Canadese, joined by the Italian Immigrant Aid Society, provided a core of organization for the postwar years. On the other hand, the Sons of Italy (Figli d'Italia) and their anti-fascist breakaway rivals, the Order of Italian Canadians, had less influence in the postwar period.

The campaign to regain the Casa was fraught with ironies since most of those involved, as well as the Canadian officials they consulted with, agreed that eventually the building should be returned, not to the community but to the Italian government. (In fact the matter was more complex than that since the Canadian wartime custodian had sold the building to the Canadian government; the Mounties, who used the building were loathe to move out, and the Italian community found itself lobbying through influential friends like the local member of Parliament, later senator,

David Croll, to retrieve the building for the Italian government, which at that time seemed to express no interest in the matter.) By 1958 when the Canadian government agreed to give up the Casa, the geographical focus of the *ethnie* had moved considerably northward, and the emotional focus of the ethnic group was about to settle on the issue of exploitation of Italian labour in the city. The site of the Casa, an old mansion – once elegant but by then decrepit – in an area which has since become Toronto's Chinatown, no longer recommended it as a symbolic centre of the Italian *ethnie*. In fact when the Italian government did decide, after almost two decades of hesitation, to use the site as a consulate again, one of those Italian-Canadian leaders who had earlier fought to retrieve the building described it to the *Corriere Canadese* as an unacceptable place to represent the "più vasta comunità etnica di Toronto."[16]

For such men, the building later of Villa Colombo and the Columbus Centre – eight miles or more north in the heart of the newer Italian settlement area – would serve as a symbol of the ethnic group's success. I cannot ascertain whether the Italian government's decision to accept the old Casa site, far from the current community, had any symbolic weight – a consul's work goes beyond his *colonia* after all – or simply represents a decision to take advantage of the opportunity to be housed in what is again an elegant and centrally located downtown mansion.

The campaign to retrieve the Casa had two important results. The first came as an almost accidental solution to the question of what use the Casa would be put to until its future was decided. The building was occupied in 1962 by COSTI (Centro Organizzativo Scuole Tecniche Italiane), a new skills and language training centre for immigrants which for many years represented all that was best in the *ethnie*'s and the Italian government's sense of responsibility to Italian immigrants and to the larger city.[17]

Sometime in the mid-1950s mainly as a result of the campaign to reclaim the Casa, an umbrella organization was created to represent the *ethnie*'s interests. (An effort to organize around the postwar Aid for Italy movement had begun as early as 1947.) The organization took the form of a federation of associations known as FACI (Federation of Canadian Italian Associations). Member associations included benevolent societies such as the Fratellanza and the Società Italo-Canadese, regional clubs such as the Famee Furlane, Circolo Calabrese, Società Trinacria, a Marchegiano club, as well as *paese* clubs for Vitese and Pachinese from Sicily and Monteleonesi and Modugnesi from Puglia. The Italian local of the Amalgamated Clothing Workers, the Italian Immigrant Aid Society, the Italian Canadian Recreation Club and several Holy Name societies were also members. The Figli d'Italia lodges and those of Order of Italo-Canadians seemed to have had associate status.

By 1956 the presence of the new Italian migrants with their different ways and different agenda could be felt in the federation. The *Corriere Canadese* reported a 1956 meeting at which one prewar patriot, a steamship agent, gave an impassioned speech about the return of the Casa. He was followed by a new member, representing a recently formed *paese* sports club who rose to complain that he could not follow the issues being raised about the Casa because the federation's meetings were being carried on in English! He and other newcomers felt excluded.[18] In 1957 the federation, realizing that some bridge between old and new associations was necessary if it were to retain and representative quality as an umbrella organization, put out a call to "all newly formed Italian Societies at present in existence in Toronto" to join. The organization was still healthy enough in 1960 to be at the centre of the controversy over the disposition of the Casa. Then with the labour troubles of the 1960s and the shift of settlement northward, this first federation, if not its constituent associations, vanishes from the record.

In 1969 when a new FACI (the acronym this time significantly in Italian, Federazione delle Associazioni e dei Clubs Italo-Canadese) with fifty-eight member associations was born, no mention was made of the first FACI, even though the president of the first FACI, now among the few prewar leaders active in the *ethnie*, was involved. The lack of acknowledgement of that first attempt, made mainly by Italian Canadians of prewar immigrant origin to create a united front for the *ethnie*, in effect to begin the process of ethnicization, seems to confirm Gramsci's observation that *gruppi subalterni* – for what else are ethnic groups in North America – are condemned to seeing their history episodically and to having it so written.

A May 1960 headline in the *Corriere Canadese* asked "Perchè La Casa d'Italia Mantiene Le Porte Chiuse."[19] The newspaper then sought counsel as to whether the building should become a cultural, a social services, or a recreational centre. The newspaper's editor called on the following people to answer the questions posed. They were club officers, the clergy and leaders of associations (*dirigenti della FACI, il Clero, esponenti delle Associazioni, Clubs, Confraternite,*

Società italo-canadesi. If he had included consular officials, the editor's list would have perfectly defined the cultural and political elite of Toronto Italia.

Something about the apparently unabashed elitism of his request caused me to step back from the narrative and gave me a chance to notice a jarring distance of tone and preoccupation between headlines about an *Inchiesta Sulla Casa* and a small item two pages farther into the paper which recorded donations, often of only a few dollars by workers and contractors, to a fund for the families of six Italian labourers killed in a tunnel cave-in while digging the Toronto subway line.

I had been drawn along by one group's view of what comprised the significant chronicle of events in Toronto Italia. There were underway other serious narratives such as that of the struggle of migrant workers for safer conditions and better pay – which I had slighted. Obviously I needed to think more carefully about the elite the editor had inadvertently defined and its role in creating the record I was relying on.

This elite and the nascent organic intelligentsia around it divides, I believe, into four groups, each with a view of, or definition of, the *ethnie*, the meaning of the ethnonym Italian and an attitude toward the "ethnic project" of Italians in Canada in terms of the meaning of the passage from the old country, the processes of change and final destiny of the group and its members in the New World. Each group fosters its own sense of the true and significant narrative of Toronto Italia, 1945-85, and the contours of each account differs markedly. The differences begin with the various ways each viewed the people of the *ethnie*. For one group, the immigrants were workers and the children of workers emigrated abroad (*lavoratori e figli dei lavoratori emigrati all'estero*); for the second, they were new Canadians; for the third, Italian Canadians or Canadian Italians; and for the fourth, they were an immigrant cohort at any given time responding or acting upon family, fellow townsmen (*paesani*) and mixed national loyalties and perhaps even nascent class ones.

Of the elements mentioned by the editor, the clergy, perhaps because of their own diversity of origin, did not hold as a collectivity to any single view. Some priests, such as the Italian-American Franciscans active in Toronto, saw the immigrants as Italian Canadians. Other clergy, however, especially those directly from Italy and from various forms of non-parish activism, viewed the immigrants as essentially *lavoratori* abroad, migrants or guest workers like those in western Europe.

This latter view seems to have been held – with varying degrees of mitigating good sense – by Italian government officials and the organic intelligentsia around them, from FILEF, ACLI and Ferdinando Santi representatives to those immigrants who remained absorbed with, and in allegiance to, Italian political parties. Such a view of the newcomers has among its consequences the corollary that the *ethnie* is best understood as a *colonia* and that leadership should come naturally from the consulate. Of the four or five standard types of emplotment for narrative – romance, tragedy, comedy, epic and farce or satire – the one most appropriate to this view is tragedy. The story of the *ethnie* becomes the story of a culture lost, or rather a people lost to their culture, of an Italian government opportunity to influence fumbled, of the fear of being accorded low status in the eyes of the Anglo-Saxon hosts, of a world in which, to quote a famous earlier consul in the United States, Luigi Villari, there were "a thousand trifling, provincial, and local animosities" and an "army without officers commanded by corporals and sergeants."[20] There are also among the organic intelligentsia of the Left who serve "workers abroad," some who see the narrative as centred on exploitation of workers, and the essence of the tragedy lying in the failure of the *patronato* to protect adequately. But more often than not, they too measure the situation in terms of partisan politics. The more traditional Italian representatives seem to favour a narrative which emphasizes events and facts which redound to the national honour of Italy, reflect her unique cultural status in Europe, or the innate skills of her *oriundi* (descendants).

The second view of the immigrants as new Canadians derives ultimately from Canadian authorities, though its agents were and are often the children of the immigrants themselves turned into cultural bureaucrats and school teachers. In this view, the real story of the Italian immigrants, of all immigrants, lies in their contribution to Canada and the aptitude with which they adjust to Canadian ways. The proper literary form for this view is romance, a tale of men and women in a new land which they help to build. Ethnoculture and ethnic identity are here treated as transient values, worthwhile devices by which to ease one's way into full-fledged participation in Canadian life or as quaint "cultural baggage" to be celebrated in the mosaic.

The third group of the elite corresponds roughly to those who lead or man the larger ethnocultural organizations, who are themselves ethnoverted and believe that the hybrid identity, Italian Canadian or Canadian Italian, represents a reality and a collective value which may persist in the New World indefinitely. It is this group that now dominates what little history – in the sense of controlling the record of events and the writing of the narrative – exists in the *ethnie*. This is so not least of all because this elite disposes of the funds or the political access routes to Canadian government funds upon which much of the immigrant or ethnoverted organic intelligentsia survives. In its least guarded moments, a narrative they encourage becomes a collective biography of those who have achieved prominence since immigrating, "uomini di successo Italo-Canadesi." Their approach shares the church view that it is nice to have saints so that lesser men can have models of comportment to admire and emulate. On that one point their understanding of the "ethnic project" and that of Italian officialdom converge. Respectability for the ethnic group, for the homeland (*madrepatria*) and for the parvenu (several of whom *cafoni arricchiti*) are reinforced by the sort of filio-pietist research which finds a pantheon of great Italians such as Caboto, Bressani and Marconi in the Canadian national past.[21] Modern social scientific history is seen as either mean-minded or as thinly veiled Marxist hostility to those who succeed in capitalist society. Their preferred narrative form is also romance with traces of the mock epic when the notables dare or good taste fails.

Some of the younger leadership, educated in North America, are embarrassed by the lack of sophistication in this approach. They have moved toward an incorporation of the fourth interpretation of community, the folk view common to those in *paese* and regional clubs and to those who find cultural satisfaction in sub-national associations, dialect and the living vagaries of *Italiese* and change in the collectivity. This narrative about the *ethnie* verges on a shared folk memory and is a mixture of comedy and popular epic. Stories usually involve using peasant cunning to outwit naive or officious Inglesi (Anglo-Saxons), to humble *"trombette"* (self-important leaders), to avoid ideological conflict. They cherish paesanism and regionalism at the same time as they assert the fundamental *fratellanza* of all Italians in the *ethnie*. Such immigrants are the most susceptible to the new tentatives being made by regional governments in Italy, especially Friuli, Molise and Calabria, to have influence among those overseas. In fact, immigrants' lives in this narrative are seen as the small folk epics they are, with emphasis put on the courage to migrate, years of austerity, overwork and exploitation, as well as the satisfactions and cultural uncertainties which come with time in the land and advancing years. In this narrative, the personal sense of time and accounts of work history as well as recollections of changing attitudes about ethnoculture coincide, for the most part, with the real sequence of migration, building of the Toronto·infrastructure and prosperity and show little awareness of the political and organizational dramas which are part of the ethnicization process and other elite narratives.

Each of the four groups highlight different moments and different clusters of emblematics which rally the ethnic group, which turn, or try to turn, the collectivity into a community. Such moments can revolve around public issues or be simply celebratory. A careful analysis of them may provide a chance to describe the different ways of being Italian Canadian. In other words such an analysis may make it possible to use the ethnonym with sufficient subtlety to be able to see when and why some segments of the group mobilize for communal activity while others do not.

Several recurring categories of rallying situations and emblems exist. They are: Italian national tragedies, e.g., earthquakes, floods, the death of Aldo Moro; celebrations, e.g., the World Cup victory, the opening of Villa Colombo or other facilities, the appointment of Italian Canadians to high office, the coming to town of popular figures, e.g., Pavarotti, Gina Lollobrigida, or a professional soccer club such as Juventus. These rallying points can release a pent-up sense of the need for community, but none of them bring unanimity. What healthy human entity would wish to have unanimity? A careful eye can discern one or the other elite definitions of the *ethnie* at work in a preference for Pavarotti over Loren or Lollobrigida as visitor, or disdain for all of them as vaguely "mangia-cake" and preference for visits by the likes of Dolci, Calvino, or Bassano. Of course, acquiring a show of Da Vinci drawings for the Italian cultural centre transcends such cultural bickering.

Sometimes differences over emblematics arise between immigration cohorts rather than elites. The postwar immigrants are not inclined to support the prewar impresario Johnny Lombardi's annual "Italian Day" at Toronto's Centre Island, which features spaghetti-eating and bathing beauty contests. The question of whether the Dante Alighieri Society should watch contemporary Italian films or hear lectures on Leopardi has elements of elite competition. Even the toponymy of the newly ethnicized core can be a bone of contention. One of the first Canadianizing elements is sharing anti-Americanism, and so many Italian Canadians view the Columbus cult as too Italian American. The new old age home is named Caboto Terrace and that is seen, by those who care about it, as proper repatriation of a process which had previously created Villa Colombo rest home, Columbus Centre, Columbus Day week. Even the communal sense that arises with the effort to help regions of Italy after major earthquakes, precisely because they occur in only one region at a time, has its frayed edges. Several other more contrived forms of rally have some success in making the collectivity momentarily a community. Slurs upon the reputation and good name of the Italian Canadian community such as imputations of widespread organized crime-especially when made by national agencies like the Canadian Broadcasting Corporation or by Toronto police officials – stir some general demand for a B'nai B'rith style anti-defamation organization. (For some reason, much of the filiopietist historiography which searches for "respectable" Italian descent heroes in the Canadian past or indulges in the celebration of immigrant achievers has as its first impulse a response to myths of organized crime.)

More precise issues can on occasion mobilize large numbers of people, often from different segments of the *ethnie*. For example, the struggle for the right to learn Italian as a heritage language in the public schools has replaced the struggle against the "streaming" or "tracking" of Italian immigrant children into vocational and commercial rather than university preparatory courses, and it draws support from the same substantial cross-section of the community as the earlier battle. Another form of rally – against unfair labour practices, to improve the workers quality of life and to deal justly with the problems of injured workmen – can mobilize, with the help of the *Corriere Canadese* and, more consistently, the *Forze Nuove*,[22] as well as Italian and non-Italian trade union officials and politicians, some in the *ethnie*, into a continuing and chastening counter-point to the emphasis which exists at the core on capitalist success and on cultural problems at the expense of social issues. In the changing of emblematic heroes – from Columbus to Caboto to Marconi – in the fact that almost as much to-do could be aroused in the 1970s over the need for the University of Toronto to create a separate Italian Studies department (Italian had been taught previously in an Hispanic and Italian department) as over responding to the Green Paper and other government initiatives to make immigration more difficult, one may choose to see either the transition from the preoccupations of an immigrant settlement to those of an ethnic group competing for status in North America, or the victory of the bourgeois hegemony, through uses of its "organic intelligentsia," over the *ethnie*'s real daily life and project, improving the quality of life.

It is remarkable, given the fact that the mass of migrants arriving after 1951 joined the construction industry work-force and played such a central role in the city's development, that a serious historiography has not emerged in or outside the *ethnie* about Italians, the economy, the labour movement and the parts of the political spectrum dependent on labour support. In those decades of rapid development and economic expansion – the 1950s and the 1960s – the unbridled capitalism of developers and contractors (among the latter some of the new immigrants) was matched by the willingness of immigrant labour to work hard, long and unsafely in order to maximize their *gruzzolo* – nest-egg – either to return to Italy or to bring over family. Men died, were exploited, persevered and succeeded. That was the beginning of the socio-economic history of the *ethnie* – a time in which neither ethnicization nor acculturation had much meaning – and detailed study of that process would be the necessary underpinning of any valid history of postwar Toronto Italia.[23]

As some emerged as *contrattori*, others returned to Italy as casualties or men with savings. At the same time, wives joined the work-force, often for the first time, as *sartini* – cleaning ladies and factory hands. Their absence from the home, particularly in the years before older dependent relatives arrived to help with children and household tasks, undercut both the *Italianità* and the sense of well-being of the home. The rate of differentiation of wealth, if not always of status, in those years among men who had begun as equals must have been astonishing. Since petty capitalist success was as often based on entrepreneurship and cunning as it was on varying levels of willingness to work hard and differences in skills, the changes must also have been troubling. It is likely that the folk memory's assertions of camaraderie and the insistence on the primary non-class based *paesani* groupings by those first labourers represents an attempt to avoid looking too closely at those times. That this labour and socio-economic history has not been even begun reflects the inadequacy of Canadian labour history, especially in settings where proletarian status is not accompanied by proletarian sensibilities.[24]

It also reflects a conscious or unconscious suppression of the "mean" labour history of the group by those who do not find it an acceptable potential narrative for a respectable *ethnie*.

In a brief commendable attempt in 1975 to suggest the need for such a history of the Italian labour movement, the former director of COSTI provided a frame for future study.[25] He saw the period, 1945 to 1960, as one when non-Italian union representatives made sporadic attempts to organize the new work-force and when various branches of government, enamoured with rapid development, were not inclined to step in to protect the work-force. Then from 1960-75 there was a period of labour violence, union organizing in the heart of the Italian community, rapid enrolment of Italians, proliferation of locals and the emergence of Italian-Canadian union officials as well as the appearance of powerful, heavily Italian, umbrella organizations such as the Labourers Local 183. (By 1971 the *Italo-Canadian Directory of Toronto* listed about twenty unions, mainly in construction, service and food trades – all of which had Italian officials.)

The central moment of this labour history arrived in 1960 and 1961. Since bad or pop history seems always to flow to places where serious history is overdue, the critical events of 1960-61 have been described in a book called *Sweethearts: the Builders, the Mob and the Men.*[26] In an account which makes a confused story incomprehensible but carries its readers with innuendoes about organized crime and political corruption, the author describes the attempt in 1961 by Bruno Zanini and others to organize the Italian immigrant workers to protect themselves from falling wages, which their own competition partially caused, and to change inadequate safety conditions at residential construction sites in Toronto. The rising death rate from industrial accidents, a *Toronto Telegram* campaign against the callousness and corruption of contractors and developers, combined with the recalcitrant bigotry or inability of traditional union leaders in the face of the Italian work-force, led to the events of 1961 which included a summer of strikes and labour violence. At the outset of the trouble over 2,000 workers gathered in Brandon Hall – the site of the Italian Canadian Recreation Club and also an informal centre for Italian contractors – to follow Zanini into battle.

The results of that season of violence were:
- the emergence of clearer lines between organized labourers, some skilled trades and contractors, as well as between

- commercial and residential construction work;
- the intervention of the Government of Ontario to end the worst excesses in employment practices and enforce work site safety;
- an eventual Royal Commission on Violence in the Construction Industry which sought to exonerate capitalism by rediscovering the Mafia. The leader of the movement, Zanini, who had shown charismatic quality in his ability to read and control the workers but inconsistency of character, disappeared from prominence; no one like him has since arisen. Nonetheless, two thousand Italian workers, without tutelage from either the consulate or the respectable elites, had met and found common cause and through a concerted effort had begun to change for the better the very bases of their material life in Canada. Someday, one hopes, it will be possible to write the narrative of Italian-Canadian labour in the rich detail it deserves.

By the beginning of the 1970s, the outlines of a new attempt to organize the collectivity into a community were emerging. Some men who had prospered in the 1950s and 1960s now turned inward to the *ethnie* out of a sense of gratitude and service, or as their critics saw it, a need to legitimize their status as *prominenti*. They encountered two pools of ethnoverted organic intelligentsia ready to serve and anxious to find a sinecure *posizione*. The first were drawn from that inevitable trickle of white-collar immigrants that comes with the mass flow. This group included a number still tied to one strand or another of Italian politics, a number of former priests with political beliefs ranging from the radical to Demo-Christian conservatism. As sometime journalists, students, editors, "researchers" *ricercatori*, etc., this migrant intelligentsia found a leadership often unsure of its culture, always unsure of its Italian language, ready to encourage the growth of an organic intelligentsia as long as it occasionally served as flack for their virtue, made justification for the elite's wealth and power, in fact, created a hegemony. Young Italian-born graduates of Canadian universities, many of them thwarted by lack of access to professional schools or buoyed by the emergent bureaucracy of multiculturalism and recognizing the difficulties, even illogic, of pursuing the study of Italian language and literature as a career in Canada, provided a natural pool of talent for the new positions opening up in umbrella Italian-Canadian institutions. This leadership responded to and husbanded the process of ethnicization, conforming to multiculturalism and asserting the growing group and individual respectability of Toronto Italia.

As before there were emergency issues such as earthquakes to draw the collectivity together, but there was also emerging a central "ethnic project," of the sort that affects all immigrant groups undergoing ethnogenesis. That project can be seen in its concrete and in its more notional way as:

- the building of "institutional completeness" with Italian-Canadian organizations and sites which can serve the *ethnie* from cradle to the grave;
- the aura of respectability and status as an ethnic group within the larger civic competition of ethnic groups, which comes with accomplishing such institutional completeness and which, as corollary or result, ends a perceived "bad" reputation in terms of organized crime or humble origins.

This is not to suggest that the ethnic group's accomplishments are less remarkable because they are done with an eye to their effect on the image of Italians in Canada, nor are they less valuable because a capitalist host society requires men of wealth and influence to accomplish, if not necessarily reign over, such communal goals. The idea that such efforts do not spring from the interior history of the group alone but have to do with a heightened sense of being watched by others may, however, help one trying to read a narrative into events such as the creation of the second FACI in 1969 and then of a National Congress of Italian Canadians in 1975 or the building of Villa Colombo and Columbus Centre. It may also help one to understand that groups in the elite hope, without either much manipulation or reflectivity, to impose a pattern for narrative on the future historian.

The new FACI of 1969 took much the same form as the first umbrella organization of the 1950s.[27] There were initially fifty-eight member associations ranging from the small in size, a radical association like the Risorgimento Club, or intent, the Puglia Sports Club to the CIBPA (Canadian Italian Businessmen and Professionals Association). Most of the constituent organizations were by this time clearly representative of the postwar migration, but a few prominent prewar leaders were also present. Although welcomed into existence by the Ontario government, which was by its own admission anxious to "obtain a responsible, responsive, and representative viewpoint of the Italian community in Metro Toronto," FACI's affairs did not prosper. There were deep divisions in the leadership, accusations of favouritism based on regionalism and an apparent tendency to look with great intensity to the emblematics such as organizing Columbus Day week rather than to issues such as a community response to the new immigration policies emerging in the Green Paper, or the new policy on ethnic groups emerging from Vol. IV of the great Royal Commission on Bilingualism and Biculturalism.[28]

A fair history of FACI would have to include an analysis of the variety of Toronto's Italian collectivity – as large as Florence and drawn from much more disparate parts of Italy – which the new umbrella organization has to represent. It is unfortunate that with one eye always cocked to the boundary to see how others perceive them, spokesmen, leaders and organic intelligentsia have always mistaken variety for factionalism and debate for a sign of a unseemly lack of shared ethnic project.[29] That differences between one leader of Sicilian descent, Protestant faith, small business origins and Conservative politics with another leader of Milanese origin, university educated and Liberal politics should be seen as divisive or shameful rather than as a healthy starting point for debate and dialogue may speak to a deeper problem both in organizing the *ethnie* and its history. Things should not be expected of a people in migration that are not expected of them in their homeland.

While the FACI appeared to founder in search of a purpose, a growing interest in creating a rest home, Villa Colombo, for the Italian-Canadian elderly rekindled energy. In the mid-1970s the effort to raise funds for the building of Villa Colombo, like the earlier Casa d'Italia campaign, had the side effect of drawing the collectivity toward community. The fact that some of the ideological Left claimed to see in the Villa a device by which the rich earned merit in the *ethnie* while providing for their parents and those of very few others seems to have had the effect – now that the Villa, Columbus Centre and Caboto Terrace are the heart of community culture and social service agencies – of neutralizing elements critical of the mainstream leadership structure. The ethnicization process and the building of the physical plant were meant to reflect what that leadership believes to be the success and respectability of the ethnic group, and they have.[30] Some tactic beyond petulance and litigation would be necessary to demonstrate that these good communal results are both too limited and an artifice.

One side of the *ethnie*'s story which could be told with more consistency is that which deals with the role and attitude of the

Italian government toward Toronto Italia. Until more documentation and research is available, this narrative too remains episodic. Rumour and gossip thrive where there is no history. There are, in Toronto, myths of good and evil consuls, a memory of one which verges on the hagiographic, a newspaper literature about another which is scurrilous. The historian has little possibility of knowing how much truth such folk views have or whether they merely represent ideological conflicts. What is true is that the relation between the consulate and the community can arouse passion. A *stornello* (type of Neapolitan broadside song) written for one consul included the verse – *chi ha l'allergia, per tutto quello ch'è democrazia* [had an allergy to everything that was democracy].[31] Another newspaper expressed the hope that *il prossimo Console arriva senza etichette politiche* [that the next consul argues without political party affiliation].[32] The consulate has not been good at telling its side of things. At the same time, and regardless of the obvious ideological or personal venom of some of the attacks on Italian representatives, there is a consistency of theme in the polemic which suggests that the *ethnie* chafes under too direct an influence from Rome. Enough nasty jokes about education experts who did their training in Eritrea being sent to Toronto circulate that the Italian government would be wise to encourage a non-ideological, social scientific history of the consular service, its recruitment, attitudes, decision-making, etc.[33]

It is interesting, for example, to see how difficult it is to measure the significance of Toronto Italian participation in the great Rome Congress of Emigration sponsored in February 1975 by the *Comitato Consultivo Italiano all'Estero*. Although many entities with their *sede* in Rome sent delegates, and at least one Toronto intellectual went as representative of an Italian political party, those who attended were for the most part a strangely distinct part of the elite, men who were seen by the rest of the community, perhaps clearly for the first time, as more Italian than Italian Canadian.

One of those who attended came back – possibly for ideological reasons that had to do with which political currents were likely to have most influence on the consulate and *patronato* – to carry on a vigorous campaign against efforts to increase the influence of the *madrepatria* (homeland) on the *ethnie*.[34] "We Italo-Canadians live in a climate of multicultural tolerance and to us the Italy of political party factions constantly in conflict with one another seems a bit far away." He went on to write that Toronto Italia welcomed help but preferred the concept of "co-ordination" to that of "tutelage," and he expressed the hope that Italian representatives would "respect the history and personality of our Italian Canadian community." These remarks appeared in a magazine published by individuals who were representative of the new leadership in the Italian Canadian Benevolent Corporation and the later National Congress of Italian Canadians (NCIC). The negative reports in Canadian *Mosaico* were less a declaration of hostilities than an assertion that Toronto Italia had passed a critical point from immigrant *colonia* to North American ethnic group in the progression of its reality and attitudes; a new relationship to Italy would have to evolve. *La Gazzetta* of Windsor described an ideal new relationship between Italian and Italian Canadian institutions in a 1978 editorial. All those entities with *sede* abroad which affect the collectivity "from FILEF to the Dante Alighieri Society" will have "to be convinced that they must recognize *Il Congresso* and collaborate with it in various sectors; schools, culture, the press, social welfare, youth, accident, etc."[35]

I believe that a detailed study of events and attitudes in the mid-1970s would show a true revolution of sentiment and identity, only dimly perceived at the time, which brought the ethno-community to maturity. Ironically but typically this very North American process of ethnogenesis coincided as well with high levels of personal slippage (assimilation) and still higher levels of acculturation. The period is characterized:

- by rapid institutional expansion – Villa Colombo, the expansion of FACI into the NCIC;
- political success – the appointment of Peter Bosa as a senator, the role of Charles Caccia in the federal Liberal government, the presence of three NDP members of the provincial Parliament – all of these politicians, postwar immigrants;
- the emergence to "middle management" and professional status in the *ethnie* of Canadian-educated children of immigrants; and
- a rallying around an ethnic identity as Italian Canadians at the expense of excessive regionalism, Italianness and Canadianness, *sans epithète*, and even, in the instance of squabbling over whether Caboto or Colombo deserved to be honoured as the group's Adam, at the expense of Italian Americans.

The discrete events of the period, so diverse in nature, all seem to serve this process of ethnogenesis, which was all the more quickly propelled by latent self-disesteem (*atimia*) and civic competitiveness, i.e., concern for the good name and reputation of the Italian group among their Canadian neighbours. Accounts of the accomplishments of those years always carry with them this sense of artifice and of performing, even competing on a multicultural stage. Thus at the fund-raising dinner for Villa Colombo while the Catholic archbishop spoke of goodwill and the minister of State for Multiculturalism emphasized the importance of giving "old folks the opportunity to continue to live as a group," a different theme emerged among the Italian Canadian celebrants. Charles Caccia, MP, described the Villa as "an example of love, tenacity and organization which was able to be given to Canada." Madonia, the president of FACI, described the Villa as "the way in which the community is able to demonstrate that it is capable of excellence." The final speech by Joseph Carrier, who had been president of that first FACI which fought to acquire the Casa d'Italia, described the "importance of this project to the Italian community."[36] The *Corriere Canadese*, covering these events, noted that "also communities numerically much smaller than the Italian, such as the Chinese and Japanese, have their own old age homes. Why not us?"[37]

In 1971 the Italian Canadian Recreation Club found it advantageous to advertise its lack of *campanilismo* (regionalist spirit) and its commitment to a new Italian Canadian *comunità*: "All'Italo Canadian Recreation Club siamo innanzitutto italiani... [there followed the names of all regional groups from Abruzzesi to Veneti]... le nostre porte sono aperte a tutti"[38]. This sort of self-conscious assertion appears over and over again throughout the 1970s. In the midst of the magnificent response to the plight of Friuli after the devastating 1976 earthquake there, Toronto Italia spokesmen/intelligentsia celebrated less the humanity of the moment and more its imposition of community on the collectivity. The Canadian *Mosaico* reported that for the first time in Canada, "tutti gli italiani si sentono fratelli." A newspaper editorial by Sergio Tagliavini identified the Friuli tragedy and the subsequent decision to send all the money gathered (almost $700,000) from the annual Mother's Day fund-raising telethon for Villa Colombo to Friuli as the moment when the Italians of Toronto found a new dimension; when they became and felt "veramente tutti italiani di fuori di ogni barriera regionale."[39] A year later the flyer announcing the establishment of the NCIC, *Cosa e'il Congresso Nazionale degli Italo Canadese?*, included eighteen principles, the first and last of which, as well as many in between, referred to safeguarding the interests of Italian Canadians and upholding the prestige, dignity and good name of the Italians. The process of ethnicization seemed to be leading Toronto Italians into the sort of concern with ethnic identity, inter-ethnic standing, boundaries which, especially in the United States, often seem to outstrip interest in the ethnocultural stuff supposedly being nurtured.

In fact then, Toronto Italia, still the most immigrant of North American Italian settlements, has ripened, perhaps under the hothouse influence of multiculturalism, into a North American *ethnie* in less than two generations. The people of the *ethnie*, for the most part, have achieved a quality of life which could only have been a dream when they arrived in the 1950s. At the heart of the collectivity lie institutions which in their physical size, their relative architectural grace and the "institutional completeness" they shelter, should still even the slightest flutter of the heart of those who suffer from *atimia*, fear bogey-men such as factionalism, criminality and familism.

If all that is a triumph of a sort – and it certainly is for the humble labourers who flooded into Toronto in the 1950s and their children – it is not an answer to questions posed about the "collective project" and the destiny of those who have left Italy for good. The Italian Canadian identity and ethnoculture continue to be best studied as a process – a progression neither moving necessarily farther away from Italy nor toward full acculturation. It is also important for the historian not to succumb to the "naturalness" of ethnic persistence even in a multicultural society. There are constantly moments of cultural uncertainty within the *ethnie* which reflect choices of identity and a species of *ethnie* or "nation building" under way. Such moments remind us that the *ethnie* is both a construct and a process. When the cultural centre acquired its original Da Vinci drawing, it hired a local security agency to guard it. During the day a middle-aged sirdar, a former Sikh soldier in a uniform which was a rumpled and pathetic parody of a police uniform guarded the drawing. At night during the cultural ceremonies, two former *carabinieri*, decked out in the melodramatic garb of the Italian federal police, flanked the drawing. In the morning the sirdar would return for he, and not the *carabinieri*, reflected the daily life of Toronto Italia.

Notes

1. Unless otherwise noted, all statistics are taken from C.J. Jansen and L. Lacavera, *Fact Book on Italian Canadians* (Toronto, 1981).

2. Interview in the *New York Times*, Sunday Literary Magazine, 1 September 1985, p. 9.

3. H. White, "Historical Text as Literary Artifact," in *Topics of Discourse. Essays in Cultural Criticism* (Baltimore, 1978), pp. 83-86 & 67.

4. For a list and discussion of the postwar Toronto Italian press, see G. Grohovaz, "Toronto's Italian Press after the Second World War," in *Polyphony*, Vol. 4, no. 1 (Spring/Summer 1982).

5. G. Grohovaz (ed.), *1932-1985, the First Half Century/Il Primo Mezzo Secolo* (Famee Furlane Club).

6. Beyond the Jansen and LaCavera, *Fact Book*, the following contain useful demographic data: W.G. Marston, "Social Class Segregation within Ethnic Groups in Toronto," in *Canadian Review of Sociology and Anthropology* 6, no. 2 (1969), pp. 45-79; A. Richmond, Immigrants and Ethnic Groups in Metropolitan Toronto (Toronto, 1967); L. Tomasi, "The Italian Community in Toronto: a Demographic Profile," in *International Migration Review* 11, no. 4 (1977).

7. See R.F. Harney, "Toronto's Little Italy," in R.F. Harney and J.V. Scarpaci (eds.), *Little Italies in North America* (Toronto, 1978).

8. Analysis of Italian Canadians in the 1941 Census can be found in Immigration Branch (Government of Canada) 1949-50, *Historical Background*, RG 76, Vol. 131, File 28885.

9. *Annuario Statistico Italiano* (Rome, 1960), Tavole. Espatri di emigrati per via marittime, 1951-59.

10. Although regional origin is not the same as regional sentiment, the existence of a coherent regional or sub-national group such as the Friulani – with their early presence in the city (the Famee Furlane was founded in 1932), numbers, separate *sede*, distinctive language, visible economic success, good political connections (including one of the two Italians in the Canadian Senate and close ties, in fact honourary rights, at the Fogolar for the only federal minister of Italian origin – a northerner if not a Friulian), their Canadian children at once culturally dutiful in terms of language retention, Furlan and Italian, and

often regional endogamy, yet possessed of high levels of education and assimilation – creates a situation in which a species of intra-*ethnie* civic competition arises. Certainly efforts by the Calabrese, both in Toronto and in the regional government are premised on a sense of the advantages of asserting sub-national networks and cultures.

11.   *Italian Canadians: a Cross Section. A National Survey of Italian Canadian Communities* (Ottawa, 1978).

12.   The Multicultural History Society of Ontario holds several hundred hours of taped interviews with postwar Italian immigrants in its sound archives. The interviews are structured generally in the manner suggested in R.F. Harney, *Oral Testimony and Ethnic Studies* (Toronto, 1978).

13.   W. Kalbach and A. Richmond, *Factors in the Adjustment of Immigrants and Their Descendants* (Ottawa, 1981).

14.   Franc Sturino, "Outside and Inside Views of Upward Mobility: the Case of Canada's Italians," paper delivered at the Canadian Ethnic Association conference in Thunder Bay, October 1983.

15.   A *busta* of letters between officials of the first FACI and Canadian government officials, legal documents and newspaper clippings referring to the Casa d'Italia can be found in the Donato Di Giulio Papers at the Multicultural History Society of Ontario, Toronto.

16.   *Corriere Canadese*, 14 April 1975, p. 4.

17.   About thirty archival feet of COSTI papers are also held by the Multicultural History Society. Those who founded the institution, especially Charles Caccia, MP, and Joseph Carraro, should be interviewed and a serious history of COSTI begun.

18.   *Corriere Canadese*, 26 October 1956, p. 14.

19.   *Corriere Canadese*, 10 May 1960, p. 3. One reason an elite was recognizable may have been willingness to pay for the privilege to lead. The vice-president of FACI wrote back to the editor that "persons who wish to elevate the state of the Italian community must be ready and willing to pay for the privilege... to give to the less fortunate what the public wishes but is denied the luxury of having."

20. L. Villari, "L'Emigrazione italiana negli Stati Uniti," in *Nuova Antologia* CXLIII (190-), p. 298.

21. R.F. Harney, *Dalla Frontiera alle Little Italies* (Rome, 1984) for a discussion of *atimia* and filio-pietism.

22. *Forze Nuove, Il Giornale dei Lavoratori Italo-Canadese* has been for a some years the voice of a number of Italian-Canadian radical and socialist intellectuals. It provides an important counterpoint to mainstream thinking and news coverage. It is difficult to measure its impact or readership, but it has been more successful and of higher quality than the short-lived communist paper, *Nuovo Mondo*.

23. There does exist one useful scholarly study of those years. It is the doctoral dissertation by S. Sidlofsky, "Postwar Immigrants in the Changing Metropolis with Special Reference to Toronto's Italian Population," (Ph.D. diss., University of Toronto, 1969).

24. One younger historian who has begun to do excellent work on this topic is Franca Iacovetta. See for example her "From *Contadina* to Worker: Southern Italian Immigrant Working Women in Toronto, 1947-62," in *Looking into My Sister's Eyes: an Exploration in Women's History*, ed. by Jean Burnet (Toronto, 1986).

25. J. Carraro, "Le Unioni e La Communita Italiana," in *Canadian Mosaico*, Vol. 2, no. 2 (February 1975).

26. C. Wismer, *Sweethearts: the Builders, the Mob and the Men* (Toronto, 1980).

27. Papers relating to FACI on deposit at the Multicultural History Society.

28. *The Cultural Contribution of the Other Ethnic Groups*, Vol. IV of the Royal Commission on Bilingualism and Biculturalism (Ottawa, 1969).

29. For an excellent discussion of how an ethnic group perceives internal dissent, see Raymond Breton, "La communauté ethnique, communauté politique," in *Sociologie et Sociétés* XV:2 (1985):23-37.

30. There is an extensive debate on the appropriateness of Villa Colombo, Columbus Centre and the Italian Canadian Benevolent Corporation – the organization created to raise funds and control the development of the ethnie's core – in *Corriere Canadese, Il Giornale di Toronto* and *Forze Nuove*. There was also unseemly litigation over statements made in that coverage.

31. *Communità Viva*, IX, 8-9 August 1980, pp. 5-9.

32. *Forze Nuove*, June 1980.

33. In the wake of the difficulties in the 1970s several changes occurred in the
     1980s. The economic and political success of Italians in Toronto and the
     emergence of scholarship about the group helped to encourage an
     ethnogenesis that transformed the group from an immigrant and ethnic
     enclave to a mature and self-confident community. With these changes fuller
     cooperation and dialogue occurred in the 1980s between the Toronto
     community and the Consulate.

34. L. Pautasso, "Il Punto di Vista di un Italo-Canadese," *Canadian Mosaico*, Vol.
     2, no. 4, April 1975. The same author published the periodical *Quaderni
     Canadesi*, which ran a number of articles comparing the Italian government in
     the 1970s with the *consolarfascismo* of the 1930s.

35. *La Gazzetta* (Windsor), June 1978 editorial by Professor W. Temellini.

36. V. Ariemma, "Update on Villa Colombo," in *Facts and Opinions*, CIBPA,
     (November 1974).

37. *Corriere Canadese*, 1 June 1974. One can be forgiven, I hope, for seeing some of
     the same *atimia* in this matter as that expressed by the pastor of St. Clement's
     Church in Toronto in 1920 whose fund-raising speech ended with, "... we have
     shown we are not degenerate Latins... We will build our new church in this
     city and remove the blemish from the good name of Italians," Parrochia di San
     Clemente (Toronto) *Annuario 1920*.

38. See advertisement for Italian Canadian Recreation Club in *Italo-Canadian
     Commercial Directory* 1971, p. 55.

39. Sergio Tagliavini editorial in *Corriere Canadese*, 11-12 May 1976, p. 1.

Photo Multicultural History Society of Ontario

4

Undoing the Risorgimento: Emigrants from Italy and the Politics of Regionism[1]

I was seized by a strong desire to tell you of my valley, of my folks, of my native town. I love my valley and my folks as myself. I know their soul which is my soul. Bartolomeo Venzetti (from death row, 1926).[2]

*T*he role that *campanilismo* and regionalism have played in the lives of Italian emigrants is referred to so often in popular discourse and scholarship on both sides of the Atlantic, that it has achieved iconic status in the canon of migration studies. The *contadino* immigrant is portrayed as the ultimate xenophobe, one who believes that anyone who comes from beyond his *paese* is a potentially dangerous stranger. After travelling extensively in the United States and Canada at the turn of the century, Aldolfo Rossi, an official of the Commissariat of Emigration, described the immigrant's state of mind and sense of identity.

> In them is a profound and tenacious tie (*vincolo*) to family, in their hearts, after their affection for their own family comes their attachment to their village; so that after their relatives they are most attached to their fellow villagers (*compaesani*), then their relatives' friends, then those from their region (*comprovinciale*). At that point begin the strangers, *l'indifferente*, the men whom the south Italian instinctively distrusts.[3]

Such a view of the immigrant usually appears as the interpretive base for any description of the welter of *paese* clubs, chains of migration, sub-neighbourhoods and networks of opportunity based on *paesani*, as well as of the "fractionalism" that thwarted priests, consuls, ethnic politicians, businessmen become *prominenti* who sought to organize a coherent *ethnie* among the migrants.

Beginning a quarter of a century ago with Rudolph Vecoli's influential article "Contadini in Chicago: A Critique of the Uprooted," scholars of the Italian-Americans began to graft their picture of the Italian migrant onto the sacred texts of American immigration such as M. L. Hansen's *Atlantic Migrations* and O. Handlin's *The Uprooted*.[4] At first glance, the string of studies inspired by Vecoli's article – his subtitle was an overt riposte to Handlin's Pulitzer Prize winning work – such as H. Nelli's *Italians in Chicago*, J. Briggs' *An Italian Passage*, and D. Cinel's *From Italy to San Francisco* modified, seemed to invalidate the themes of uprooting, of undergoing a sea change, of hungering to be American, of mobility and acculturation that had formed the American canon. Although Nelli failed to see beyond a generic cohort of "Southerners," the other authors (I should add parenthetically followed bravely in Canada by Harney, Ramirez, Zucchi and Sturino) revelled in demonstrating the "rootedness" of the Italian migrants, dwelling on their *campanilismo*, the economic advantage they derived from *paesanism*, their sojourning mentality, their "double consciousness" i.e. active interest and concern for the *terra natale* (a sufficiently vague geographical term no matter how evocative to spare one from explaining the difference between *paesanism*, regionalism, and patriotism). Affirming the image of the first North American Little Italies as places "of a thousand trifling provincial and local animosities" where the idea of *paesani*, although a *"fecondo creatrice di nuclei coloniali*, defeated every attempt at thinking on a larger scale, of renewing or changing the moral (and political) atmosphere,"[5] the historians demonstrated that most migrants from Italy were most definitely not "uprooted" from their primary loyalties.

Most also agreed that not just Americanization, but also ethnicization took place. Within a generation, the institutional life and rhetoric of the migrants, often when they were on the very threshold of acculturation and assimilation, moved from *campanilismo* and regionalism toward a pan-Italian and Italian American sensibility. From a vantage point, looking across three generations of Italian Americans, scholars could see the objective conditions in North America – geographical proximity to migrants from many parts of Italy, Italian "national" parishes, shared encounters with prejudice, competition against other ethnic groups for a "piece of the (political and economic) pie" and for reputation, the relentless assault on the migrant audience by the nationalist preachments of *prominenti*, consuls, and some clergy, ironically combined with a decline of real knowledge of Italy and a rise of nostalgia – that had conspired to encourage the development of a sort of Italian national consciousness among the immigrants. Drawing upon these North American realities, different historians have pointed out different causes for the decline of *campanilismo* and regionalism and the growth of national feeling, a sense of shared ethnicity, to use the jargon of North American social science, among the immigrants and their Italian American descendants.

Some saw bigotry and exploitation, – or, if one emphasized the degree to which Italian Americans were petty capitalist *contadini* rather than permanent proletariat, of barriers to mobility – as playing a major role in forging an Italian identity among the migrants. For example, Vecoli ascribed the tendency of Italians on Minnesota's Iron Range "to remain within their group" as partly a matter of choice but also as "a reaction to ostracism by the dominant Anglo-Scandinavian element." He added that "one consequence of this exclusion was that the Italians gradually came to recognize that their common identity as a nationality group was more important than regional differences and that only through unity could they challenge the entrenched WASPs." Others saw the decline of particularism, ethnicization, and the rise of Italian American national consciousness as a product of the rhetoric of World War I and of Fascist propaganda efforts to *"italianizzare"* the immigrants. Cinel characterized the mental journey that San Francisco Italians made in a century thus: "They started with *campanilismo* and ended with Americanization." With chapters entitled "Italian regionalism in San Francisco" and "From Regionalism to Nationalism," Cinel left no doubt that he accepted a model of identity negotiation which began with *paesanism*, moved on to regionalism, then to *Italianità*[6], and then to the Italian-American ethnic group, or to fuller acculturation and assimilation. Although few Italian American scholars have shown sufficient distance to study the matter yet, it is clear that a renewed nationalism, or ethnicism, with accompanying jeremiads about the consequences of lack of ethnic cohesion, has also been nurtured by the "status anxiety" of the 1960s and 1970s which led some Italian Americans to embrace the "new ethnicity" in the face of WASP hegemony and Black mobilization.

In Canada, John Zucchi's work has illustrated the dynamics of *paesanism* and emergent nationalism among Italian immigrants before World War II in more detail and with more subtlety than has the American literature on the subject. According to him, the new realities that the earliest migrants to Toronto faced such as the need to create a national parish, common business interests, the need for expanding mutual aid insurance pools, the scarcity of suitable marriage partners from a given *paese*, and the sharing of neighbourhood with migrants from many regions, fostered a continuum in which loyalty to *paesani* was not xenophobic *campanilismo* but rather a necessary building block toward a sense of *Italianità*. Zucchi concluded that "loyalty to the hometown group therefore did not preclude loyalty to the larger Italian population of the city... It was through the hometown that the immigrant began to identify with an Italian community in the city." Zucchi has gone on to demonstrate the "nationalizing" role played by various elites within the pre-Second World War Toronto Italian collectivity. Reinforcing the theme of ethnicization, i.e. that the migrants from the Italian peninsula became Italian, or were forged into an Italian ethnic group, in North America, are thoughtful studies on parallel ethnic groups, such as F.M. Padilla's recent work on the development of a shared Latino consciousness among Mexicans and Puerto Ricans in Chicago.[7]

What is striking about all these accounts of prewar Italian immigrants in the United States and Canada is how closely they resemble the "exceptionalist" myths of earlier American historiography that they claim to subvert. In the end, the Italian American literature enriches the canon with ancillary texts without changing its essence. Certainly the image of the "uprooted" peasant is modified by accounts of migration chains, *paesanism* and sojourning mentalities. Certainly Handlin's Crevecourerean assertion that migrants crossed the sea questing to escape oppressive European ways and landed on the shore anxious to become American, is modified by the ethnicization thesis and the idea that immigrants developed Italian national feeling even as they acculturated to North America. Such revelations are only exegesis to the canon's original texts which claim that immigrants arrived as "men of their village" and ended as Americans whether Anglo-conformists, products of the melting pot, or partisans of the "new ethnicity."[8] In all these texts, the American vector toward the future is confirmed; migrants come from an identity of origin and move – after a period of felt and ascribed hyphenated ethnonational identity – toward their American identity of destiny. That odyssey of sentiment is viewed as in lockstep with objective social reality, especially geographical and economic mobility and acquisition through experience or education of the mainstream culture.[9]

The diachronic form the American canon takes leads to historicism. Put simply, since the story of immigration and ethnicity is seen exclusively as part of a national drama of becoming or failing to become the America of the dream, any synchronic sense that conditions and sentiments change in the homeland, that the natural patterns of immigrant pre-selection change, that the post-industrial world's sense of *paese* and *madrepatria* change, that the political culture and social ideas and conditions of the homeland continuously intrude and shape immigrant identity becomes irrelevant. It is true that some American studies have dealt with the impact of World War I patriotism, of Fascism, and of the War Years on Italian American identity, and one, A. DeConde's *Half Bitter, Half Sweet* is, if not a synchronic study of Italy and Italian-Americans, at least an effort to deal systematically with "double consciousness among immigrants from Italy in the United States. However, the idea of studying the immigrants and their American children as sharing a continuing history with their country of origin and with those they define as part of their global diaspora living in other target countries, the idea of viewing political and cultural change in the old country as an integral part of immigrant history, of listening to the dialogue between immigrants and their homeland would seem to contravene orthodoxy and lie outside the canon.

It would be a silly and visceral anti-Americanism to argue that the exporting of "exceptionalist" myths about immigration is the fault of the thoughtful scholars who tried to create the most elegant models for explaining Italian American immigrant history only to be incorporated in those myths. Nonetheless those who study the Italian experience outside of the United States, especially the new and larger phenomenon of post World War II migration need to comprehend how the mass migration of the turn of the century became mythopoeic in American thought.[10] It is a mistake, for example, for historians of post war Canada, Australia, and even the United States, to assume the applicability of the scriptural account of the prewar migrant's sentimental journey from particularism to Italian national feeling and then assimilation and/or the "new ethnicity" which dominates the American canon. At least, we cannot do so without testing it against the contemporaneous reality.

In the same year, 1964, that the appearance of Vecoli's "Contadini in Chicago" signalled the beginning of rigorous study of the place of Italians in American immigration myths, I began teaching the history of Italy and of immigration at the University of Toronto. Since then, the American literature has informed much of my work and that of some of my students. The idea of immigration history as a vector of progress from localism through ethnonationalism to acculturation served admirably as a way of describing prewar Toronto Italians who were, after all, merely an outrigger of the flow of labour to capital that went on so massively in the United States. However, I have become increasingly uneasy about applying diachronic ideas, with their emphasis on ethnicization fading into acculturation – and their untidy dependence on concepts like "ethnic rediscoverers," the "need for roots" and the "third generation return" to account for anomalous instances of renewed ethnicism – to postwar global migration and to the Italian collectivity in greater Toronto specifically. Too many things have changed in the world for a model that fits the 1900s in the United States to explain the choices which immigrants make in Canada in the 1980s.

Before mentioning some of those changes and suggesting how they may affect interpretation of the immigrant's world, I wish to describe the nature and magnitude of the Toronto Italian collectivity, one of the largest and most vibrant outside of Italy, and one, unlike American Little Italies, dominated by immigrants rather than North American-born ethnics. (Indeed the very magnitude of Toronto Italia may skew my interpretation. Perhaps what I am about to describe could only happen in so large a collectivity.) About six out of every ten Canadians of Italian descent live in southern Ontario, four of ten in Metropolitan Toronto. Between 1951 and 1981, the population of Toronto has doubled from a little over a million people to its current two and a half million. The source of that growth is revealed by the fact that in the 1981 Census, 43% of the city's population was listed as foreign born and that, after immigrants from the United Kingdom, the largest group of newcomers came from Italy. While the city's population has doubled in those thirty years, the Italian descent group has grown almost tenfold, from under 30,000 to well over 300,000. The immigrants come from all regions of Italy with the largest contingents, probably in descending numbers from Calabria, Abruzzi and Molise, Friuli and Treviso, Lazio, Puglia, and Lucania. This new concentration of Italians, generally in one broad corridor of settlement throughout the west end of the city – with a second predominantly Sicilian and Foggian collectivity in the east end – has an *ambiente* and "ethnic institutional completeness," an immediacy of ties to both the Italian state and "high tradition" as well as to hundreds of sending *paesi*, unmatched anywhere in the world. According to the 1971 census, the Italians of Toronto were 54% immigrants and 28% the children of immigrants. Only 17% were the children of the Canadian-born. Over 50% of the migrants had come to Toronto in one great wave between 1951 and 1961. In 1971 only 6% of the group had both parents in North America. The Italian-born continue even now to outnumber the Canadian-born, especially among adults. It is significant though that some of the leadership is passing from the prewar *prominenti* and those who came as young adult workers to those who came as dependent children after World War II.[11]

No discussion of the magnitude of the Italian immigrant collectivity in greater Toronto can possibly impart a sense of its variety and of the mercurial pace at which the psychology of ethnolinguistics, associational life, loyalties, culture, and identities move. Toronto, after all, has as many Italians as Florence, drawn from many more parts of the peninsula and freed, some might say confused, by the conditions of being migrant and of having exchanged the yoke of one hegemony for another. That should be kept in mind when one judges the influence of consuls speaking of a *colonia*, of NCIC officials who refer to the community, or of young Italian-Canadian politicians who invoke a bloc vote. To paraphrase D'Azeglio, Toronto Italia may exist *"ma bisogna ancora fare gli italo-canadesi."*

In fact, it seems to me that Toronto Italia defies the definitions imposed upon it by those seeking hegemony over it in the same way that its present and its future cannot be contained within the simple model borrowed from prewar American experience. For me, looking at the history of Toronto Italia as an episode without predetermined vector, analyzing synchronically the sentiment, behaviour, and political and cultural choices made here as part of a *fenomeno coinvolto* that ties together immigrants in Toronto, returnees and people left behind in the *paesi*, and migrants from those same *paesi* in colonies around the world, is a necessary antidote to North American cliches about immigrant history and ethnic group life as well as to the tendency to accept as reality the definitions of community preferred by competing "agents of articulation" and contenders for hegemony over the immigrants. I am convinced that a more deeply textured narrative of the immigrant collectivity's history is possible. We need to learn from literary criticism, especially discourse theory, and from social anthropology, especially the Geertzean idea that one can find a nexus of significance and a cultural narrative through "thick description" of communal occasions, in order to comprehend Italian-Canadian history in process. We need to be open to the possibility that:

- changes in the migrants themselves,
- changes in Italian political culture,
- the slow growth of a pluralist alternative to assimilation in the receiving countries, and
- the revolution of transportation, communication, leisure, and interlocked service economics in the Atlantic world make it unlikely that postwar migrant settlement history will repeat that of the 1900s.[12]

Obviously I could spend much time delineating the nature of change in each of the categories mentioned above. The new migrants to Canada, unlike their Umbertine great grandparents who had rarely participated in the political process, are the products of first a unified, then a fascistized Italy, and finally of the clientele systems or ideological patterns of mass democracy. A century long migration tradition informed their choice of migration targets and defined their migration projects. Although many have come from the less developed regions of the country, the *paesi* they left behind were not isolated but rather the vital labour supply periphery of a fully industrialized Europe with all that implies in terms of their knowledge of job opportunities throughout the world and their levels of expectation. Return migration, annual seasonal return, return for specific ritual occasions, sending Canadian-born children on visits to Italy are along with marriages and new household creation a central preoccupation in Toronto Italia. The reason for this are many and intertwined. They include the availability of low cost, rapid and comfortable transportation; the comparative well-being of the *paesi* – itself a by-product of successful migration strategies – ; the social safety nets of the modern Italian state; the constant coming and going of migrants within the European labour market; decisions in the *paesi* to encourage mondialization (*apaeseamento*); the neo-capitalist system's fostering of both tourism and periodic leisure time for workers.

If the migrant's sense of the consequences of the act of migration have changed, so, slowly, has the receiving society's sense of who the migrants are. The existence of guestworker systems that discourage permanent settlement and assimilation provide both Italian migrants and Canadian and Italian authorities with models of behaviour that undermine the view that the prewar American experience will repeat itself here. Although most of the objective conditions which draw immigrants toward acculturation – or at least toward formation of a sense of self and group in keeping with their real condition – pertain in Canada, there are new conditions as well. The declared policy of multiculturalism, state support for heritage language teaching, the pandering of political parties to the ethnic groups as potential bloc voters, encourage a sense of ethnicity and group persistence. The multicultural policy, especially, seems to imply penalties for any group of migrants who do not mobilize, form an *ethnie* and show sufficient ethnoversion to impress the host society and the government with their political potential.[13] That is one reason why an observer can detect a tone of voice, a sense of competitive performance among those who call for an active and coherent Italian Canadian *ethnie*, very reminiscent of the Risorgimental intellectuals' embarrassed laments about the Italian peninsula's disunity, the low national consciousness of the people, and the nation's failure to be a great power in the mid-19th century. If the Jewish and Japanese ethnic groups can build magnificent cultural centres or homes for their elderly, if Ukrainian Canadians can exercise so much political influence, etc. why can't Italian Canadians? Or, shouldn't we?[14] So far, the forces favouring ethnicization, followed by acculturation, would seem to be dominant, especially when one adds to the formula the impact of an English-speaking host culture which is little inclined to make regional distinctions about Italians. Indeed, as Ontario becomes more multiracial, there have been occasions when representatives of visible minorities refer to all the white populace including Italian Canadians as Anglosaxons.

Among the most interesting juridical, political and sentimental changes affecting the postwar Italian emigration is the emergence of regional government as a force in the lives of migrants overseas. When the 20 regional juntas, promised in the republican constitution of 1948, finally came into being in 1970, many might have agreed with the assessment that saw the creation of the regions as a cynical effort by the mass parties, denied power at the centre, to build their clientelist systems on the periphery. A few analysts were acute enough, even then,[15] to see that while part of the populace would fret over another level of government as bringing "more taxes, more political officials, and more bureaucrats to harass the citizenry" others would understand the "concrete benefit to determinate individuals which more government can provide." Few could have predicted the special helix of mutual need that seems to be emerging between regional politicians and those from the region overseas, or how the combination of tourism and well-healed *rientrati* may become for regions what remittances once were for *paese*.

Since the emergence of regional governments in Italy, immigrants overseas or in western Europe have been offered an alternative rally of loyalty and way of seeing themselves to that of citizens of a unitary nation or to the particularist view of themselves as *paesani*. The complex needs of politicians and intelligentsia in Italy to find status, employment and justification through regionalism meshes nicely with the need of immigrants or their children to identify with an area and population less obscure than the hometown and less impersonal than the nation state. Regional authorities find in the tourist and trade, possibilities of increased ties with emigrants, a financial resource which should more than compensate for the decline of remittances which comes naturally with the maturing of a migration cohort overseas. In the nostalgia for "home" and search for "roots" which often signal the completion of the migration process, many immigrants are a natural audience for regionalist texts in the ethnic discourse. They can imagine themselves as fellow members of a regionalist community, and since all communities larger than a village must be based on imagination rather than face to face contact, such imagined community, with the proper nurturing, can grow in relevance.

Although it tries to ally itself with and use efforts at mondialization (*apaeseamento*) also underway in Italy and in the *colonie*, this new political regionalism is different from traditional forms of *paesano* loyalty as expressed in the idea of *campanilismo*. Political regionalism battens on the technological and psychological forces which make mondialization possible, especially the flow of people and news back and forth and the proliferation of "little magazines" and newspapers among the *paesani*, but its agenda and its goals are not about the small towns of emigration.[16]

In the remainder of this discussion, I wish to look at three topics in order to comprehend the appeal of regionalism for some "agents of articulation" and a portion of their audience within the *ethnie*, and to encourage closer study of the daily conversation and discourse that goes on there. The three topics are

- the nature of the discourse within the *ethnie* – who are the speakers, what are the texts, and who are the readers of texts (as well as and what are the fora within which the discourse takes place),
- what is the special appeal of regionalism to emigrants from Italy in southern Ontario now, and

- a case study of the forging – I use the word with the mischievous double meaning that Yeats intended when describing the rise of Sinn Fein in Ireland – of a regionalist "national identity," in this case among the so-called "Molisani" in Toronto.

To begin to hear the discourse and the daily discussion in the *ethnie*, we need to abandon definitions of ethnicity, or nationality, based on descent rather than consent. Ethnicity is a North American process; it is a continual negotiation of identity within a context of the concentric circles of loyalty and patriotism toward family, friends, town, region, country of emigration, as well as nascent loyalties to his new friends, neighbourhoods, cities, and country of immigration. Ethnocultural communities, or *ethnies*, only to a certain extent, are the logical consequences of immigration, settlement and diglossia. They emerge first as natural shelters from the violent forces of prejudice, exploitation, and acculturation that surround migrants and their children. Ethnic groups in the end, unlike immigrant collectivities, are made, not born; they are artifices, quasi-polities within which clergy, politicians, notables, middle class brokers and entrepreneurs, visiting old country intellectuals, consuls and government officials from the sending countries, and organic intelligentsia of the Left and Right struggle to attain hegemony over the emergent ethnocommunity's discourse. The immigrant often lives in a whirl of conflicting or mutually unintelligible written, spoken, and semiotic texts which guide him in his choice of loyalty, identification with group, and intensity of ethnoversion. The existence of the ethnic group is, to paraphrase Renan, "a plebiscite of all the people, every day." The fluidity of ethnicity is reflected in the situational way in which people respond to the questions posed in a polyethnic society like Canada, questions such as *Who are you?*, *Where do you come from?*, *What language do you speak?* Questions which, of course, deserve and receive different responses when they are posed in English, Italian, or dialect. It is this situationalism that gives ethnicity a historical life and makes the borrowing of earlier historiographies problematic.[17]

The question posed in the paper's title "When is an Italian Canadian" reflects the migrant's changing situational sense of primary membership, a sense described by labels such as Italian, Italian Canadian, Italo-Canadese, Calabrese, Consentino, Canabrese, and new Canadian. This variety of adjectives is the inheritance of the struggle within the discourse, the hierarchy of discourse in the city, the clutter, misreading (*méprison*), and slippage which characterize a group of people who possess so much freedom of choice, leisure, and access to mass communications, a group of people who, in the same month, may have to access their relationship to a fund raising effort encouraged by the Italian embassy to build a museum in honour of Marconi, the quasi-regal visit of the president of the Abruzzi region to Toronto, the visit of the president of the Italian Republic – Prime Minister Mulroney of Canada breaking bread with both presidents, the *feste* of several hometown saints. The catalogue can seem endless and the ink, air time, sermons, as well as the gossip in the little storefront *paese* clubs, dedicated to such events, excessive. In fact, it seems unlikely that any regnant ideology could be imposed on the people who live in Toronto Italia. Until recently, three regimes of truth, which I characterize as the colonial, the proletarian, and the "coming Canadian" have dominated the interpretation of who the immigrants are, or who they are supposed to think they are.

In the first view, the migrants are seen as Italians in danger of losing their *Italianità* in Canada – or as an embarrassment to the ethnonational intelligentsia because they have never been carriers of Italy's urban "great tradition". With variations, Italian officials posted to Toronto see the *colonia* that way, while those in the various party-based parts of the *patronato* such as FILEF and ACLI often describe immigrants as *lavoratori italiani emigrati all'estero*. In this view, there is little sense that immigration is permanent or that primary political loyalty might shift to Canada. There is also a tendency, reflected in the recent legislation on *comitati consolari* to see the collectivity as a *colonia* or community to be directed from Rome and to view *paese*-based or regional clubs as quaint, or perhaps as a source of advisors, courtiers, or agents for combatting fractionalism or lethargy and indifference in the collectivity.

Texts in the discourse have location as well as audience. As Toronto Italia moves northwestward, the consulate remains in the older downtown. In Toronto, as in Montreal, the *Istituto Italiano di Cultura* is located near the premier university, not in the community. That is not mere accident, for as one official put it: "If I bring in a major Italian theatre company, for instance, it would be wrong to drag everyone to some building on the city's periphery." One can hear echoes of older Italian struggles between urban and rural culture in such remarks.[18] Clearly the texts about group identity and culture one would hear or read at the *Istituto* or the consulate,

define the *ethnie* differently from those present on a given cultural
or social evening at the Famee Furlane or the community-run Villa
Colombo rest home and Columbus Centre; and as Luciani has
pointed out, not only the texts but the medium would be very
different in the dozens of *paese* clubs and "soccer-supporter"
cafe/billiard parlors where "one speaks only the dialect of the
region, with linguistic variations which characterized such and such
a village." An ethnoculture to exist has to be embedded in a coherent
sub-society.[19] Toronto Italian can hardly be said to have such a
basis.

Of course, the effort to make Italian national identity the
primary loyalty of the immigrants receives powerful boosts from the
same sorts of events and crisis which cause patriotic surges in the
homeland. It is a truism that when nationalist texts can be grafted
onto latent patriotism or *amour propre*, fractionalism declines. The
response to slurs directed at the community, especially those that
trade in the mafia mystique, and to moments like a World Cup
soccer victory leave no doubt that the collectivity always has latent
pan-Italian national feeling. Thus community response to
earthquakes in Italy transcends regionalism. At the time of the
Friulan earthquake in the mid 1970s, journalists in the community
marvelled that *"tutti gli italiani si sentono fratelli"* and that they
moved *"fuori di ogni barriera regionale."*[20]

In the second view, the immigrants are seen, not in
ethnonational terms or as sojourning guestworkers, but in a
Canadian socio-economic context. They are peasants turned labour
migrants, faced with the difficulties of insertion into an industrial
economy, victimized either by bigotry and capitalist exploitation or
by their own diglossia, in need of political mobilization to protect
themselves. That mobilization, of course, should, in this view, be
under the aegis of a Canadian labourers' party such as the NDP. The
problem for these speakers in the discourse is that, while their texts
had great relevance for the first generation of migrants, and for those
who are the continuing victims of the migration process and
Canadian industrialism, it seems to appeal less and less to that large
segment of the immigrant cohort who came as labourers in the 1950s
and 1960s and who have participated successfully in the Ontario
boom, and who have satisfied many of the very petty capitalist
impulses which inspired their original decision to migrate. Another
part of the organic intelligentsia competing for hegemony and to
impose their texts on the *ethnie*, is the clergy. Depending on their

own background, length of time in the land or pastoral sense, priests in the collectivity adhere variously to the view of their parishioners as exploited labour migrants, *paesani* in need of the religious and local cultural *ambiente* of their towns of origin, or Italians who face the loss of their culture from the onslaught of secular media, a Protestant or religiously indifferent host, and an Irish Roman Catholic hierarchy.

Finally there is the view of the Italian immigrant which sees them as hesitant new Canadians, as people in search of economic improvement, opportunity for their children, and about to be swept into the Canadian mainstream by mobility and acculturation. The maintenance of aspects of a *via vecchia*, of *paese* clubs, of close-knit neighbourhoods, of the Italian language or of various dialects are, in this view, which is mainly held by Canadian "caretakers," barriers to full participation in Canadian life, or, at best, ingredients for symbolic differentiation and folkloric celebration of heritage through which "multiculturals" – the lexical monstrosity often preferred now in public circles to use of the word "ethnics" – contribute to the Canadian mosaic.

The truth is that, if ethnicity is processual and situational, a negotiation of every day, then all of these "regimes of truth" claiming to define the migrants have their moments of relevance or explanatory power. A fourth "regime of truth," which is how the migrants see themselves in relation to their act of migration and to the various speakers and texts competing to tell them who they are, emerges from an attempt at a more demonic intellectual history of the *ethnie*, that is intellectual history as the history of the immigrants and their children's thinking. That fourth "regime of truth" has an increasingly regional idiom.[21] Michael Kenny's study of Spanish migrants abroad offers a view of the relationship between ethnonational texts and regionalism that usefully suggests the competition of speakers and hierarchies of discourses inherent in shaping an *ethnie*. "Regionalism is artificially preserved and indeed exaggerated abroad by a kind of mouth-to-mouth network of mutual aid and celebration of "little traditions." Over this transplanted regionalism, Kenny describes a superficially grafted "great tradition" and nationalism which, he believes is "arbitrarily universalized into ethnonational holidays and group causes.[22]

I believe the case can be made that such a grafting of the "great tradition" and nationalism – despite committees to celebrate Columbus Day, to put Caboto on a stamp, to build a Marconi museum and despite less symbolic efforts to manipulate migrants as potential voters in Italian or Canadian elections or to emulate the more ethnoverted communities of refugees from eastern Europe in demanding group recognition and a "piece of the pie" in terms of appointive offices – generally fails in Toronto Italia. There is, in effect, the same lack of a true *"azione sui contadini"* that which characterized the Risorgimento and made of it a *"rivoluzione passiva"* incapable of revolutionizing the sentiments of the mass of people.

The absence of this central mobilization into an ethnic community bothers those who involve themselves in the discourse at the level of ethnonationalism. Thus an influential newspaper editor, significantly one of the few educated Milanese in the migration, called as early as 1959 for a *"piccolo parlamento di una grande comunita"* which could "give the Italian Canadian community a center, a direction, a program."[23] In such a context, manifestations of regionalism are only tolerated if they can be translated into a confederal basis for ethnonationalism. At the first meeting of the *Circolo Calabrese* in 1956, the president called for the club to expand its activities "to the advantage of all Calabresi residents in Toronto. An influential businessman who played an intermediary role with the host society interrupted from the floor to endorse the work of the club and to suggest that "it would be more desirable if all the activities of various regional clubs *confluiscono* into the activities of a bigger and all encompassing *circolo italiano* (Italian Canadian club). Two decades later, the need to break through regionalism to develop an ethnonation was described in much the same way. "The community," wrote the journalist, "lives like an island, or perhaps an archipelago formed by many little islands: the Sicilians, the Calabresi, the Abruzzesi, and Friuliani and so on... " He went on to observe that *"paese* or regional clubs are important and no one wants to diminish them but in the nature of things they do not help the community show a common face to outsiders... "[24]

"A common face to outsiders," the ethnonationalist's plea for solidarity at the expense of factionalism can seem harmless to some and has the ring of an unthinking parody of Italian nationalism from Crispi to World War II to others, but it has left room for the emergence of regionalism, no longer seen as crippling or irrelevant in the new world context. As a new "regime of truth," regionalism sees the immigrant squarely as a man of a region, nurtured by a regional government, an active member of a regionally based club or federation in Canada, tied to a confederation of such clubs throughout the diaspora. Such a man may be Canadian in citizenship, replete with latent patriotism for Italy, but regionalist in his sense of fellow feeling, his networks of acquaintance, his culture, and his dialect (which may, in this view, be a mark not of ignorance of the *lingua dantesca* but rather possession of a nascent national language.) In some synchronic sense, such a man is not a migrant from Italy, not merely *un paesano* but a part of Molise, or Calabria, or Friuli *nel mondo*. The idea of being primarily identified as from a region and the ideology of having to act on the existence of that idea are different stages in consciousness and mobilization.[25] Thus being an emigrant from near Cosenza in Calabria can be variously read as being a Rendese, a Cosentino, a Calabrese, or an Italian. Increasingly the texts – written, oral and semiotic – that cause some of the migrant readers to describe themselves in regional terms grow in appeal.

In Toronto, one especially powerful, and in many ways misleading, semiotic text available to those from the regions created in 1970 is the success and coherence of the migrants from Friuli. (The group's experience is misleading because Friuli as a region has had autonomy since the 1940s, has an ancient sense of being a nation, and its migrants in Toronto have often had the advantage of having the right physical characteristics to please the sensibilities of a racialist north European host society.)   With their separate hall (*fogolar*), distinct language,[26] economic success, relative endogamy and their ability to be Friulian, Canadian, and yet exercise group power within the Italian-Canadian entity, the Friuliani trigger what a leading analyst of modern European ethnonationalisms, Walker Connor, labels "the demonstration effect" among submerged peoples.[27] If they can persist or assert themselves as a people, we can and should too."

To understand how regionalism may be affecting the ethnicization of Italian-Canadians and subverting some of the texts of Italian officials and nationalist intelligentsia on the one hand and of the *paese* associations on the other; we need to look more closely at how an ethnic group is made, what lies beyond the adjective *Italian* in the Canadian census and the assertions of leadership that mobilized ethnic group, or ethnocommunity as opposed to a simple collectivity of migrants, exists. I suspect that regionalism among the immigrants works like a virus or "worm" lurking in a computer program, either flaring up to dominate the discourse or slowly changing the agenda. It does this by subtly altering the texts of true *campanilismo* and intruding into the various fora (clubs, *circoli*, weddings, picnics, etc.) where *paesani* gather. At the same time, it insinuates itself through the party structure of the *patronato* and through regionalist participation in the official and semi-official *giro di propaganda* into the Italian government's work with the *lavoratori emigrati all'estero e i figli*. The number of regional delegations, politicians, and entities paying visits to Toronto in the last three years seems to grow exponentially. In the last year or so, I have myself attended or been invited to attend Abruzzese, Molisan, Friulan, Calabrian, Sicilian, Trentine, and Puglian affairs where the machinery of the regional government was apparent. In a city that lacks large numbers of immigrants from urban northern and central Italy, the numerically strong contingent from the Abruzzi have often managed to seem to represent mainstream *Italianita*. That perhaps obscures the fact that for many years the regional government of the Abruzzi has been the most active in Toronto.

"Agents of articulation" for the regional governments are busy creating what the historian David Potter has called the "two psychological bases" of nationalism: "the feeling of common culture and the feeling of common interest."[28] One sees the changing emphasis in the discourse everywhere. It can be a telephone call from a speechwriter, unwilling to identify himself, in search of a line from a regional poet suitable for a Canadian politician or the president of a regional club to quote a banquet speech. The proliferation of new publications such as *Il Laghetto dei serresi nel mondo* or *Guzzura. Mensile d'informazione dei Santonofresi nel Mondo*, and the even more significant efforts to "regionalize such *paese*-based discourse with new magazines such as *Dimensioni Calabro-Canadese*, *Cisiliute*, and *Molise*. Other magazines or newspapers such as *Cisiliute*, *L'Eco d'Abruzzo*, and *Giornale di Sicilia* play some of the same roles for Friulians, Abruzzese, and Sicilians respectively. All such publications encourage a view of the region as a shared homeland, an "imagined community."[29] Along with efforts to suggest that the *paesi* should be allied in regional efforts, such publications introduce the extension of some of the values of fellow-feeling felt about *paesani* to *comprovinciali* and then to those from the same region. In this, of course, they reinforce some of the North American realities of proximity, smaller numbers, mobility, and recycled regional barriers of bigotry that had already begun to conflate family into *quasi-parenti*, into *paesani* into fellow *Calabresi*, *Molisani*, and occasionally into *Italiani* as well.

Content analysis of texts such as those in the magazine and newspapers mentioned above would show that they also contribute to the other base of nationalism that Potter refers to, that is community of interest. Advertisements in such publications give a sense of the range and power of the regional descent group in Canada, imply the advantages of business networks and patron/client relations based on regional fellow-feeling and the fact that people from the same region "understand each other and speak the same language," and show that successful immigrants are unembarrassed by their regional ties. In fact, dialect-speaking can move from a reason for exclusion from the "high tradition" to a diacritical mark allowing membership in the new and more comfortable world of the region. Recreation, accessible culture, *intermediarismo*, work opportunities and clientelism can go on within an *ambiente* more familiar to most immigrants than that offered by Canada or by those representing official Italy and its culture. Not just *anomie* and a growing sense of alienation from the more massive and impersonal world of the state or the ethnonation, but also a species of resentment, of the periphery getting even with the core, is at work. Certainly it is not surprising that some migrants who feel they have been told repeatedly that they speak a crude dialect and that they come from the margins of Italy's urban cultural mainstream can enjoy being described as the heirs of *Magna Graecia* or as speaking Italian with Sannitic influences rather than with the dialect of Campobasso. Such filiopieties are no truer and no more ignoble than the texts of the speakers of the "high tradition" that imply that the individual talents of Dante, Galileo, or Columbus are national traits, or of the Italian Canadian speakers who see Marconi or Caboto a more illustrious ancestor than their immediate ones.[30]

I would like to conclude with a foray into social anthropology about emergent Molisan regionalism in Canada. (I think one could do this for Calabria or Friuli as easily, but I find the Molisan case more charming and whimsical.) To help "defamiliarize" the texts and cultural artifacts further, I will describe the phenomenon as the rise of Molisan national feeling, or nationalism. Although I suspect that Azoreans, Basques, Bretons, Croats, Frisians, Friulians, Ladinos, Macedonians, Scots, Slovaks, Welsh – maybe even Genovese – will all have nation states of their own before *Molisani* do. I see no way to predict that such a thing could never happen. As Ernest Gellner puts it, too cynically to be sure, "Nationalism is not the awakening of nations to self-consciousness: it invents nations where they do not exist." An historian has to believe it possible that the modern unity of the Italian peninsula may prove episodic, that the unitary state is merely a long Mazzinian or Savoyard detour from Cattanean or neo-Guelf ideas.[31] Perhaps we should even take heed of the Jamaican dub poet who defines the national language as the dialect the army and bureaucracy speak. And if one insists that Molisani are not potentially another people but merely variant Italians, Walker Connor points out

> "one of the oddities of our period (in large part a response to the quality and quantity of communications networks) is that as the cultures of various groups are becoming more resemblant of one another, the saliency of feelings of ethnic distinction is also growing. What would seem to be involved here, then, is not the degree of cultural similarity. It is psychological and not cultural assimilation with which we are dealing... "[32]

The two cultural artifacts that I will draw on are a Molisan-Canadian banquet that took place in Toronto last year and the international symposium on Molise that took place at Campobasso last summer. I also wish to discuss two texts, one is the new newspaper, *Molise*, the periodical of the "Associazione Molisani Canadesi" and the other is the two volume cookbook, *La Cucina Molisana* which appeared in 1986. Clifford Geertz defines a cultural artifact – "whether suttee among Balinese or baseball in America as analogous to a dream or a Freudian slip... If properly addressed, it will tell an important story about the collective mental life of the people among whom it is found."[33] Banquets staged for one pretext or another are pervasive among migrants from Italy abroad; they are just such a cultural artifact.

I am not clear about the relationships that exist between the tentatives of the Molisan regional government and the efforts of some migrants from the Molise in Toronto to raise regionalist consciousness through the creation of a *Federazione Associazioni Molisani Canadesi*. It is one of those subjects that requires more synchronic study, or perhaps like all nationalist movements, its origins are shrouded in mystery. In 1986 the announcement of the creation of ARMA (*Associazione Regionale Molisani d'America*) appeared in Italian North American newspapers.[34] The bellicose sounding association was created, according to the newspaper, to "break the grip of the enemy that has kept us silent for centuries: *accidia* (lassitude or sloth), the natural ally of isolation and solitude." The newspaper added that ARMA would be a constituent part of *l'Associazione Molisani nel Mondo.* Such a cultural entity, the reader was told, existed for nearly all the other regions of Italy.

It is impossible to know the exact number of migrants from Molise who have entered Canada since World War II, especially since they were statistically lumped with those coming from the Abruzzi. The figure probably is close to 25,000. It would be even more difficult to determine how many of that number saw themselves primarily as *Molisani* rather than as first men and women of their *paese* or province such as Casacalenda or Campobassan, or even Abruzzese or Italian. If "words provide clues to attitudinal states," then the infrequent use, indeed absence, of the substantive noun *Molisani* in any Toronto-Italian publication until the 1960s should suggest that there was no primary loyalty to region among the immigrants, or at least remind us of Apter's point mentioned earlier that being from a place and feeling the need to act on that fact of birth ideologically are two different things, a point akin to the usual sequence preferred in nationalism studies: that people progress from nationality to national feeling to nationalism.[35]

What is common to the regionalist banquets and the International Symposium on Molise in the summer of 1987 is an effort, either conscious or unconscious, to assert the existence of a people called the Molisani, who have common traits, common past and common destiny. The Symposium was intended to be, and I am sure was, scholarly. (So, of course, were the many Congresses of Italian Scientists, held throughout the 1840s, that preached Italian nationalism under the very noses of the Habsburg overlords.) The blurb for the Symposium calls for scholarship but a normative and filiopietist note does creep in. "Both the successes and failures of the emigrants will be noted: needless to say, attention will center on some Molisani and their progeny who did enormously well as measured by any standard, and who achieved fame and recognition."[36] Moreover, the Symposium is clearly seen as a vehicle for helping *Molisani* in the world see themselves as *Molisani*, learn about their fellow-regionalists in other migration target cities, and recognize the commitment of the region, or regional government to drawing them into its own species of modialization. "Consequently the ties between Molise and America are like the bonds that a mother feels for her children who have gone off into the world and have not been heard from for a long time." The migrants and their children are to be transformed from *paesani* dispersed in search of work opportunities to *Molisani* in diaspora with all that term implies for shared destiny and eventual reunion. Thus while a number of sessions in the Symposium are entitled *Molisani* this and that or in such and such a city, only one has the name of a *paese* in the title. At the same conference, the designated *vate*, or Molisan national poet/prophet, in this case the novelist Giosue Rimanelli, significantly teaching "in exile" in America, played a central role in the program.

The banquets of the *Molisani* in Canada provide more semiotic texts than written ones. A popular priest from the region says grace and is seen to bless the regional tentative. Caterer and hall are owned or managed by a *Molisani*, giving special meaning to Potter's idea of common interest as one of the bases of nationalism. The presence of displays of Molisan food, industrial and folk art products such as Colavita oil and La Molisana pasta suggest a commerce of regionalism. At least one *piatto* in the catered meal is duly described as a Molisan food specialty and sign of regional/national genius. The presence of politicians from the Regional junta, leaders of clubs made up of *paesani* from the many Molisan towns of emigration to Toronto, and of mayors of various *paesi* on the *giro di propaganda* of town modialization promise that things will get worse after the meal. They will be introduced at length and will speak, usually at great length, about the ties that bind and that survive the Atlantic crossing. What Eric Hobsbawn calls the "invention of tradition" is in the air. Whatever form it takes, one can be sure that it will begin with antiquity, with a time when the Sannitic tribes were the cultural or political equals of Rome, it will include reference to recently discovered traces of a past greatness (unfortunately the *Molisani* have not yet found or invented anything to match what the *bronzini* of Riace do for Calabrian national pride.) If the official speeches are in Italian, almost all other conversations go on in dialect or English. One feels a certain tension between the *paese* leaders and the regional politicians and speakers. The officers of each *paese* club are introduced; young people in the distinctive costume of various provinces or towns, are paraded through the room to rounds of applause. For the regionalist agenda to work well, the various *paesi*, especially those with large contingents must be portrayed as *tessere* within the regional mosaic, part of the glory of Molise. There is no question that those who attend the banquet leave with a heightened sense of being Molisani together.

For an awakening nation, no text is innocent. A good example of that is the two volume cook book *La Cucina Molisana* published at just about the time ARMA was formed. Beyond setting the boundaries of the "imagined community" through the compilation of a large number of recipes defining a distinctly Molisan cuisine, the cookbook is overtly "nation-building." "The identity and existence of Molise," write the cookbook's authors, "has been left in question because of the long isolation and the relative recency of regional autonomy." The authors conclude that, not just isolation and economic backwardness, but "the fragile and intermittent nature of cultural discourse, the not always adequate promotional efforts of public institutions, have left in the shadows for a long time, relevant moments in regional history that would have been able to sustain attention and respect for the name Molise."[37] In one such sentence from the cookbook, we have seen perfectly parodied Fanon's statement that "while politicians situate their actions in daily life, men of culture take their stand in history" as well as an affirmation of the old Mazzinian adage that revolution can only follow insurrection, that is that only after the mechanisms of the state are in the hands of nationalists can the people be educated to their national identity.

The nation-building role, intended and incidental, of the new *Federazione Associazioni Molisani Canadesi* publication, *Molise*, is even more manifold.[38] The advertisements of businessmen and professionals of Molisan descent, lists of Molisan *paese* clubs and all their officers, lists of candidates of Molisan descent (*candidati molisani*) for Canadian public office, lists of the members of the regional government and mayors of towns in Molise dominate the pages of the paper. The lead headline in boldface reads *Convegno comunità molisana in Canada e Molise*. That same *comunità molisana* is described in an advertisement as *"numerosa e laboriosa."* There is as well a two page socio-economic profile of Molise containing a large map of the region/nation. A list of titles of books held in the new *Federazione's* library also suggests the malleability of history and how the new regionalist texts have proliferated. The books include a multi-volume *Il Molise dalle origini ai nostri giorni* and other books on the regions' history. (Of course there is no way of knowing from the newspaper list whether the library is talismanic or a true resource.)

The attempt to equate regionalism with nationalism may seem far-fetched, but it should at least reinforce the notion that ethnicity and nationality are a negotiation, a response by readers to texts, an artifice by speakers and leaders seeking to impose their own view of the world as a hegemonic idea on others. Regionalism – admittedly most often in the context of the continuum from family and town to the Italian nation – seems to be taking increasing hold over Toronto's immigrants from the Italian peninsula. Recently Roberto Perin has raised questions about the nature of old world cultural persistence among immigrants, a central and vague tenet in Canadian multiculturalism, questions that show that he understands that ethnicity is process not inheritance and that the tension that exists between speakers for the "high tradition" and those who carry the culture of Italy's small towns is a form of hegemonic struggle between factions of intelligentsia.[39] "What is to be retained," he asks, "the culture of the metropolis or that of the immigrants?" The politics of regionalism suggests the question need not be put so baldly. The strategies of regional government, the inadequate or half-hearted efforts at an *azione sui contadini* by the officials of the central government and the organic intelligentsia of the "high tradition," and the psychological needs of *paesani* in transition to the Canadian middle classes may combine to make his question moot. Regional man will create, or retain, a space between the cultural dictates of the core and the fractured and folkloric "little tradition" of the *paese*/periphery. In a poem about Calabria, Pasolini, himself a man of the periphery who felt himself culturally oppressed by the core, saw the matter apocalyptically. "They will obliterate Rome/ and upon its ruins/ they will sow the seed/ of ancient history."

Notes

1. Letter of Bartolomeo Vanzetti to Mrs. Russell (18 Sept. 1926) in M.D. Frankfuter and G. Jackson (eds) *The Letters of Sacco and Vanzetti* (New York, 1956).

2. This paper was written in 1987 for a book entitled *Immigrant History of Molisani*, but was never published.

3. A. Rossi. "Per la tutela degli italiani negli Stati Uniti" in *Bollettino dell'Emigrazione* no. 16 (1904) pp. 20-21.

4. M.L. Hansen. *The Atlantic Migration* (New York, 1961); O. Handlin. *The Uprooted* (New York, 1951); a good attempt to describe the development of the canon is M.Passi. *Mandarins and Immigrants: The Irony of Ethnic Studies in America Since Turner* (Ann Arbor, microfilms, 1972). For the logic of its origins, see E. Saveth. *American Historians and European Immigrants, 1875-1925.* The Italian American responses and additions include R. Vecoli. "Contadini in Chicago: A Critique of the Uprooted" in *Journal of American History* (Dec.

1964); H. Nelli. *The Italians in Chicago, 1880-1930. A Study in Ethnic Mobility* (New York, 1970); J. Briggs. *An Italian Passage* (Yale, 1978); D. Cinel. *From Italy to San Francisco.* The Immigrant Experience (Stanford, 1982). Some newer studies that have a more sophisticated approach to the migrant vector and suggest the canon may be changing are Wm. O. Douglass.1 *Emigration in a South Italian Town. An Anthropological History* (Rutgers, 1984); D. Gabaccia. *From Sicily to Elizabeth St. Housing and Social Change Among Italian Immigrants, 1880-1930* (Albany, 1984), and G. Mormino and G. Pozzetta. *The Immigrant World of Ybor City. Italians and Their Latin Neighbours in Tampa, 1885-1985* (Illinois, 1987).

5. C. Panunzio. *The Soul of the Immigrant* (New York, 1921) pp. 78-79: A. Bernardy. *America Vissuta* (Rome, 1912) pp. 323.

6. R. Vecoli. "Italians on Minnesota's Iron Range" in R. Vecoli (ed.) *Italian Immigration in Rural and Small Town America.* (AIHA, 1987) p. 186; R.F. Harney. "Toronto's Little Italy, 1885-1945" in R. Harney and J.V. Scarpaci (eds.) *Little Italies in North America* (Toronto, MHSO, 1981) pp. 52-58.

7. J. Zucchi. "Italian Hometown Settlements and the Development of an Italian Community in Toronto, 1875-1935." in R.F. Harney (ed.) *Gathering Place. Peoples and Neighbourhoods of Toronto, 1834-1945* (Toronto, 1985) p. 140. See also J. Zucchi. *Italians in Toronto. The Development of a National Identity* (McGill-Queens, 1988); F.M. Padilla. *Latino Ethnic Consciousness. The Case of Mexican Americans and Puerto Ricans in Chicago* (Notre-Dame, 1985).

8. For example, Handlin's *The Uprooted*, chapter 7 "In Fellow-Feeling" actually predicts almost everything that is contained in the newer ethnicization and overcoming of parochialism thesis, but perhaps treats the subject too much as an episodic breathing space rather than a processual stage that can be prolonged indefinitely by circumstances.

9. This is not the place to analyze the literature of the "new ethnicity" in the United States. In general however, lamenting the deprivation of culture of origin as the price of acculturation, leads only to a normative rather than a factual questioning of the validity of the vector that is central to the canon.

10. Only a very few volumes by American historians try to combine into a single narrative and analysis the history of prewar and postwar, of white and non-white immigration. See D. Reimers, *Still the Golden Door* (New York, 1985) and T. Archdeacon, *Becoming American* (New York, 1983).

11. C. Jansen and L. LaCavera. *Fact Book on Italian Canadians* (Toronto, 1981).

12. C. Geertz. "Thick Description. Toward an Interpretive Theory of Culture," in *The Interpretation of Cultures. Selected Essays.* (New York, 1973).

13. R.F. Harney. "So Great A Heritage As Ours: Immigration and the Survival of the Canadian Polity" in *Daedalus* (Fall,1988) pp. 63-87.

14. An early indication of the impact of competition on *ethnie*-formation can be found in O. Bressan. *Non Dateci Lenticchie. Esperienze, Commenti, Prospettive di Vita Italo-Canadese,* (Toronto, 1958) who urges his fellow migrants to emulate the Chinese and Jews of Toronto in building and ethnocommunity.

15. The reality is more complex. Five special border regions had received autonomy at the time the Republican Constitution was promulgated in 1948. The remaining 15 (Abruzzi and Molise were separate entities in 1963) held their first regional elections in 1970. See N. Kogan. "Impact of the New Italian Regional Governments on the Structure of Power within the Parties" in *Comparative Politics* (April, 1975) pp. 393-394, and P. Allum and G. Amyot. "Regionalism in Italy: Old Wine in New Bottles" in *Parliamentary Affairs* 24:1 (Winter 1970) pp. 53-78.

16. A good description of the continuum of loyalty from the local to the provincial to the regional and how the terms of that continuum can be manipulated can be found through vague usages such as *terra natale* can be found in R. Berdahl. "New Thoughts on German Nationalism" in the *American Historical Review* #77 (Feb. 1972) pp. 65-80.

17. It is for this reason that I have borrowed the title of this essay from an anthropological study of minorities in the Balkans. M. Schein. "When Is an Ethnic Group: Ecology and Class Structure in Northern Greece" in *Ethnology* (Jan. 1975) Vol. XIV:1; see especially page 83.

18. U. Kareda. "The Not So Dolce Vita of Francesca Valente," in *Toronto Life,* (May 1987) p. 10.

19. G. Luciani. "Les immigrants d'origine italienne au Canada anglophone," in *Annales de l'Universite de Savoie* (1983) p. 73.

20. An editorial by S. Tagliavini in *Corriere Canadese,* 11-12 May 1976, p.1. The recriminations and accusations of fraud, inefficiency, and egomania that seem invariably to follow these Italian Canadian efforts should be analyzed. Certain "hidden injuries of class" among men who started as humble labour migrants together and have experienced different success rates as well as revived regional hostilities seem to inspire such post-mortems.

21.   See L. Levine. *Black Culture and Black Consciousness: Afro-American Folkthought from Slavery to Freedom.* (New York, 1977) p. iv.

22.   M. Kenny. "Which Spain? The Conservation of Regionalism among Spanish Emigrants and Exiles" in *Iberian Studies* V:22 (Autumn 1976) p. 47.

23.   See editorial by A. Scotti in *Corriere Canadese* (14 Nov. 1984).

24.   On the Circolo Calabrese, see *Corriere Canadese* (Oct. 26, 1956) p. 14; for the journalist's remarks, see *Corriere Canadese* (11 May 1979) editorial entitled. "Columbus Centre: un voto per il futura della communita."

25.   D. Apter. *The Politics of Modernization* (Chicago, 1965) p. 314.

26.   A few years ago there was a serious debate in *Cisiliute* among the Zovins Furlans (Friulian youth) as to whether the Italian hegemonic language would wither away among them in the New World to be replaced by English and French as well as their own Friulian language.

27.   W. Connor. "Ethnonationalism in the First World: The Present in Historical Perspective" in M. Esman. (ed) *Ethnic Conflict in the Western World* (Cornell, 1977) pp. 22-23.

28.   D. Potter. "The Historians Use of Nationalism and Vice-Versa" in *American Historical Review*, 67 (1961-62) p. 937.

29.   B. Anderson. *Imagined Community. Reflections on the Origin and Spread of Nationalism.* (London, 1983).

30.   For more on this phenomenon, see D. Rodnick. "Group Frustration in Connecticut" in *American Journal of Sociology* XLVII:2 (1940) pp. 159-60.

31.   G. Carbone. "The Long Detour: Italy's Search for Unity" in F. Cox et al (eds.) *Studies in Modern European History in Honour of F.C. Palm* (NYC, Bookmans, 1956) pp. 49-80.

32.   Connor. "Ethnonationalism" p. 29.

33.   See P. Robinson's review of C. Geertz. *Local Knowledge. Further Essays in Interpretive Anthropology* (New York, 1983) in the *New York Times Book Review* (25 Sept. 1983) p. 11.

34. "Angolo del Molise" in *La Gazzetta del Niagara e di Hamilton* #3:3-4, p. 31 (Natale 1986).

35. C. Hayes. *Nationalism. A Religion* (New York, 1960).

36. For an attempt to do a content analysis study of the adjective that accompany a given ethnic or regional identity such as Molisano, see D. Knobel. *Paddy and the Republic. Ethnicity and Nationality in Antebellum America* (Wesleyan, 1986). For the ways in which regionalism resembles or becomes ethnicity, see J.S. Reed. *One South. An Ethnic Approach to Regional Culture* (Baton Rouge, LSU, 1982).

37. A.M. Lombardi and R. Mastropaolo. *La Cucina Molisana two volumes* (Campobasso, 1986) pp. 11-16.

38. Molise Periodico a cura della Federazione Associazioni Molisani Canadesi. Anno I:1, (October, 1988).

39. R. Perin. "The Immigrant: Actor or Outcast" introduction to R. Perin and F. Sturino (eds.) *Arrangiarsi*, (Montreal, 1989). If there are choices to be made in "making a future from our past" as the Ontario government's Heritage Branch puts it, the role of speakers in the discourse, or organic intelligentsia, will be crucial. No studies such as W. Beer's excellent analysis of Basques and Bretons entitled "The Social Class of Ethnic Activists in Contemporary France" in Esman (ed.) *Ethnic Conflict*, or even J. Higham (ed.) *Ethnic Leadership in America* (Baltimore, 1978) have been done about Italian Canadians.

5

Commerce of Migration

*B*etween national unification of Italy in 1870 and the First World War, millions of Italians migrated to the Americas. In Italy that emigration became part of a national polemic on both the need for colonies and the problem of the South. In America the immigration became a sub-theme in urban and ethnic historiography. The differences in perspective and concern of those who view the migration as emigration and those who see it as immigration obscure the continuities in the migrant society. This paper is about an aspect of that continuum, the mediating and exploiting role of the middle classes in Italy and America.

American observers saw misery and hunger driving South Italians overseas. J.F. Carr wrote in *Outlook* that "through whole districts in this overcrowded land Italians have to choose between emigration and starvation."[1] Some Italian advocates of emigration like Senator Nobili-Vitelleschi felt that without mass migration "the land would strangle in its own excess population *soffocare nella sua pletora*, and everyone would have to eat one another to survive... "[2] On both sides of the Atlantic, stereotypes and self-images colluded to make Italian emigration seem inevitable. The South of Italy was poor, over-populated and misgoverned. America was a land rich and underpopulated, ergo migration. In such a human flood, differentiation of classes and roles, distinctions between natural and artificial uprooting appeared insignificant. It was assumed that misery drove men from Italy and *La Miseria* was so total that the perils of migration, the hostility of "Anglosaxons," and the difficult struggles ahead could not deter the peasant.[3] The prefects of Southern Italy overwhelmingly attributed migration to misery.[4]

Unfortunately, misery was exactly what North American historians saw as Europe's peasant condition, the misery of potato famine and the hungry '40s, the misery of the Russian Pale and pogroms. The plight of Southern Italy seemed to be of the same order. In the *Uprooted*, Oscar Handlin confidently generalized about the European situation. "Year by year, there were fewer alternatives until the critical day when only a single choice remained – to emigrate or to die.[5] But misery in Italy did not really mean to "emigrate or to die." In 1906, about 435,000 left Italy for America;

in the same year, 158,000 returned to Italy. Some came back for good, others, like the *rondini* (swallows), were simply commuting from harvest to harvest, from Autumn in Piedmont to Spring in Argentina.[6] There is no way to compare return rate with that of the Irish and Germans of the hungry "40s or the Jews of the Pale, but the answer, even accepting changes in transport, is self-evident. R.F. Foerster observed of the Italian emigrants in 1919 that though "the notion of flight is rudimentary... Rarely if ever does it alone govern the man's conduct." Most Southerners had a "notion, however vague, of a tangible positive gain to be secured, a notion that generally depends upon the evidence of other's success."[7]

Interpretations of Italian emigration stressing the volition of the migrants and the role of a secondary group of caretakers, exploiters and agents have taken a number of forms. Emphasis on agents and sub-agents has often been a conservative device in Italy used to deny or obscure the real plight of the South or to justify the policing of emigration in the interest of the land-owning classes.[8] South Italian radicals condemned the legislation of the 1880s that sought to regulate the activity of South American state recruiters, control steamship companies and reduce the numbers of official subagents. Since such critics of the government saw the roots of the problem in the backwardness and suppression of the South, analogies to the negro slave trade, phrases such as *commercio di carne umana* (trade in human flesh) or *i negrieri* (slave traders) and *merce/uomo* (men as goods), came easily to their tongues. Legislation against agents, they felt, was either a conservative ruse or the product of a naive devil theory.[9] Grazia Dore, in her *La Democrazia italiana e l'emigrazione* in America (1964), remarked that the term *agenti* was employed by the government both as a perjorative and to imply the artificial nature of emigration. She added that some of the Southern bourgeoisie, seeing easy profit in the emigration trade, served as sub-agents for steamship companies, labour contractors and South America *white settler agents*.[10] Unfortunately, Dore's concern was political history; she ignored the natural role of the middle classes as mediators between the literate and illiterate, between countryside and city, between the individual migrant and the alien government.

In North America, following the lead of the Congressional Commission of 1911 (referred to henceforth as the Dillingham Commission), historians have uncovered two "unnatural" stimuli in Italian migration, the steamship agents and the *padroni*, or contract labour boss. In its most pernicious form – peasants seduced by a labour contract from their European village and virtually in thrall to a boss in North America – the *padrone* system had a brief if lurid career. With the growth of Little Italy communities, exploitation began to take more subtle forms.[11] In 1888, the Italian vice-consul reported that there were no longer *padroni* in New York City.[12] A recent historian of the Chicago Italians even claims that the bulk of pre-paid passages were probably paid for by relatives rather than labour contractors.[13] However, the Dillingham Commission, sensing the limits of its definitions and investigation, was not naive enough to count the *padroni* out completely. The Commission noted that immigrant bankers' offices (often travel agencies as well) had a way of serving as hiring halls and labour bureaux.[14]

Other villains in the piece were obviously the big steamship companies who encouraged uprooting, winked at the illegal practices of their sub-agents, and were pleased when the emigrant failed because it assured them of an eastbound cargo in the lucrative Mediterranean trade.[15] One line, the Inman Steamship Company, was reputed in 1892 to have 3,500 agents in Europe. Drumming up steerage trade was "a business which can be almost indefinitely expanded by vigorous pushing. A skilful agent can induce any number of simple and credulous peasants of a backward European country to emigrate, who had scarcely had such an idea in their heads before."[16] The Fagin-like qualities of men who ran strings of bootblacks from the Basilicata, the *padrone* and *negriere*, and the callous approach of the steamship companies filling their steerage quotas were all real but they turned a socio-economic situation into a morality play. The study of the role of intermediaries remains too political in Italy and too moral and too fragmentary in North America.

The new interpretation of Italian emigration, identifying the role of chain migration, ethnic receiving neighbourhoods, and continuity of kinship ties from Italy to the receiving country improves upon the devil theories about *padroni* and agents. The Australian demographer, J.S. Macdonald, presents a model for emigration "in which prospective migrants learn of opportunities, are provided with transportation, and have initial accommodation and employment arranged by means of primary social relationships with previous migrants."[17] The "chain migration" interpretation has an easy answer to the charge that South Italians are "amoral familists" who distrust everyone beyond their nuclear family. Emigration itself brought more extended kinship and friendship systems out of desuetude because they were needed. This is the contention of an excellent study of Buffalo Italians by V.Y. McLaughlin. Stress on family ties and the anthropological approach have advantages, but one obvious drawback is the tendency to observe the strength of the immigrant family and to see ethnic neighbourhoods as primitive idylls, where money, class and terror – all realities of the Italian countryside – do not penetrate. McLaughlin, for example, discusses the number of boardinghouses in Buffalo and remarks that many boarders were *paesani* of the homeowners. There is no mention of the possibility of their paying rent, let alone of their being gouged or exploited.[18]

The process of migration was not as familial and "paesano" as "chain migration" theory implies, or as episodic and rapacious as the literature about *padroni* would suggest. Often ignored is the impact of class structure in Southern Italy, in the migration itself, and in the Little Italy receiving depots. "Middle class brokers" served and preyed upon their countrymen from Calabrian village, along the railways, to Naples, and finally in New York, Buenos Aires and Toronto. Neither in Italy nor in America was this so-called *borghesia mediatrice* (middle class go-between) class a caste. Just as people known as *generetti* (little big people) or *mercanti di campagna* (merchants of the countryside) emerged in the South of Italy after unity, so too the business of emigration made other emigrants rich or richer in America. In that world of pre-industrial social groups, petty transactions and literacy as "white magic," the role of the middle classes is ill-defined. If one accepts the view of Antonio Gramsci that "the South was reduced to a semi-colonized market of the North,"[19] it is possible to see that a natural product of such an economy is men. The *slavetraders* may have been a few *padroni* in America or the sub-agents and agents of large steamship companies in the Italian South, but all the middle classes gained from the commerce of migration.[20]

Money and socio-economic structure were at the heart of emigration. To understand the role of middle-class intermediaries, we must enlarge our definition of agents, and look for all the parts of the process of migration where services were rendered and money exchanged. The agents were all those who stood between the parochial, rural lower classes and the larger society, those who mediated between feudalism and modernity.

The steamship, as the intrusion of modern technology into the South, allowed the middle classes a role in migration to North

America and in the process of urbanization itself. They responded to the enlarged economy, with their only product, men. When, for example, the government in the 1900s, tried to reduce the number of official sub-agents to one for each district with more for those areas recognized as remote, almost 2,000 communes petitioned to be classified as remote areas.[21] Men obviously encouraged emigration for the *senseria* (steamship company bounty) alone, and in towns like those that petitioned, most of the non-peasant structure saw profit in emigration. Prime Minister Crispi defined agents inclusively in his 1888 legislation.[22] Article Six of Crispi's Law promised jail and a fine for any unlicensed person "who, for financial gain, counselled or excited the peasants of the nation to emigrate, who furnished and procured ships passage for emigrants, intervened as mediators between the emigrant and the steamship lines, or who transported them to the port of embarkation, or to the place of destination, or in any way, personally, or by means of others, with verbal, written or printed information set out to promote emigration."

Sensing perhaps the blurred line between cash transactions, favour and patronage in such a setting, Article 7 added a fine of 1,000 lire for clergy, mayors and communal officials who, using written or verbal exhortation, promoted emigration *"anche senza fine di lucre."* (even without a profit motive). In fact, the problem faced was a simple one and endemic in the South. The government intended to use the wolves as shepherds for the flock. In the various legislative efforts to regulate emigration and to mitigate the harsh conditions of emigration, the people made responsible were those for whom migration had become a lucrative trade. An Italian senator, supporting legislation that made local committees of notables responsible for the emigrant's well-being saw the problem. "And when one speaks of local authority, we mean to speak of all; from mayor to pharmacist, from tax collector and doctor to field guard – all must treat the peasant differently." Yet any addition to the rules increased the power of go-betweens.[23] Bureaucrat or businessman, the middle-class brokers, stood between the less literate and the newly enlarged state and economy.

A case in point is the Royal Decree of 1901 requiring the prospective emigrant to apply in writing or orally to the mayor of the commune for a passport.[24] The latter would investigate and, if he approved, forward a *nulla osta* (no obstacle) to the prefect who would judge the case. To receive the *nulla osta*, the emigrant had to guarantee that he was leaving no dependents; that he was not under age; that he was not an ex-convict; and that he was not enmeshed in Italy's military conscription and reserve system. If all went well, the emigrant would receive his passport for two or three lire. With the problem of illiteracy and the peasant's assumptions about government corruption in mind, let us examine the possibilities of this minor and well-intentioned piece of legislation.

It is here one should question the concept of "amoral familialism" and "chain migration" in the *Mezzogiorno*. How will the emigrant move through the maze of unknown regulations; can he do it through emigration-wise relatives? Perhaps. The "war of all against all" has in the South of Italy, as in any capitalist society, a logical extension. What cannot be done through the family can be done with money. Money insures that services rendered are in the self-interest of both parties: a little "bustarella" (a small envelope full of lire) for the mayor, even if he is an honest man; some votive candles bought for the Church when the priest writes a letter to a brother in Boston. Social and economic interaction in a South Italian village does not end at the borders of the family. Somewhere near those borders money could produce truces and allies in the war of all against all, and it made one man's family interest another man's family interest. In fact, what is pathetic about the South Italian conversion to a money nexus is that the peasant's understanding of it causes him to force money on those honest brokers, "caretakers" and state officials whom he need not pay. "Chain migration" and travel-wise veterans could only provide the map of whom to pay and how much to pay. If, as Macdonald claims, familialism and patronage were "the motor driving the chains which took so many emigrants from this part of Italy...," then money was the grease on the chains, and the migrants knew it.[25]

Our emigrant, then assuming that government is a thing of *foreign thieves*, must take the first steps toward the American shore through a maze of papers, extortion and hostility. Let us see how many ways he can spend his money. He might perhaps hire a notary to write up the petition to the mayor for a *nulla osta*; his own illiteracy, the fact that the notary is the mayor's cousin, and the tendency of the genteel classes to treat him as a beast of burden make that a wise precaution. Now what if he had dependents or had been convicted of a felony, might he not pass the line of legality and, *bustarella* in hand, sally forth to buy the necessary approval. If he were too young, he could pay a notary or lawyer for signed statements that he was of age, and if there were complications in his military status, he could expect to spend both legal and illegal money. Then he waited for his passport, fearing, as only the illiterate can, the places he had marked his name, and the papers he had seen passed. In the very act of leaving, he may have tied himself down. "The sale of his cottage or farm hut, the mortgaging of a few goods to procure money for the trip" or the outright deal with a loan shark were not things that freed him from his *paese* but tied him to the local "middle class brokers."[26] The man called a *mercante di campagna* in one source may simply be a loan shark in another, and if a Verga novel can be trusted, he may often be an uncle as well. Money borrowed against property ran as high as 60 per cent. Tribute to the middle class and its full scale commitment to profit as intermediaries is the fact that by 1913 interest on mortgages and loans was down from 50 per cent to 3 or 4 per cent, and the day was gone, according to one source, when "a single agent in a single year in not too big a town, could make 25,000 lire."[27] The ship's bounty, even at 50 lire, was but the beginning; it was only the most obvious transfer of money in the migrant process. The *via dolorosa* of Oscar Handlin's uprooted peasant of the 1840s was, by the 1890s, an organized and mechanized *via commerciale* for South Italians.

"The inevitable decorations at every train station [were] the placards of sailing and steamship companies," and in the harbour area of Naples more banners, agencies with confusing names, and men with as much chance of being fleeced as of embarking. "The region around the harbour [was] thronged with steamship ticket offices, often flying the American flag and with emigration agencies, and the line between the two [was] frequently very difficult to draw."[28] The importance of "chain migration" lay in the fact that they "had folk knowledge of the obstacles and pitfalls ahead." For example, peasants from a certain village in Basilicata could resist the gaudy advertising for Lloyd Sabaudo or the German steamships because they had been told by a veteran migrant that "on English ships, one always eats more civilly.[29] Even though forewarned, the migrants travelling from village to town to Naples were subject, before they reached the port, to such a *camorra* of *sensali, incettatore, viaticali, grande, piccoli, minuti commercianti*, – all names for go-betweens – that one can describe the trade as having primary and secondary benefits. Naples, a somnolent port, grew rapidly and that growth was based on the trade in men. In 1900, the port of Naples represented only 8 per cent of the total port activity of Italy but was first in third class passengers.[30] The port too was embarkation point for wine, olive oil, garlic, cheese, macaroni and other products for growing Italian colonies overseas. Returning migrants – the successful *Americani* travelling first class, the failed *cafoni* in steerage – remittances, ship provisioning, kept the port expanding. After humans, the coal for the new railways was the most important cargo coming in. Narrow gauge track networks spread out from Naples.[31] No one has studied their development and relationship to emigration, but the small coaches and the routes chosen suggest that they were an integral part of the commercial network of migration.

Only local area studies will fully explain the ramifications of emigration. For every account of fields left fallow and gentry left without peasants, references exist about refurbished villages along the railway right-of-way. A Sicilian mayor claimed that only American remittances kept most small holders from losing their property for non-payment of taxes.[32] Still, it is clear that bureaucrat, notary, lawyer, innkeeper, loan shark, *mercante di campagna*, runners in the harbour city, agents, even train conductors depended on the emigration trade. On the other side of the ocean, the scale of remittances, uninterrupted traffic of emigrant and repatriate, all the auxiliary food trades, seasonal migrants, and the network of financial and commercial exchange justify treating Southern Italy and Italy overseas as one society and one informal economy; and parallels to the rural/urban migration become more trenchant. No Italian city, least of all Naples, provided enough urban employment for the Southern masses, but when New York, Chicago and Pittsburgh are treated as part of a whole, then a useful picture emerges. Replace agents in Italy, *padroni* in America, not just with "chain migration and ethnic neighbourhood," but with the thought that the same social relations and class structures (allowing ecological variants) existed on both sides of the Atlantic. The expansion of employment for peasants in the industrial world outside of Italy meant expanding opportunity for the pre-industrial middle class in Southern Italy. According to Isaacs, "at all times a relatively large number of capitalist immigrants has soon joined the ranks of the destitute while others, after starting without any means, become highly successful within a relatively short time." As one old emigrant put it: "The big fish always follow the minnows that they feed on."[33]

Paeans to American opportunity such as one finds in Nelli's study of Italians in Chicago – "Over the years newcomers and their children moved up the economic ladder, progressing from unskilled labour into commercial, trade, and professional lines" – obscure the

social structure and economy of emigration. In an earlier riposte to
The Uprooted, Vecoli observed that most immigrants came from or
near a "rural city" not "simple communities of agriculturists... their
social structure included the gentry and middle class as well as the
peasants."[34] Even if more new men were apparent in a Little Italy's
elite, they had *arrived* in the same way as the middle-class *generetti*
in Southern Italy. The trade that made them successful was a trade
in men and in handling the problems of less literate countrymen. Let
me give, before I go on, some impression of the magnitude and the
intercontinental nature of that trade.[35]

Most contemporaries noted the steamship companies' preference
for the South European passenger trade because of the high rate of
returnees.[36] The flow of people in a peak year like 1907 – about
250,000 returnees and 300,000 outward bound – provides a sense of
the scale and the unity of the emigrant business. Money went and
came with the migrants. The Dillingham Commission estimated that
85 million dollars was sent to Italy in 1907; 52 million of that was
processed by immigrant bankers. The Cashiers Office at Ellis Island
as a depository of alien funds held as much as $500,000 monthly. An
"Immigrant Clearing House" of the Trunk Line Railroad Association
on Ellis Island often handled $40,000 a day in cash ticket sales.[37]

Remittances were made to relatives for the support of the young
or the old, for sisters' dowries, as bride prices, or as passage money
in cash or in the form of pre-paid tickets. Money was also sent home
to pay mortgages contracted to make the original trip or to invest in
new land.[38] All such transactions passed through the sticky hands
of brokers on both sides of the ocean. Profit ranged from the staid
and honest 2 or 3 per cent on every transaction taken in by the sub-
agents of the Banca di Napoli, to that of "shrewd speculators
acquiring vacant land parcels at low prices, in anticipation of the
return of emigrants, then breaking them into cultivable units, and
selling them in advance.[39] The process of departing and the process
of remitting served the long-range purposes of those who since the
Risorgimento had seen the land as a commodity and not a
patrimony. The mortgaging and selling and the rebuying of small-
holds, the consolidation of arable property, beyond providing
endless opportunity for notary, lawyer, banker, pawnbroker and
local bureaucrat, continued a process begun against the impecunious
nobility by the *mercantile di campagna*. In Italy overseas, ethnic realtor,
"immigrant banker," broker, and travel agent waited to perform
similar functions. The continuum was noticed by an Italian senator

writing in 1905.[40] He observed that, though the crops and employment situation in the South were no better or worse in 1904 than other years, there was a decline in migration, new mortgages and land sales. He reasoned that the decline had to be the result of a crisis of confidence, engendered by the presidential campaign in the U.S. and the bloody strikes with Italian involvement in Colorado and Pennsylvania. One economic pulse beat for the Italian South and for Italo-America.

Earlier, the short life of the real *padrone* structure was mentioned. The term itself, conjuring up both too much *padrono* and too much ward healer, has not died. Although disinclined to see the role of brokers and the money economy in the *family* process of emigration, "chain migration" theorists have not completely given up the *padrone*. Macdonald, for example, includes under the heading "employment agents, sweatshops, subcontractors, bankers, landlords, foreman, scribes, interpreters, legal advisers or ward bosses."[41] Two American historians have provided an interesting study of a man whom they label a "padrone."[42] His career included the following occupational sequence: 1891 – grocery business, notary public and steamship agency, 1893 – general contractor and ultimately political notable. The progression in this *padrone*'s career suggests that he was a general go-between, a *mediatore*, that he began as a labour boss simply reflected the mediation needs of the first migrants. His later career grew from serving as broker in the variety of encounters that immigrants had with the Old and New World governments and economies. In other words, he provided the same services as his middle-class counterparts in the Italian South. In the same way, his pretensions to power in the Republican Party ran parallel to the *generetti*'s attempt to join the older *signori* of the South.[43] All in all, it would be better to drop the attenuated term *padrone* and recognize the ethnic middle class.

Using the less equivocal term "immigrant banker," the Dillingham Commission tried to explain the intermediary role of the immigrant middle class in turn-of-the-century New York. The need for intermediaries in North America was as great or greater than in Italy. Instead of a Tuscan bureaucrat or Piedmontese *carabiniere*, one might have to face an Irish *cop* or Yankee customs officer. High illiteracy rates created an equally high dependence on scribes, notaries and interpreters. Now the neologisms bred in the strange new world of migration increased dependence upon the *middle-class paesano* who spoke English, Italian, dialect, and the new Italo-

American language of *setaiola* (city hall) and *grosseria* (store).[44] The handling of money, bureaucratic problems and minor legal questions, some loan sharking, and problems of transport were the main business of the go-between on both sides of the ocean. On both sides, dependence on a literate *paesano* was the lesser evil in the face of officials assumed to be thieves and known to be outsiders. Familialism and patronage in simple anthropological terms are just not compatible with the number of notaries and quasi-lawyers in the South Italian global village. Of 47 Italian immigrant bankers investigated by Dillingham's Commission, all served as agents for steamship companies: 34 carried on other business as well;[45] 20 were notaries; 6 realtors; 8 employment agents; 9 postal sub-stations; and 7 grocery stores.

Imagine the immigrant broker's storefront and look at a contemporary Toronto ethnic travel agency: "all available space is filled with steamship posters, money-changing notices, and many coloured placards, alluring always in the inducements they present." There above the door, it says *Banco Italiano-Notario-publico-agente marittimo*. The affairs that go on inside the door affect the economy of two continents. The notarized papers, pre-paid tickets and mortgage agreements have their counterpart in Avellino, Benevento, Campobasso, in all the cities of the South. The banker takes 3 per cent on your remittance, but speaks your dialect. He buys your lire at a 5 per cent discount and sells at 3 per cent, but even the *Banco di Napoli* agent cannot understand your problem, fails to stay open in the evening, and he does not know where your home town is. Your remittance may change the cadastral structure of your village, make your sister marriageable, or fix your mother's cottage roof, but a percentage of it at both ends falls in myriad and wonderful ways to the middle-class brokers. Why should the ethnic neighbourhood be different from the home town, and why not continue to accept the evil one knows over the unknown evils of American or Piedmontese bureaucracy?

Although there are obvious changes in the *ambiente* and ecology of migration, the idea of a *commerce of migration* and of a *borghesia mediatrice* can be pursued in contemporary Toronto.[46] The most important changes are probably,

- the aeroplane,
- the increased consciousness of Italian nationality and increased literacy in the post-Fascist period, and
- the presence in the Canadian-Italian migration of more Northern Italians and more urban people.

Despite these changes, the *commerce of migration* in Canada, it seems to me, provides better comparisons for research with the old migration than does the contemporary United States where two generations of nostalgia have softened the image of exploiters, relatives and *paesani*. Most groups of Italo-Americans now unconsciously or pridefully overemphasize the extended family and its patriarchal strength. Healthy family structure is, after all, one of the criterions that they use to distinguish themselves from more recent Latin and Black migrants.[47]

The Italian community of greater Toronto numbers almost half a million people. The continuity between this Italo-Canada and Italy is less tentative than in the earlier migration. The technical acceleration of communications, the competition between CP and Alitalia for the airborne version of steerage is obvious. The new immigrant, more literate and attuned to a mass consumption economy, is followed to Canada by more than the cheese, oil and occasional musical *maestri* that came after the Umbertine peasants who migrated to the United States. Phonograph records, clothing styles, packaged foods, Fiats, follow and create a merchant class to profit from and distribute them. Even a construction worker who winters on unemployment cheques among the mandarin oranges and prickly pears of their *paese* does his part for the social and economic continuity.

Despite higher literacy and the benign welfare state, the emigrant still seems to need a "middle-class go-between." Mistakes at airports, before government agents, and in banks can be just as costly as they were in Naples in 1895 or New York in 1910. Signing the wrong papers can bring anything from unwanted aluminum siding to deportation. It was estimated in 1961 that 25 percent of the Italians in Toronto spoke no English at all. Many others were surely functionally illiterate in English; most are more comfortable in dialect than in Italian itself. In his book, *Non Dateci Leticchie*, O. Bressan, a *leader* in Italo-Toronto, notes that his countrymen have "a pessimistic concept of public officials in general and of state and parastatal officials in particular."[48] The same structure of illiteracy and distrust of government agencies that characterized life in the South of Italy exists in contemporary Toronto. Naturally then, intermediaries emerge or follow the migration. "Caretakers" and "intellectuals" dedicated to serving the migrants also proliferate. Toronto has political groups, religious and educational institutions and philanthropic organizations for the immigrant community.[49] To the extent that the middle classes – those who are *civile e gentile* in the eyes of the migrant – dominate these institutions, they are little different from commercial intermediaries like banks and travel agencies. "The claim of any person or institution to be inspired by zeal for public rather than private advantage will be regarded as a fraud."[50] In observing this, Banfield mistakenly considered peasant distrust of the middle class as an aspect of amoral familialism's "war of all against all." However, distrust is the heritage of how expensive dependence on one's "betters" in Italy has been, especially since the advent of the cash economy. Can you really trust a man who offers to translate for you at an immigration hearing, or to make out your tax returns without charge? What is his game? Since the end of feudalism, or at least of the Risorgimento, the common people have paid in cash and deference for their inferior social and educational status, and they are used to it.

There is in Italo-Toronto, dependence on middle-class "Brokers" ranging from ethnic driver education schools and realtors to consulting only doctors from one's *paese*. The most typical broker in the community is probably the travel agent. The Italo-Canadian Commercial Directory for 1971 lists about fifty travel agents in Toronto, although the number would be far greater if it included formal and informal sub-agents.[51] Toronto agencies often have business or familial ties with sub-agents in Italy, and some also tend to serve a specific *paese*; for example, the Trinacria agency for Sicilians, the Venezia agency for people from the northeast of Italy. The pattern follows that of the "immigrant banks" of New York in the 1900s. The agent serves as go-between for his immigrant client in almost all conceivable encounters with the outside world.

A travel agency advertisement in the Italo-Canadian Commercial Directory almost duplicates the immigrant banker's advertisements addended to the Dillingham Commission reports of 1911. After mentioning the travel part of the business, the agency offers "servizio Contabilita, Bookkeeping service, Income Tax, procure [proxies], atti notarili, cambio valuto, servizio per il publico [sic] fino alle ore 9:00 pm." Another travel agent offers "prenotazioni e biglietti per ogni destinazione" but also "pratiche di ogni genere, rimesse di denaro... "[52] The following, in order of frequency, are the services that first-generation Toronto Italians expected a travel agent to render:

- Tickets, pre-paid tickets for relatives in Italy and other travel arrangements,

- Arrangement of passports,
- "going to Immigration,"
- Remittances,
- Helping with unemployment insurance,
- Making out Income Tax forms,
- Dealing with the Workman's Compensation Board, OHSIP, Old Age Pensions, and
- Dissolving partnerships and other notarial work.[53]

After doctors and lawyers, travel agents ranked highest among Italo-Canadian professionals and semi-professionals in the minds of immigrants. Some people, in fact, expected to pay a fee for visiting a travel agent just as they would for visiting a doctor or lawyer. The most common remark about these agents was that they "know the right people." Although the phrase smacks of mystery and criminality, it is simpler than that. According to one immigrant, his travel agent was his "voice to the outside." That is what the intermediaries always were. Because of their assimilation to *italianità*, the money economy and the Piedmontese conquest, the South Italian middle classes stood between local society and the larger polity. The "immigrant bankers" of the American East Coast dominated their countrymen because they were already bourgeois or Italo-American while the newcomers were still greenhorns and peasants. In Toronto, the intermediaries are also men between cultures. They may support ethnic radio stations and Italo-Canadian newspapers; they promote local Italian culture; but their role in the community comes as much from their assimilation to Canadian life as from their higher levels of literacy and sophistication.

Their humbler countrymen pay the intermediaries for the use of their literacy and assimilation. For example, it is estimated that, before the introduction of the currant points system, 80% of the migrants to Toronto from Italy were "sponsored." Sponsorship constitutes the most obvious form of chain migration. Yet, 60% of the people interviewed had consulted travel agents about sponsoring relatives, and some had depended upon agents to find them sponsors. All had paid for the services rendered over and above the price of pre-paid tickets. When asked why he had consulted an agent about sponsorship, a veteran migrant showed the resignation and skepticism of those who depend upon intermediaries. "You may not need a travel agent to get to Canada;" he said, "then again, you may not need a priest to get to heaven."

All this is not intended to suggest the existence of a criminal bourgeoisie or to justify the *waspish* response of those who have always dismissed immigrant problems as the exploitation of one "dirty foreigner" by another. It does maintain that coherent class analysis can cross oceans in a way that the random and episodic study of separate kinds of exploitation cannot. And, now that it is not fashionable to see the immigrant as an uprooted and disoriented countryman, the alternative view should not simply be an anthropological idyll where smiling people use their sense of kinship to cope with modernity. Modernity existed in migration in the form of *lire, denari, soldi* and dollar bills. A semi-professional, commercial and bureaucratic bourgeoisie was and is as much a part of an Italian ethnic neighbourhood or of a Neapolitan village as are religious festivals, grandmothers in black and godfathers.

Notes

1. John Foster Carr. "The Coming of the Italian" *Outlook* (1906) p. 421.

2. Sen. F. Nobili-Vitelleschi. "Espansione coloniale de emigrazione" *Nuova Antologia* (May 1902) 183:107.

3. F.S. Nitti "L'Emigrazione italiana e suoi avversari (1888) *Scritti sulla questione meriodionale* (Bari, 1959) 11:327.

4. Nitti. "L'Emigrazione." II:333-334 for a breakdown of the prefectoral reports. G. Dore. *La Democrazia italiana e l'emigrazione in America.* (Brescia, 1964) p. 45 suggests that the phrasing of the questionnaire sent to the prefects encouraged *miseria* as an answer.

5. O. Handlin, *The Uprooted.* (New York, 1951) p. 37.

6. F. Thistlethwaite. "Migration from Overseas in the Nineteenth and Twentieth Centuries" in H. Moller. *Population Movements in Modern European History* (New York, 1964) p. 77. *La golondrina* left Italy in November and went to Latin America for the summer there. In 1904, 10% of Italian migrants entering the United States had been there before. The aeroplane has made such seasonal migration from Italy to the Americas even more common.

7. Robert F. Foerster. *The Italian Emigration of Our Times.* (Cambridge, Harvard, 1919) p. 416.

8. The best account of the politics and legislation of emigration if F. Manzotti, *La Polemica sull'emigrazione nell'Italia unita.* (Milano, 1969).

9. F. Nitti. "L'Emigrazione". pp. 305-307; Manzotti. *La Polemica* pp. 69-76.

10. Dore. *La Democrazia italiana,* pp. 38-42.

11. *Reports and Abstracts of the Immigration Commission,* 41 volumes, Document No. 747 61st Congress: 3rd Session (Washington, 1911). Cited henceforth as the *Dillingham Commission.* The padrone system and the legislation directed against it are discussed in Volume II of the Abstracts, pp. 375-408. The Commission apparently felt that the system was so moribund by 1910 that it did not deserve a separate report. For a warning against the uncritical use of the Commission's Reports see O. Handlin. *Race and Nationality in American Life.* N.Y., 1957.

12. C. Erikson, *American Industry and the European Immigrant, 1860-1885.* (Cambridge, Harvard, 1957) pp. 85-86.

13. H. Nelli, *Italians in Chicago, 1880-1930. A Study in Ethnic Mobility.* (New York, 1970) pp. 55-87.

14. *Dillingham Commission.* II:419.

15. *Dillingham Commission.* I:26.

16. H.P. Fairchild. *Immigration.* (New York, 1913) pp. 148-149.

17. J.S. Macdonald. "Chain Migration, Ethnic Neighbourhood Formation and Social Network." *Millbank Memorial Fund Quarterly.* XLII (Jan. 1964) p. 82.

18. E. Banfield. *The Moral Bases of a Backward Society.* (New York, 1958). V.Y. McLaughlin. "Working Class Immigrant Families: First Generation Italians in Buffalo, New York". Paper delivered at Organization of American Historians (April, 1971) pp. 6-7 and 11-13.

19. A. Gramsci. *Sul Risorgimento.* (Roma, 1967) p. 103.

20. The term *negriere* (slave trader) was used by F. Nitti "La Nuova Fase della emigrazione d'Italia" (1896) in *Scritti sulla questione meridionale* II:387. A. Mosso. *Vita moderna degli italiani.* (Milan, 1906) used the phrase "commercio di carne umana" p. 76.

21. Mosso. *Vita moderna*, pp. 77-78.

22. Quoted in Nitti. "L'Emigrazione" pp. 304-305.

23. See V. di Somma. "L'Emigrazione nel Mezzogiorno" *Nuova Antologia* (May, 1970) CXXIX:517.

24. Royal Decree of 1901 in *Dillingham Commission*, IV:211. On illiteracy rate see *Annuario Statistico* analysed in *Dillingham Commission* IV:186-187. The chief migrating areas of the Italian South – Abruzzi, Campania, Apulia, Basilicata, and Calabria) had about 60% male illiteracy and 80% female illiteracy. Illiteracy in Sicily was probably higher. Since emigrants came usually from the more rural parts of these areas, the rate of illiteracy among them was probably even higher. V. di Somma. "L'Emigrazione" p. 514. "In 1905, in a commune of about 2000 people, of 22 inscribed for military service, only 2 presented themselves, all the others had emigrated."

25. J.S. Macdonald and L. Macdonald. "Italian Migration to Australia. Manifest Function of Bureaucracy versus Latent Function of Informal Networks." *Journal of Social History* (Spring 1967) p. 254.

26. A. di San Giuliano. "L'Emigrazione italians negli Stati Uniti d'America" *Nuova Antologia* (July 195?) CXVIII:89-91. See G. Verga. *I Malavoglia*.

27. Amy Bernardy. *Italia Randagia attraverso gli Stati Uniti* (Torino, 1913) p. 313. However, H.P. Fairchild, *Greek Immigration in the United States* (New Haven, 1911) p. 222 suggests that the weight of remittances lowers the mortgage rate. In either case, the middle class receives its share.

28. Bernardy. *Italia Randagia*, p. 311; Fairchild. *Immigration*, p. 151.

29. Bernardy. *Italia Randagia*, p. 312.

30. G. Aliberti. "Profilo del Economia napoletana dell Unita al Fascismo" *Storia di Napoli* X.L. Fontana-Russo, "La Marina mercantile e l'emigrazione" Rivista coloniale (May-June, 1908). Foerster. *Italian Immigration.* pp. 467-468.

31. F. Benedetti. "Ia Strade ferrate della Basilicata e della Calabria" *Nuova Antologia* (June 1902) 183:500-512. This article describes the railroad development but sees no connection with migration.

32. Mosso. *Vita moderna*, p.114, and L. Bodio. "Del l'emigrazione italiana e della legge 31 gennaio 1901 per la tutela degli emigranti" *Nuova Antologia* (June, 1902) 183:533.

33. J. Isaac. *Economics of Migration* (London, 1947). p. 232.

34. H. Nelli. *Italians in Chicago*. p. 20. R. Vecoli. "Contadini in Chicago: A Critique of the Uprooted" *Journal of American History* (Dec. 1964) LI:3, pp. 408-409.

35. Foerster. *Italian Immigration*, p. 15 on emigrants; pp. 19-20 on repatriation. Isaac. *Economics of Migration*, p. 63 estimates a 40% return rate. Foerster points out the limits of the statistics which were based on passports issued and emigration from Italian ports plus LeHavre. Since passports were good for three years, three seasonal migrations as well as any illegal (draft-dodging) migration could go undetected. See also F.P. Cerase. "Nostalgia or Disenchantment: Considerations on Return Migration: in S. Tomasi and M. Engel (eds.) *The Italian Experience in the United States*. (Staten Island, 1970). See PhD. thesis on Italian repatriation and remittances written for NYU by Betty Boyd Caroli.

36. Mosso. *Vita moderna*. pp. 72-74; *Dillingham Commission*, I:26.

37. *Dillingham Commission*. II:427. Vol. 37, Chapter V of the Commission reports had a detailed analysis of Italian remittances and the practices of immigrant bankers. See esp. pp. 271-285. For Ellis Island statistics, the memoirs of the Commissioner E. Corsi. *In The Shadow of Liberty. The Chronicle of Ellis Island*. (New York, 1935), pp 123-126.

38. Isaac. *Economics of Migration*, pp. 244-245; Bernardy. *Italia Randagia*, p. 314, and Mosso. *Vita moderna*, p. 114.

39. Foerster. *Italian Immigration*, p. 451.

40. A. di San Giuliano. "L'Emigrazione italiana", p. 91.

41. J. Macdonald and L. Macdonald. "Italian Migration to Australia, p. 257.

42. I. Iorizzo and S. Mondello. *The Italian Americans*. (New York, 1971) p. 143. The career is that of Thomas Marnell of Syracuse. The authors describe him as "a classic example of the small Italian businessman's struggle for economic and political power for himself and his people."

43. The mayor in G. di Lampedusa. *The Leopard* is an excellent example of a Sicilian *generetto*.

44. Bernardy. *Italia Randagia*, pp. 89-93, on new dialects.

45. *Dillingham Commission*, 37:211 and 311; on immigrant banks generally pp. 197-350.

46. The impressions of Toronto's Italian community in this part of the paper are drawn mainly from two sources. For eight years, students in my Italian history course at the University of Toronto have written one of their two term papers on "anonymous immigrant history" subjects. Palmacchio Di Iulio, pre-Law Student, helped in the interviewing of over a hundred first generation Toronto Italians.

47. For a scholarly example of this emphasis, see L. Tomasi *The Italian American Family* (New York, 1972) p. 8.

48. O. Bressan. *Non Dateci Lenticchie. Esperieni, Commenti, Prospettive di Vita Italo-Canadase.* (Toronto, 1958) p. 26.

49. For the use of the term "caretakers" as dogooders see H. Gans. *The Urban Villagers. Group and Class in the Life of Italian-Americans.* (New York, 1962) pp. 142-162. There is a list of *Associazioni assistenziali e culturali* in *Italo-Canadian Commercial Directory*, 1971 (Metro Toronto) (Toronto, 1971) p. 8.

50. Banfield. *The Moral Bases of a Backward Society*, p. 98.

51. *Italo-Canadian Commercial Directory*, pp. 50-51.

52. *Italo-Canadian Commercial Directory*, pp. 51 and 52: Compare these advertisements with the examples in *Dillingham Commission*. 37:340. Appendix VI.

53. Of a hundred people interviewed, 90% expected services 2 and 3 from a travel agent; and about 70% expected service 4, and 40 to 60% expected the other services. To the migrant, the phrase "going to immigration" meant that the agent solved a problem or "arranged" a difficult case. The agents seemed to protect their role as mediators by affecting an air of mystery about the nature of such transactions.

6

Men Without Women:
Italian Migrants in Canada, 1885-1930

*I*n July of 1908, the lead article of the *Rivista di Emigrazione* described emigration as the "greatest social phenomenon of our epoch whether one is speaking of the demographic impact on the country, its economy, its moral condition, levels of criminality, state of public health, in fact, of any aspect of the people's life."[1] Since that time, both in countries of emigration and in immigrant receiving countries, historians have created a rich literature about migration's demographic and economic impact. From Robert Foerster's *Italian Emigration Of Our Times* (1919) to recent studies of remittances and *ritornati*, we have been shown the way in which emigration affected class structure in the Italian South.[2] Much less has been said of emigration's impact on the people's morale.

The reasons for this silence are numerous. Having seen the damage wrought first by racists and restrictionists and then by a few insensitive social scientists, the historian is disinclined to emphasize the disruption and pathological aspects of migrating. It is far safer to describe migration as simply the first step in the journey to assimilation or as an orderly advance by means of which families and villages adjust traditions in order to maintain their commonweal.[3] However, not since the turn of the century debate on emigration in Italy which generated writings like that of Fortunato, Nitti, Pasquale Villari, Adolfo Rossi, Amy Bernardi and Leonello DeNobili, has the Italian migrant himself been at the centre of study.[4]

In the *inchieste*, polemics and studies of those writers, the abnormality of leaving one's home place and the caprice of the world economy which moved men about was demonstrated. Such writers understood that the social history of the European agrotown or village was one with that of the history and vicissitudes of the migrants in North America. Somewhere that integrity of view has been lost. Preoccupied with issues of assimilation, the North American historian has worked within a framework which limited debate to questions of uprootedness and persistence of ethnicity. The sojourner's physical commitment to the place from whence he had come needs to be revived.

This essay concentrates on the Italian emigrant as a man of his family and of his *paese* (agrotown or village). It suggests that his intentions when he began his sojourn in North America defined whether or not the length of his stay caused extraordinary stress on him and also on those he had left behind. For, just as the hometown remained at the centre of his concern, so too the migrant did not lose his place in the social organization of the village or in the inheritance structure and plans of his family. The debate over the role of nuclear and extended families in South Italian life is tedious, but all would agree that family members were expected to suppress their individualism and to work for what Constance Cronin has labelled a synthetic person, the family.[5] Such a view of the family is not, of course, uniquely Italian. The family as a functioning economic unit occurs in most rural and pre-industrial settings. Boguslav Galeski puts the point most simply. "For the rural family is a collective producer, sometimes also a collective entrepreneur and common owner of a small plot."[6]

The decision to migrate then was not usually made by the individual, particularly not if he was a young man. "The actual decision itself is thrashed out in the nuclear family."[7] (The corollary then should be that the decision to end a sojourn abroad will also not be the result of individual decision.) In fact, the migrant, like the cash remittances and the *ritornati*, was a constantly accounted-for unit of the family and town which he left behind.[8]

The mayor of a small town in Basilicata informed a parliamentary committee in 1907 that "the population (of his town) was 2400 souls of whom about 600 were in America." At first glance that is an extraordinary view to take of the fact that one quarter of the population, and probably at least half of the productive men and boys, were residing in foreign lands.[9] But the mayor did not see those men as future Canadians, Americans or Argentinians. They remained in his mind the husbands, sons, fiances, and fathers of the women in his town. In this essay, we try to share the mayor's perspective. The role of the migrants as cheap foreign labour and potential Canadian or American citizens has been studied; their role as wage earners and sources of "cash money" for the Italian South is receiving more attention now. Here we look at the impact of emigration on family life, on morals, health, and the state of mind of the migrant himself and his people.

Italian critics of emigration felt that it engendered that most pompous and portentious of Italian crimes "delitti contro il buon costume e l'ordine delle familie."[10] Perhaps if we look more closely at the personal and family issues raised by migration, we can see what truth lay in that charge. The so-called "target migrant" – the man who goes abroad or to the city in search of cash money for a specific family objective – expects certain things of his sojourn away from the village and plans to be away for a certain amount of time. In turn, his family and dependents expect things of him and have at least a rough estimate, based on local folk wisdom, of how long it should take him to achieve those objectives.[11] Obviously, a sojourn which goes beyond the customary time causes anxiety for all involved. The daughter awaiting a dowry, the empty conjugal bed, aging parent, or just a Mediterranean spring missed – all put pressure upon the migrant. In this essay we will be dealing with migrants betrayed, thwarted in their schedule by the Canadian economy, by dishonest men, and by harsh winters. The betrayal turned seasonal migration into long term sojourning and turned momentary success in achieving the financial goal of migration into new depths of indebtedness. Unexpectedly long separation brought disruption and perhaps some of the social pathology which the critics of emigration feared.

How long could commitment to family obligations survive the great distance and increasing time that lay between the sojourner and his origins? One Lithuanian who came as a migrant to Canada in the 1920s told me that, when he returned to Vilnius after fifty years in Canada, he went immediately to his sister in order to apologize for failing to send her dowry money to her a half century earlier.[12] Did young migrants from Calabria have a less filial or familial sense of duty than that?

A tradition of happy endings has grown up to obscure the disruption and pain caused by long sojourning abroad. The *ritornato*, the rich *cafone*, the *Americano* with the diamond stick pin who returns to buy the land that he once sharecropped and to marry the girl of his dreams or take up with the wife whom he has not seen for many years – both the latter as virginal as when he left for America – is migration study's version of the Western melodrama.[13] In the same genre, of course, are the happy vineyard owners who send to Italy for brides who have been fluttering expectantly for many years: "In his absence, members of the extended family or clan will provide protection and supervision for his immediate family. He can return at any time, assured of a physical home, a social niche, and least some income."[14] How does that sanguine view of the modern migrant correspond to De Nobili's survey of Calabria in 1907? "Adulteries, infanticides, and vendettas are the order of the day – manifestations of that abnormal social state brought on by emigration and the consequent disequilibrium of the sexes." One critic clearly understood the difference between inheriting the earth and losing one's soul: "The country is covered with houses, the houses of the new landowners, but from their houses and those of the former owners is banished an ancient heritage and an ancient nobility – the moral integrity of the *focolaio*."[15] The same cash money which confused and brought mobility to the social and cadastral structure also deeply affected family structure.[16] However the physical absence of the migrant himself, especially if it was unexpectedly prolonged, ravaged any dream of a well-ordered future for South Italian families. It changed the distribution of inheritances, the meaning of marriage alliances, and the feelings of people toward one another.

Canada had a higher percentage of "target migrants" in its Italian immigration after 1900 than the United States did. There were sound economic reasons for that, but there was also terribly fraudulent advertising of work and exploitation of migrants, so Canada also had a very high percentage of seasonal and "target migrants" trapped into longer sojourns. The gap between the intention of the sojourner and his fate seems particularly great when one looks back at Canada in the 1900s. In that sense, it becomes an especially fruitful setting for the study of the impact of long term sojourning.

One reason that Canada had more migrants and fewer immigrants than the United States was that neither the Dominion nor the Italian government encouraged settlers from Italy. The Italian Commissariat of Emigration issued several *bollettini* on conditions in Canada which pointed out that the country was not suitable for colonizing except by wealthy peasants. In 1901, the Italian consul in Montreal went so far as to fault "the lightheartedness with which the Canadian government seeks to people the desert plains of the Dominion." He concluded that Canada was no place for "experiments with our peasantry."[17] Nor did Sifton, the Dominion's powerful Minister of the Interior view Italians as useful immigrants.[18] So the climate of opinion was as frigid as the climate itself. Nonetheless a well organized system of seasonal migration to Canada developed at the beginning of the century.[19] Before World War I, thousands of Italian labourers, particularly from Calabria, the

Abruzzi, Basilicata, and Friuli were induced to migrate to Canada. There is little doubt that most of those who came through this network fit the definition of "target migrants". They came intending brief sojourns, usually hoping for summer's work in the railway, timbering and mining camps of the Canadian North.[20]

False newspaper reports were printed in Montreal and distributed throughout Calabria. Workers were led out of Italy overland through Chiasso and Switzerland and then on to the Channel ports and England where they made the crossing on Cunard, CP, and Beaver lines ships. They were escorted by a variety of sinister labour and travel agents, and so they reached Canada much in the manner of migrants travelling with a foreman to seasonal work on the European continent. Solimbergo, the Italian consul in Montreal, "found out that of all Italian emigrants who were already in Canada not one thought it of any use to become a colonial... the emigrants are going to Canada in order to find work."[21] At first the seasonal work offered by the great Canadian labour-intensive employers such as the railroad, mining, and lumber companies served the interests of the "target migrants" well.[22] Struggle for control of the labour pool, though, led to dislocation in the system. Every year a certain number of seasonal migrants became a winter residue in the country. In some years, for example, 1901 and 1904, simply too many migrants were brought over.

Men who had come for single "campaigns" found that crooked bankers, foremen, boardinghouse keepers, and late thaws made it impossible to hold to their family and community schedule for migration.[23] The same commerce of migration which made the system efficient and drew the "target migrants" also led to cutthroat competition between *padroni* and dishonest labour bureaux. That in turn led to imbalances in the labour supply and lost time for migrants. In 1901, a correspondent for the *Corriere della Sera* accompanied a group – "almost entirely young men, representing the best portion of our country population of the South". He soon learned how the system could fail the "target migrant" and his family plans. His group was met in Montreal, where they had been promised work, by agents of the Donnor Emigration Company which had sponsored their crossing. The migrants were told that they could only have work in British Columbia. Most had no idea where that was. "Those who refused the terms were abandoned. Those that remain here," he went on, "seek to house themselves as best they can. Many found their way into different houses, and when it came to paying were driven into the streets as they had no money, their belongings having previously been retained."[24]

Canadian immigration statistics are virtually useless for the study of return flows to Italy, so it is difficult to estimate the number of migrants caught in the country each year as winter approached.[25] If a man did not get home at season's end, it was quite likely that he would not do so for another year and perhaps for many more. The boardinghouses were run by *padroni*, the camp commissaries were exorbitant and dishonest, and there was little or no work for foreigners in the winter except city snow removal. Some were lucky and found factory work or steady work in street railway construction; many others never escaped the seasonal cycle of work and consequently found their sojourn becoming a form of exile.[26]

It is a truism of migration studies that people who regard themselves as sojourners, regardless of how long they dwell in a host country, continue to think of the problems and needs of their hometown as paramount.[27] Translated into national assimilation measurements, the same idea is expressed in Eisenstadt's statement that "the analysis of the immigrant's motive for migration and his consequent *image* of the new country is not of historical interest alone, but is also of crucial importance for understanding his initial attitudes and behaviour in his new setting."[28] If it is true that the sojourner was preoccupied with what he had left behind, then we should study him not just as an urban problem or a potentially assimilable immigrant, but also in his own existential frame of reference. Italian migrants were, first and foremost, men away from loved ones and familiar places. They were men entrusted with responsibilities who sensed the proximity of failure, usually failure to bring family levels of existence into harmony with rising expectations. They were men with the increase and natural suspicion that things would not be, indeed could not possibly be, as they should be when and if they managed to get back home.[29] The abnormality of their own existence had to have, they thought, its mirror image in the *paese*.

This essay speculates on the impact of separation and uncertainty on the sojourner. It does not matter whether each migrant eventually became a rich and respected *ritornato* with many children and a Fascist party card or sent for a wife and became part of the Italian-Canadian bourgeoisie. Any seasonal or "target migrant" who did not return after the first season slipped into an abnormal existence; so did the people left behind.

One reason historians have shied away from studying the turn of the century in terms of migration disruption is distrust of the sources. We do not have much chance to employ the survey and interviewing techniques used by the anthropologists and sociologists who study contemporary migration.[30] Only bits of oral history material survive, along with risky inferences from migration statistics, to suggest the migrant's real frame of mind. What we are left with is the very suspect literature of those opposed to emigration in Italy and the missionaries, social workers, and restrictionists in North America. Obviously with such sources it is too easy to paint a picture of emigration and the migrant's life as pathological. What follows is not a vindication of such literature, but the modest suggestion that it makes sense to think of the man separated from his people as in an abnormal situation and to use the questions raised by the anti-immigrant literature to propose avenues of research.

We know the economic consequence of the migrant's commitment to his hometown – that willingness to be crowded in cheap boardinghouses, to depend on *padroni*, to show little interest in the host country, and to risk no "cash money" on North American situations. Now we must look at the migrant's frame of mind itself. Let us begin with his hometown world which concerns him so much. His failure to return after a season's work may have been eased by remittances (although more often than not, it was lack of funds which made him stay in Canada). Then too there are things money can't buy. If he was a young man, the girl of his choice may not have waited. If he was a father and husband, he worried about the virtue of his womenfolk.

Anti-emigration literature concentrated on the impact of sojourning on sexual morality. As migration increased, there apparently was an increase in cuckolding and bastardy in the Italian countryside, as there was of prostitution in the cities.[31] Giuseppe Scalidi, writing about Calabria in 1905, claimed an absolute correlation between emigration rates and the increase of "delitti contro il buon costume e l'ordine delle famiglie." Another moral opponent of emigration put it more bluntly. "It is a sad fact but one well known to everyone who knows the regions of heavy migration that the wives and fiancees of the *Americani* take the place of prostitutes." In fact, in a grand analogy to the "commercio di carne umana" which exploited the menfolk, the author goes on to describe such women as "ignorant, inexperienced and impoverished, who sadly *si gettano nel grande mercato della carne femminile.*"[32]

What is one to make of such evidence? Obviously such writers believed that emigration caused massive social disruption. Their writing also reflected an old Mediterranean assumption that healthy people left alone copulate, and that women particularly are helpless in the face of temptation. "Modesty is not natural in women but imposed on them. (Il pudore è atteggimento più coattivo che spontaneo della donna.) The emigration of men, fathers, brothers, husbands, lovers, eliminates the coercion and lets natural and unbridled instincts emerge."[33] The author's view of women and their instincts was primitive, but one can wonder whether it was more so than that of young, under-educated, rural men and jealous husbands who were the migrants themselves. Moreover, one can also assume that, among men thrown together in work gangs, camps, and boardinghouses, such a view of women became accentuated. The coarse jokes, thwarted young appetites, the dreams of women left behind and inaccessible women seen in the host country, the banter about *cornuti*, the fragmentary news from home, all colluded to paint a picture of the hometown which would increase the migrant's tension.[34] The reality of the impact of migration on the countryside hardly mattered as much as the imaginations of those abroad in causing tension and misunderstanding.

It is unlikely that simply the absence of men would destroy the inbred, umbertine and Catholic values of most peasant women. Moreover, few towns or families were so completely decimated by migration that some older guardian of the family's good name was not about to cluck over impropriety.

> "Even the logistics are impossible. Overpopulation is not conducive to trysts. When husband and wife share their room, often their bed, with their children, and grandmother sleeps just the other side of the partition, it is hard to have a private fight, let alone arrange a secret meeting. On the few occasions when the street is empty there is always an old woman peering through the cracks in her *dutch* door. Empty fields do not exist... Where becomes almost unsolvable."[35]

So the possibilities of family disintegration, cuckolding, and dishonour haunted men whose sojourn grew uncontrollably and the phantom that lived with them was, at least in part, created by fear and guilt about how well they were fulfilling family obligations.

Of course, not all the migrants had the same social and familial stress upon them. Many young men had only limited responsibility and had in some sense been ejected from the family inheritance structure with a cash settlement which paid their fare to the New World. (If, however, they were beyond puberty, they might already have had pressure from a potential bride and need to meet the property conditions of forming a new nuclear family.) Nonetheless, some young men clearly fit Osborne's category of "escaping" rural migrants,[36] and many married men had become such multiple migrants that they managed to return once a year, beget children, settle family affairs and thus mitigate the burden of uncertainty that came with long term sojourning.[37]

All sojourners were under some pressure and the Commissariat of Emigration doctors saw that as a cause of insanity in *ritornati*.

> Il disagio economico, l'ansia della ricerca del meglio, la preoccupazione dell'ignoto, associati all'strapazzo fisico alle privazioni alle fatiche e disagi de ogni sorta e in fine assai de frequente alle delusioni piu amare, sono il doloroso fardello che di solito accompagna l'emigrante nella sua odissea.[38]

There is no need for us to believe that large numbers of men buckled completely under such pressure in order to make the case for the abnormal life style of the migrants.[39] One index of the changes which came with leaving the village was the degree to which one could conceive of and practice marital infidelity or be promiscuous.

The Italian critics of emigration, just like racist restrictionists in North America, saw the male sojourner as a dangerous and amoral beast preying upon North American women. The fear and jealousy of the sexual prowess of strangers along with an almost colour racism against Italian bachelors makes it impossible to study this aspect of the migrant's life through layers of prejudice in North American sources. For example, Toronto's local muckraking newspaper, *Jack Canuck*, carried lurid accounts of Italian labourers having carnal knowledge of young girls and diseasing them.[40]

Years ago, Robert Foerster remarked that "plenty of testimony exists to show that loose living on the part of male Italians abroad is common. Our witnesses, who are generally also critics, affirm that there is often a ready frequenting of prostitutes, a class of persons all but absent from the Italian countryside and village."[41] Perhaps the Italian literature deserves more attention since it has no racist edge. The critics of emigration, as umbertine Italian gentlemen, held the rather simple physical and ecological view of sex which we spoke of when dealing with the family without its menfolk. Illicit sex would take place if physical and social barriers were not erected against it.

To the critics, the migrants abroad were men with the barriers removed. They would be unfaithful to wives and fiancées. They would spend in bordellas money earned for a sister's dowry or saved for a few *tomoli* of land. So,

> "... freed from the sexual control... which long habit and religious anathema hurled against the flesh by the clergy enforced, that the physical exhaustion of their bodies, the jealousy of the wives, and the ferocious surveillance of the gossipy village also enforced... "

they would run amok. Especially when they encountered the flirtatious American women and the free atmosphere of cities. Perhaps with an insight only possible for a conservative, the same critics remarked that this phenomenon which happened to migrants in North America was an exact analogy to the decline of respect for property.[42] The corollary was that America's negative moral and physical impact on Italy could be shown by detailing the rising incidence of madness, alcoholism, syphilis and tuberculosis in areas of heaviest emigration.[43]

No doubt travelling only with other males produced an earthy camaraderie typical of a peasant work force. Whatever the culture or education of the sojourners, life in isolated work camps brutalized them in the truest sense of the word. Men became *bestie* (brutish) under the impact of conditions, and work camp life in Canada was usually worse than in the United States.[44]

The decline into brutishness which took place was not one into unbridled sexuality. The workers were too isolated, tired, and frugal, and the host society too prejudiced against them for moral decline to take that form. Rather, the failure came in terms of personal dignity, outward appearance, and language and manner. The process enabled North American racists to remark that such conditions could only be imposed on victims who were "the sons of a backward civilization and know not what twentieth-century living is."[45]

Interviews with men who were young migrants in those isolated camps refer over and over to becoming *bestie*, to feeling inadequate and inferior not just to the Anglo-Celtic Canadians but to city folk generally. Men came to feel like the *forese*, "the man who lives *fuori*," those too poor and brutish to live in a nucleated argo-town, the unclean, impoverished shepherds and others who held their head downcast when they entered town "and in the face of *stranieri*, nearly always more educated and civil then they, felt themselves humiliated by their ignorance, as men and as Italians."[46]

They were men who had not eaten anything but stew on mouldy bread and sardines for months on end and had only eaten in the company of other men. They were men who were "deprived of the refining influence of women and the soothing touch of childhood." And their decline was not just in concern for their physical appearance.

> "Camp life is an unnatural life, and in it the coarse, vulgar elements of human nature came to the face; the indecent story, the vulgar joke and the immoral picture are introduced and passed around. If intoxicants are within reach, the men will drink and gamble."[47]

The quote may have the speech rhythm of a born again preacher or Salvation Army sergeant, but there is no reason to doubt its essential truth.

In general the brutalization of foreign migrant workers was worst in the most isolated settings. Even in those settings, though, controls existed to keep them from the immorality and sexuality which the critics in Italy assumed. First of all, the very system which drew "target migrants" to Canada kept them in groups based upon their *paese*. Employment of sub-bosses, foreman, and *agenti* from each *paese* was the way in which the large scale *padroni* in Montreal and Toronto used *campanilismo* to advantage.[48] This meant that often the eyes of the village followed the migrant into the remotest setting. If a man became a drunkard, consorted with the rare prostitutes to be found in the North, dabbled in perversion or just seemed to go crazy, word might get back to the family and town. (It would be interesting to be able to show that those who were not "target migrants" but "rural escape migrants" or immigrants fell away from scrutiny first.) As the modern students of rural-urban migration put it, "rural norms and customs are most likely to be retained precisely among those who plan to return home in the foreseeable future."[49] The other powerful force which kept most of the "sins against chastity" of the migrants at the level of fantasy was the deep prejudice toward them among their hosts. Literature about "dirty foreign navvies" abounds and would seem to imply that the migrants were unlikely to find female companionship among the natives easily or without a price.[50] A quotation about those who left the labour camps for the city has more bravado than historical detail.

> "However Toronto has little appeal for the young rugged Italian labourers without families. There were no enjoyments, no drinks during the week, and

few girls. Montreal had all that. It was the center of attraction for Italians who came from the west. Instead of facing a dull winter in Toronto they pushed on to the gay port city."[51]

The story was much more one of demeaning assaults on manhood by the natives and the constant fear of getting into trouble for offending Anglo-Saxon custom. This plus lack of confidence and language difficulties impelled the migrant toward the lowest classes of female companionship or left him at the level of vain flirtation and coarse inference:

> "Down below there was more noise than it is possible to describe. Everyone was busy preparing his bed or sleeping. Five or six were running and throwing potatoes at each other. Two German girls sleeping in the same compartment were obliged to leave shortly after owing to the stupid remarks by two Calabresi who were in the vicinity."[52]

"Stupid remarks" – the innocence of it rings true – from the first rejection of attention on the boat to the veteran *ritornato* who "come back, marry – no women in America, *ostia* – las'time I wer six year in America, work in backwood, for two year never see a woman."[53] The abnormality of life for the migrants came not from promiscuity but from total physical and cultural frustration. The same was probably true for the vast majority of women left behind in the *paese*. Perhaps the substitutions were just as debilitating for the family structure. Commissionaries in most camps sold alcohol. The U.S. Industrial Commission of 1901 claimed that unemployed Italians spent "almost all the idle time... in the saloons and in other resorts of their countrymen," a strange new image for an abstemious wine-drinking people and one, as we have seen, that the critics of emigration in Italy had been quick to notice.[54]

In the long run, the same combination of external and internalized social coercion which guarded the *villagio pettegolo*, "the gossipy village," existed in the migrant camps. The backbiting *paisano* or solicitous relative, the hostile women of the host society, combined with levels of filial piety, parental duty, and morality in the migrant to serve as a brake on his decline into brutishness. He might drink more, he might find a prostitute, he certainly became coarser and more vulgar than he had been when he left Italy, but he probably had not broken faith with the commitments which had sent him forth. He still worked to send money home for specific purposes; he still intended to marry someone from his *paese* (most often someone whom he or his family had chosen before he left), or to return to his wife.

Each migrant seems to have measured time differently according either to his nature, or to the original purpose of his sojourn, and to the situation in his town of origin. To the extent though that migration was a form of suspended animation, the sojourn had no time dimension. A young man, if he was a bachelor, was held between youth and manhood in regard to marriage, inheritance, and indeed of carrying weight with family and *paesani*. Oral history interviews with immigrants from half a dozen countries show that what Arensberg said of the Irish countrymen held true in most rural communities, "the *boy* reaches adult status when he marries and inherits the farm. The family and the land are both involved in the crucial reorganization."[55] Young men who had married but had no children before they migrated were often just like the bachelors. Their counsel was worth little and until they had saved money to start a household, would not be. Their absence was a temporary solution to problems of space and fecundity even if the larger problem of owning arable land could only be solved by a long and successful sojourn. Fathers of families worried more; they had more that could go awry or dishonour them at home. For all these men seasonal migration, repeated trips across the oceans, and even accepting immigration were options: the degree to which they entertained each option was entangled with their fortunes in America and the nature of news from home. Out of that cluster of concern emerged the real measurement of each man's sojourn time.[56]

If a man escaped the confined world of labour camps in summer and large padrone-owned boardinghouses[57] in winter and still had not found means to return to Italy or continued to have a "target" need for cash he might begin to look for a chance to become *bordante*[58] in one of the larger cities with a family from his *paese*. This meant that some of his job transience had declined and usually coincided with the transition to city street work or to factory work.[59] The value of the system to husband and wife was obvious. It provided sheltered work at home which enabled her to continue her economic role in the family. The increase in the atmosphere of "civile e gentile" for the migrant *bordante* was also obvious, but what did the system of *convivenza* mean for the moral life of the migrant and for the maintenance of his commitments to his village of origin?

In the first place, if each good-sized Little Italy was a combination of many little *paese*, the little *paese* broke down farther into houses where families took in *paesani* and relatives. Historians have long known this, but we have not thought about these homes as outriders of the goals and mores of the *paese*. It is through the households and neighbourhoods that "the high proportion of temporary migrant... often associated with large numbers or apparently *broken* or *incomplete* families and of people living with friends or relatives rather than their nuclear family"[60] began the process of reasserting the social controls of the village and some of the original goals of migration. The Italian Mission (Methodist) in Toronto 1908 complained that "there are so many homeless men in this community it makes it necessary for every woman to accommodate as many boarders as she can crowd into her house."[61]

Moving from camps and working-class hotels to live with families did not just reflect the emergence of job opportunities in the city. The price of home-cooked food and family chatter, clean clothes and a safe mailing address was that migrants themselves had to clean up, to overcome cafonism, and to make conversation without constant vulgarity. In the city, living with families or visiting families from the *paese* on Sundays marked either the settling in for a long sojourn or the beginnings of thinking about true immigration. Married men had been unable to envisage their womenfolk living near most non-urban Canadian work sites.[62] Becoming *bordante* also meant that the decline into brutishness and the constant but idle chatter about sex ended. The family with whom one boarded, particularly *la padrona*, might know the boarder's family as well as his commitments at home and his dreams. Often the lady of the house had her own dream of playing matchmaker. If the *bordante* was not betrothed or married, there was invariably a niece of the household who could be sent for as a bride. In such simple human terms the needs of the old country family and of the *paese* itself were served. No one who boarded with a landlady from his own village had much chance of being either promiscuous or exogamous.

Often the lady of the house was as young as the youngest boarders, but if they were *paesani*, they most likely addressed her as *zia* (auntie). Respect, recognition of her connection to the Old World family structure and a guarantee of propriety were all in the use of the word auntie.[63]

Probably that proximity to the occasion of sin which so exercised the critics of emigration came into play occasionally between *la padrona* and the *bordante*. Although in the home as in the village and camp, the problem of *where* remained complex. The chance arrival of husbands, children, neighbours, other boarders, visiting city nurses, water meter readers, settlement house workers, and Methodist missionaries could make a farce of the most passionate scenario. The central actors themselves also made passionate scenarios unlikely. Whether from morality and familial honour or a good sense of status and self-preservation, trysts were not likely. Amy Bernardy, one of the most insightful of Italian travellers, in her address to the first Congress of Overseas Italians at the Campidoglio claimed that she could not speak in a language fit for a congress about the fruits of the "promiscua servitù" which the system of *convivenza* imposed on Italian women in North America,[64] but that was merely rhetoric.

Short of a survey or a statistical analysis, we may never know how effective the safeguards against the "near occasion of sin" were. Certainly good order in a home with boarders had something to do with the immediacy of kinship and hometown ties between the boarder and the family. The word *paesano* is quite misleading in this context, since being Calabrese together hardly constituted a strict relationship with social safeguards built in. On the other hand, being from Cosenza and related by marriage obviously imposed reciprocal obligations.

There obviously were cases of hanky-panky, but how many? A social worker at Central Neighbourhood House in Toronto reported that "a child came with a story of immoral relations between mother and one of the boarders. Case investigated – Reported to Juvenile Court." Of fourteen other Italian social cases that day, all others refer to problems of health or rents, of four Anglo-Canadian cases, one was a fourteen year old "living an immoral life" and a second was a husband's desertion.[65] It is difficult to draw conclusions about the effect of abnormal transient lifestyle on Italian peasants from such material. Certainly there are none of the suggestions of even the practical promiscuity of the *zadruga* system among South Slavs, and certainly none of the sly humor which exists in the Hungarian-American concept of the "star-boarder" could have developed among Italians if it is true that the first purpose of accepting boarders was to find women work where there was no threat to chastity.

At any rate, the social and moral structures of the *villagio pettegolo* which had been weakened but never vanished in the all-male work camps recovered in the city's "Little Italy." The Rev. Taglialatela, Methodist colporteur to the Italians of Toronto, saw social abnormality in transience itself. "They are not under the eyes of their friends and relatives and do not feel obliged to look better and act well." He, of course, thought that they had improved with time in the city, perhaps the sense of the *paese* and its controls simply reasserted itself through family and campanilist density.[66]

Vecoli's "Contadini in Chicago," a decade ago, noted the crucial place of the family in Little Italies. "If the South Italian retained a sense of belongingness with his fellow townsmen the family continued to be the focus of most intense loyalties.[67] The point, I think, could be pushed further. Just as the village or agrotown was a collectivity of families, so potentially were the *colonie* of the *paese* in North America. A migrant or sojourner was at all times within the system whether as a potential *ritornato* or as a colonist of the new *piccolo paese*. He was also at all times a member of a family, nuclear and extended. In fact, families – new ones, old ones, broken ones, potential ones in the form of young sojourners, girls awaiting dowries, husbands, fiancees, sons with insufficient inherited land, fathers toiling abroad so that family status kept pace with fecundity – were the impelling cause of migration.

Remittances made one economic world of the village and the many far away lands where there were migrants sojourning. In the same way, families and neighbours in the New World reimposed the social coercion, jealousies and affectionate familiarity of the *paese*.

> Most of the Cinisari in the 69th St. group intended to return to Sicily. The town of Cinisi is forever in their minds: I wonder if I can get back in time for the next crop?... They receive mail keeping them informed as to the most minute details and about all gossip that goes on in Cinisi; in addition, they keep their hometown informed as to what is going on here. They write home of people here who have transgressed some custom: "So and so has married a American girl. The American girls are libertines. The boy is very disobedient." He has married a stranger... that is an Italian of another town. In this way they blacken a man's name in Cinisi so that a bad reputation awaits him on his return.[68]

We have long known about this pattern of contact between a specific *paese* and a specific part of some American city. The instances of it are very numerous.[69] Such networks of communication and transit existed between most towns of emigration and their *colonie*, but perhaps we have spent too much time looking at the remittances or prepaid tickets which were the chief items transmitted through the communication system. "Cash money" was rarely the end purpose of "target migration." Settlement of family or land questions almost always was. The abnormality of the migrant condition came as we have seen, not from decline into boorishness or unbridled sexuality, but from the suspended animation in matters of marriage, sex, and inheritance which came with separation. The logical end of sojourning was either creation of a new nuclear family or reconstitution and completion of one. This could come about by "going home," sending for a wife or betrothed, or marrying endogamously in the new land.[70] Whatever the solution, the real messages carried along the communications network were the details of family life.

> "In the old country there is no such thing as a person not married, every man he is born when he is little, he grow up he marry, then a little while and he die. I never hear of no person not marry in old country."[71]

Different cultures obviously have different tolerance levels about bachelorhood and different proper ages for marriage. It is difficult to say how much the tradition of migration affected such cultural predispositions. Certainly inheritance systems affected the age of marriage more. The ethnic groups who provided the shock troops for turn of the century industrialization – Italians, Hungarians, Greeks, South Slavs, Poles, Lithuanians, Finns and Chinese – all had tremendous imbalances of male over female in the sex ratio of their migration statistics. And the boardinghouse stereotypes of rowdiness, insobriety, ignorance of English, and transience persist to one degree or another about all these groups, but perhaps less so about the Italians than the others.

While most Italian communities in North America have a few old unmarried "uncles" and *cafoni* who are the fossils of that earlier abnormal life style, Italian culture has not been tolerant of bachelorhood.[72] Then too, despite the difficulty of U.S. and Canadian quotas and of Fascism, the *paese* to *piccolo paese* communications network which carried gossip, matchmaking, and prepaid tickets was fully interrupted only briefly during World War II. Unmarried sojourners alone or in groups were always whittled away by that family and village desire to make the future by creating new nuclear families.

If immigration was a matter of intention and attitude rather than duration of sojourn, one is tempted to suggest that true immigration did not really commence until the questions of marriage and inheritance were settled. A migrant's search was ended when he had fulfilled his target, but his target was almost always to live a normal, i.e., married life among his own kind somewhere in the psychical world of his *paesani* where he could make a living.

The ideas in this essay owe more to ethnologists and students of developing nations than to historians. This is fitting, since the study of sojourners should be centred on the people themselves. Moreover, their commitment to the *paese* may come as close as one can to "ethnicity" defining daily existence. Sex ratios in migration and other statistical tools provide a rough correlation to migrant intentions, but folk truth, acquired from the "memory culture" of the former migrants themselves, is a more useful guide to the sojourner's frame of mind.[73]

The real history of the sojourners and of Canadian Little Italies will only be within our reach when all the possible archival and statistical sources are used along with the "memory culture." Church records, minutes of *mutuo soccorso* and other benevolent societies, stub books of payment, receipts and remittances from immigrant banks, and the sparse records of *paese* clubs are the internal ethnic sources we need to use. Photographs and city directory analysis also help to show the place of the migrants and *bordanti* in the birth of a *paese's* colony.[74]

Much of this essay should be read as a plea and perhaps an agenda for further study – study of the villages and towns of emigration and study of the migrants mind set as a key to his North American experience. Until studies of such topics as changes in marriage and bethrothal patterns, cuckolding, alcoholism, mental problems among *ritornati*, endogamy rates among sojourners, and a myriad of attitudinal cultural subjects are done, plausible constructs such as this essay provide our glimpse of the men who entered Canada in the 1900s.

We have at least been freed from seeing every man in North America as somewhere on a scale of assimilation. The work was begun by those who realized that the migrant was not "uprooted" and those who, through "return flow" rates and study of remittances, saw the economic consequences of families and towns reaching out across the ocean for survival or improvement. What we must do now is study more closely the preoccupation with family and status which was the motive behind the world-wide search for "cash money." If we do so, I am sure that we will discover new and useful perspectives about emigration, about ethnic persistence and identity, as well as about the pace of assimilation. Historians, like the migrants, may take courage from some verses of a poet from my *paese*, Robert Frost, who writes in *Wilful Homing*:

Since he means to come to a door he will come to a door
Although so compromised of aim and rate
He may fumble wide of the knob a yard or more,
And to those concerned he may seem a little late.

Notes

1. Leonello De Nobili, "L'Emigrazione in Calabria". Effetti dell'emigrazione in generale in *Rivista de Emigrazione* 1:5 (July 1908).

2. R. Foerster, *Italian Emigration Of Our Time* (Harvard, 1918). See F. Cerase, *L'Emigrazione di Ritorno* (Rome, 1971) and Betty Boyd Caroli, *Italian Repatriation for the U.S., 1900-1941* (N.Y.,1973), T. Saloutos, *They Remember America* (Berkeley, 1956).

3. O. Handlin, *The Uprooted* (N.Y. 1951) and John Baxevanis, *Economy and Population Movements in the Peloponnesus of Greece* (Athens, 1972).

4. See, for example, F.S. Nitti, *Scritti sulla questione meridionale* (Bari 1959), Amy Bernardi, *Italia randagia attraverso gli Stati Uniti* (Torino 1913), G. Fortunato, *Il Mezzogiorno e lo stato italiano, Discorsi politici, 1880-1910* (Bari, 1911), A. Rossi, "Vantaggi e danni dell'emig. nel mezzogiorno d'Italia. Note de un viaggio fatto in Basilicata e in Calabria del R. Commissario dell'emig". *Bollettino dell'Emigrazione Anno 1908* #13 D. Taruffi, L. De Nobili and C. Lori, *La questone agraria e l'emigrazione in Calabria* (1907).

5. C. Cronin, *The Sting of Change: Sicilians in Sicily and Australia* (Chicago, 1970) pp. 85-89. C. Ware, *Greenwich Village, 1920-1930* p. 197. "a child would be expected to sacrifice his own ambition and advancement to the interest of the family group." Pitkin shows the obverse of this, the parents duty to "sistemare" their children's lot. See D. Pitkin "Marital Property Considerations Among Peasants: An Italian Example" *Anthropological Quarterly* 33:1 (Jan. 1960):37.

    An earlier view of emigration as disruptive to the family in N. Douglas, *Old Calabria* (N.Y., 1928) 63 "What is shattering family life is the speculative spirit born of emigration. A continual coming and going: two thirds of the adolescent and adult male population are at this moment in Argentina and the U.S."

6. B. Galeski, "Social Organization and Rural Social Change" *Peasants and Peasant Societies*. T. Shanin (ed.) (London, 1971) p. 120.

7. C. Cronin, *The Sting of Change*, pp. 58-59; Baxevanis, *Economy and Population Movements*, see especially Chapter IV, "The Decision to Migrate".

8. This, of course, can be seen from the perspective of the "stem family" or from the person's own sense of family responsibility as a "target migrant." The clearest discussion of migrant intentions that I have found is Joan M. Nelson's, *Temporary versus Permanent Cityward Migration: Causes and Consequences* (Migration and Development Study Group, MIT, 1976).

9. Response of the Mayor of Albano di Lucania to commissioners in A. Rossi's, *Vantaggi e danni dell'emigrazione*, p. 1550.

10. Dr. Angelo Alberti, "La psicologia dell'emigrati," *Rivista di Emigrazione* 1:9 (Nov. 1908) or Dr. Antinio D'Ormea, "Per la profilessi psichica dei nostri emigrati," *Rivista di Emigrazione* 11:2 (Feb. 1909).

11. See testimony about timing and length of sojourn throughout A. Rossi's, *Vantaggi e danni dell'emigrazione*. An anthropological study of a Lebanese village shows that there was both a real and ideal pattern of migration deviation and income. See L. Sweet, "The Women of Ain ad Dayr," *Anthropological Quarterly* v. 140. p. 171.

12. Taped interview with Mr. Jonas Yla, former Lithuanian-Canadian newspaper editor, (MHSO collection, 1976).

13. Typical would be the idyll in G. Fortunato's *Il Mezzogiorno* 11:502. "But the peasant, oh the peasants pick up the zappa and the vanga willingly again, happy enough to be free from the usurious slavery of rents, of being able to acquire for himself and for his a bit of his own and a piece of land."

14. J. Nelson, *Temporary Vs. Permanent Cityward Migration*, p. 37.

15. DeNobili, "L'Emigrazione in Calabria," p. 7 and A. Milani "L'Emigrazione e una partita del suo bilancio morale passivo," *Rivista di Emigrazione* 1:7 (Sept. 1908) p. 17.

16. Again the contemporary Lebanese case study echoes the many cases recorded by Nitti, Fortunato, De Nobili, etc. in the 1900s. "Then some families have land but not labour, some have sheep and goats but no land, some have both, and many receive money from overseas which aids the exchange of food and work necessities among all. Sweet, *Women of Ain ad Dayr*," p. 173.

17. Some of the more damning *bollettini* about Canada were D. Viola "Le condizioni degli opera: italiani nel distretto minerario di Cobalt nella provincia di Ontario" Anno 1910 #13; E. Rossi's, "Delle condizioni del Canada rispetto all'imigrazione italiana" Anno 1903 #4; B. Attolico's, "L'agricoltura e l'emigrazione nel Canada" Anno 1912 #5. There were also complaints in the Italian parliament in 1901 which led to the *Corriere della Sera*'s investigative reporter accompanying immigrants.

18. See D. Avery "Canada's Immigration Policy and the Foreign Navy, 1874-1914" *The Canadian Historical Association, Historical Papers* (1972) pp. 135-156.

19. The best account of this "commerce of migration" through Chiasso to Canada is in B. Brandenberg, *Imported Americans* (N.Y., 1903). His is the only account of the notorious E. Ludwig who operated on the Swiss-Italian Border as a labour agent for a number of Canadian companies.

20. The testimony of many labourers before the Royal Commission of 1904 confirms their transience and "target" intention. See *Royal Commission appointed to inquire into the Immigration of Italian Labourers to Montreal and the Alleged Fraudulent Practices of Employment Agencies* (Ottawa, 1905).

21. *Corriere della Sera*'s, report "Emigration of Italian Peasants to Canada" (March 18, 1901) includes *Solimbergo's Report*. Public Archives of Canada. Immigration Branch, RG 76 Vol. 128, File 28885:1.

22. See Royal Commission (1904) for details.

23. See reports to the *Corriere della Sera* through 1901. Some "target migrants" apparently even found themselves recruited to fight for Great Britain in the Boer War.

24. *Corriere della Sera*, "In Canada the Landing of the Emigrants New Delusion" Quebec, May 3rd and the despatch of May 5th in PAC, Immigration Branch, RG 76, Vol. 129, File 28885:1.

25. See W.D. Scott, "Immigration and Population" in *Canada and Its Provinces* ed. A. Shortt and A. Doughty VII: 561 (Toronto, 1914) for the system of counting immigrants. Since so many Italian migrants to Canada came and went through U.S. ports, the figures are particularly unreliable. The sex ratio in Italian migration to Canada in the 1900s overpoweringly suggests seasonal and target migration. In 1906-1907, 5,114 Italians arrived in Canadian ports in steerage, 17 in other classes, 4,430 were men and 384 were women. Some reconstruction of such arrivals can be made from the annual immigration reports in

Parliamentary sessional papers, but they cannot answer questions about Italian migration between U.S., "Little Italies" and Canada. Even in Toronto where there should have been more balance between the sexes, there were three times as many Italian men as women according to the Census of 1911.

26. The "memory culture" describes many South and East European bachelor migrants being caught in a cycle of inadequate summer work, winter indebtedness and thus no opportunity to end the sojourn. For some, the turn of the century "reconnoitring of North America elided with the Depression years." The impact of harsh winters on the seasonal migrant continued a traditional problem of Canadian social history. See Judy Fingard, "The Winter's Tale: Contours of Pre-industrial Poverty in British America, 1815-1860" *The Canadian Historical Assoc. Historical Papers* (1974) especially p. 67.

27. See R. Berrier and T. Wolf, *Internal Migration*, a selected bibliography (Migration and Development Study Group) MIT 1975.

28. S. Eisenstadt, *The Absorption of Immigrants*, (London, 1954) p. 4.

29. The concern could range from that for the health of a parent or of a fig tree, but it tended to involve jealousy about property and female virtue. Foerster, *The Italian Emigration* quotes Coletti as claiming that in "some parts of South Italy men who marry just before emigrating sometimes, by way of precaution, leave wives immaculate." p. 441.

30. For examples of a literature which put the migrant himself at the centre of study, see J. Berger and J. Mohr, *A Seventh Man* (London, 1975) and Jane Krame "Invandrare" *New Yorker Magazine* (22 March 1976). Ann Cornelisen, *Women of the Shadows* (Boston, 1976) is a good picture of those left behind.

31. T. Cyriax, *Among Italian Peasants* (Glasgow, 1919) pp. 216-217.

32. A. Milone, "L'emigrazione e una partita". p. 7.

33. Ibid. p. 10.

34. A brilliant, if a bit cruel, analysis of the relationship between South Italian male sexual fantasizing and banter on the one hand, and their feelings of poverty and powerlessness on the other can be found in A. Cornelisen, *Women of the Shadows*.

35. Ibid. p. 35.

36. Ann Osborne, "Migration from the Countryside in the Absence of Consent: Escape as an Alternative," *The Political Economy of Urban Development in Latin America* ed. W. Cornelius & F. Trueblood (Sage Publications #5 Los Angeles, 1975).

37. See the pattern described by V. Nee and his wife in San Francisco's Chinatown where men actually did go home only to beget sons or to bring them to America when they reached puberty, *Longtime California. A Documentary Study of an American Chinatown* (Boston 1973) pp. 60-124.

38. A. D'Ormea, "La Pazzia negli emigranti rimpartriati": *Riv. di Emigrazione* 17 (Sept. 1907). One doctor noted that not just emigration but the emigration of parents "passa gia costituire essa medesime un carrattere degenerativa." Translation of quote in text: "The economic discomfort or poverty, the worry of seeking a better life, the pre-occupation within the unknown, together with physical exhaustion from privation, fatigue, and discomforts of every kind, and finally, the frequent, bitter disappointments made up the burden which usually accompanies the immigrant in his odyssey."

39. It is almost impossible to confirm this from remittances which tend to decline with length of sojourn anyway. See Valeriote Store stub books and receipts (Multicultural History Society of Ontario collection).

40. See S. LaGumina, *Wop A Documentary History of Anti-Italian Discrimination in the United States* (San Francisco, 1973). See *Jack Canuck*, 1:12 (25 Nov. 1911) City Archives of Toronto.

41. Foerster, *The Italian Emigration*, p. 441.

42. A. Milone, "L'emigrazione e una partita," pp. 15-16.

43. E. Duse, "Pellagra, alcoolismo ed emigrazione nella Provincia de Belluno" *Revista pellagrologica italiana* (1909). See D'Ormea "La Pazzia negli emigranti." p. 99. Supporters of emigration tended to see such vices as older than emigration. See P. Villari, *Seritti sulla emigrazione e sopra alti argomenti vari* (Bologna, 1909).

44. See P. Roberts, *The New Immigration* (N.Y. 1928) for U.S. work camps. E. Bradwin, *The Bunkhouse Man* (N.Y. 1928) for Canadians. Neither account details the degradation as well as the Italian *bollettini* and some of the oral "memory cultures" do. See note #17.

45. Roberts, *The New Immigration*, p. 112.

46. Notiziario in *Rivista d'Emigrazione* 1:3 (May 1908). See John Davis "Town and Country," *Anthropological Quarterly* 42:3 (July 1969). This view was confirmed very forcefully by all the former migrants interviewed. Davis' local study is based on Pisticci which happened to be the hometown of many Italians who came to Toronto.

47. Roberts, *The New Immigration*, p 115.

48. See *Royal Commission* (1904) and R.F. Harney "The Padrone and the Immigrant" *Canadian Review of American Studies* V:2 (Fall 1974).

49. Nelson, *Temporary vs. Permanent Cityward Migration*, p. 63.

50. The limits of the "memory culture" and of oral history sources generally are discovered when one asks about sex habits among the migrants. Even the oldest survivors will talk about the heterosexual prowess of their youth, but little else.

51. A.V. Spada, *The Italians in Canada*, (Ottawa 1969) p. 265.

52. Report to *Corriere della Sera* "On board the *Lake Megantic*" 24 April 1901 PAC, Immigration Branch, RG 76. Vol. 129, File 28885:1.

53. T. Cyriax, *Among Italian Peasants*, p. 90.

54. U.S. Congress, *Reports of the Industrial Commission* (Washington, 1901), XV:498.

55. C. Arensberg, *The Irish Countryman, An Anthropological Study* (N.Y. 1968) p. 77. Interviews with Poles, Macedonians, Ukrainians, Italians, Lithuanians and Croats confirm this view.

56. J. Baxevanis, *Economy and Population Movements* writes that "Emigration is the historical solution to land fragmentation." p. 67. The point is true but not subtle enough for the Italian situation. For some "target migration," for others seasonal migration, and for others longtime sojourning were alternatives, not simply emigrating. The Italian folk song, *Quando Saro in America*, shows how complicated the matter was. See T. Cyriax, *Among Italian Peasants*, p. 196-197.

57. On the complicated question of whether the *padrone*, steamship agent, and boardinghouse keeper were one and the same, see testimony before *Royal Commission* (1904) p. 167. A comparative study between the role of women in Slavic, Hungarian and Italian boardinghouses would be very useful.

58. In North America, the usual usage was *bordante* or *bordisti* although variations of the Italian *covivenze* were used as well.

59. J. MacDonald, "Chain Migration, Ethnic Neighbourhood Formation and Social Networks" in *An Urban World* ed. C. Tilly (Boston, 1974). p. 230. The MacDonalds view the *bordanti* more as the product of serial migration than as migrants from the camps coming to the city.

60. Nelson, *Temporary vs. Permanent Cityward Migration*, p. 62.

61. *Missionary Outlook* (June 1908) XXVIII:6, p 141. "As these are not employed all the time in winter, but spend the idle hours around the house, it gives the housekeeper much extra work and makes it hard to leave and attend meetings."

62. John Davis, "Town and Country," p. 174, "and the very strong associations of women with town make it difficult for men to accept that the women should work in the country."

63. The use of terms of respect or affection for *la padrona* came out in many interviews. One of the most detailed accounts was that of Mrs. M. Caruso about her grandmother. (taped interview, 7 Dec. 1976, MHSO collection). Mrs. Gina Petroff remembers that as a young wife, she always referred to her older boarders as uncle. (taped interview 27 Oct. 1976, MHSO collection).

64. "The congestion of Italian American households is more dangerous to women and children than the factory or the street... cases of incest are more frequent than one could believe... boarders are in truth an economic resource but are also the principle cause of congestion, filth, degeneration of domestic life of the immigrant family." Bernardy goes on to blame the spread of syphilis on boarders. "Da un relazione di Amy Bernardy su l'emigrazione delle donne e fanciulli italiane nella Stati Uniti" *Bollettino del'Emigrazione* (1909). Contrast her view with that of the MacDonalds that the system of *bordanti* became popular because women could work at home and avoid the "threat to their chastity" that outside work, especially as domestics, posed. MacDonald and MacDonald, "Chain Migration." p. 231.

65. *Report of My Day* by Headworker (Sept. 23, 1918) Archives of Central Neighbourhood House, Toronto. A. Vazsony's "The Star Boarder. Traces of Cicisbeism in an Immigrant Community" in *Tractata Altaica* (Weisbaden, 1976) is a wonderful ethnological foray into the morals of Hungarian boarding-houses.

66. A. Taglialatela, "Our Italian Citizens", *Missionary Outlook* (April 10) XXX:4.

67. R. Vecoli, "Contadini in Chicago," in *Journal of American History* L1:3 (Dec. 1954), p. 409.

68. Cusumano account of Cinisi colony in New York. R. Park and Miller, *Old World Traits Transplanted*, (N.Y.), pp. 150-151.

69. See C. Bianco, *The Two Rosetos* (Indiana, 1974), L.W. Moss and S.C. Cappannari, "Patterns of Kinship Camparaggio and Community in a South Italian Village," *Anthropological Quarterly* 33:1 (Jan., 1960) and the bibliographical references in MacDonald and MacDonald, "Chain Migration."

70. Endogamous marriage to have real meaning for this essay would have to be between people from the hometown or surrounding villages. Marriage between people from the same province is really out marriage in *paese* terms. Unfortunately, priests in North America, to avoid the difficulties of following canon law – the prescription that records be sent of the marriage to the parishes where a couple were baptized – usually simply wrote "Italy" into parish registers.

71. Quoted in "Women and Settlement Work," in *St, Hilda's Chronicle* (Michaelmas, 1915), University of Toronto Archives, p. 7.

72. John Kosa's *Land of Choice* (Toronto, 1957), p. 28, describes the place of the bachelor among Hungarian immigrants. The bachelor is accepted. He may be irresponsible, gamble, drink, and play by different rules, but that is because he remains "a boy" no matter what his age.

73. In fact, we in Canada have already neglected oral sources too long and much of what one can gather about the sojourner frame of mind has to come from survivors of the 1920s migration, not the true "target migrant" of the turn-of-the-century.

74. The Multicultural History Society of Ontario has found many sources to be richer than assumed and others to be disappointing. As we noted earlier, parish records fail to give the hometown or parish of baptism of most of the Italians who married in Toronto. (Russian and Macedonian Orothodox Churches, however, kept very exact records of town or village origin.) *Paese* club records were apt to be destroyed when the secretary-treasurer's pants were washed and he had forgotten to clean his pockets. On the other hand, *banchisti*, stores, and steamship agencies kept, for obvious reasons, thorough accounts of debts, remittances, and prepaid tickets.

7

The Canadian Prairies: A Target of Italian Immigration

Canada's historians, like those of many immigrant polities, present the national past as an epic of development, a complex interplay between landscape and humans, between fertile land, timber, mineral resources waiting to be exploited and the immigrants who arrive to people the epic. At the turn of the century, the Canadian prairies, from the Ontario border to the Rocky Mountain barriers of British Columbia, was represented as just such a rich landscape awaiting its human resources. It was a land, as one Italian visitor noted, "three times greater than the German Empire and five times the size of Great Britain and Ireland."[1]

By the time of the opening of the Canadian prairies, an organic intelligentsia had grown up in Italy around the issue of mass migration. Those who contributed to the political discourse known as "la polemica sull'emigrazione"[2] or inhabited the emerging governmental or pastoral bureaucracies concerned with migration from the Commissariat of Emigration to the Dante Alighieri Society and the Italica Gens had come to believe that they could exercise control over the flow of labour to capital that they could manipulate migration in such a way as to satisfy their own objectives which ranged from using the emigrants as agents of "informal empire" to the less ambitious goals of protecting them from extremes of exploitation or from secularism and protestant evangelism. Among the earliest Italian travellers to Canada was a former member of the research staff of Franchetti and Sonnino's great *Inchiesta* on the Sicilian peasantry, one Enea Cavalieri, who published the account of his Canadian trip in *Nuova Antologia*.[3] Cavalieri quoted Lord Dufferin, Canada's Governor General, as saying of the vast new nation: "the only thing we shall want is to man the ship with a more numerous crew." For some of this organic intelligentsia, a massive conjuncture seemed to exist between Italy's needs and Canada's. Surely Europe's most prolific exporter of rural migrants had a major role to play in the peopling of the fertile and empty lands of Manitoba, Saskatchewan and Alberta.

In a 1907 *Rivista Coloniale* article,[4] one such intellectual, Goffredo Jaja, wrote of the advantages of turning away from the United States and Argentina as targets of migration and turning toward the British colonies. He drove home the significance of the Prairie to his Italian readers. The existence of the uncultivated arable soil and other economic opportunities was Jaja's text, but a subtext existed as well. It was not simply that Canada West could absorb "18 to 20 millioni di contadini", but also that the civil conditions and governance were optimum. To comprehend the importance of the subtext, it is necessary to see the question of Italian migration in the context of a discourse, what Calvino calls a library in which "each work is different from what it would be in isolation or in another library."[5] Jaja's remarks about Canada were read by intellectuals who lived within a discourse that included other publications, ranging from *Nuova Antologia* to the *Bollettini* of the Commissariat of Emigration. The presence of "la polemica sull'emigrazione" provided an Italian context, unfamiliar to Canadians, for seeing the Prairies. It also distorted the reality of Canada West almost as much as the hyperbole of Canadian immigration propaganda did. Moreover, as Canadian officials and intellectuals elaborated an ethnic and racial ranking of potential immigrants into preferred and non-preferred so too the Italian political discourse ranked the potential targets of migration in the world. Texts about the problems of Asian labour competition, public disorder, and government corruption an Italian migrant would face in Peru or the diseases that afflicted those who went as canecutters – "noi Kanakas" they called themselves – to Queensland, Australia crowded in on the Italian reader of Jaja and others writing about Canada as forcefully as did the debate among Italian officials as to whether the climate of Calgary was, or was not, more salubrious – "piu secco ed asciutto" wrote Egisto Rossi – than that of St. Paul, Minnesota or Sao Paolo, Brazil.

For those who believed the Canadian prairies offered an opportunity to create healthy Italian colonie that would maintain their ethnoculture in the manner that the bloc settlers such as the Galicians and Mennonites did, the lack of movement was disappointing. Canadian authorities had begun an aggressive campaign of recruitment of settlers and had, despite clearly preferring colonists from the United Kingdom, the United States and northwestern Europe, accepted, indeed encouraged bloc settlement of white agriculturists.[6] "Peoples of every land in the temperate zone, even Syrians, were represented there except – take note – Italians" wrote Father Pisani of the Opera Bonomelli after a prairie tour in 1908.[7] To this day, the two prairie provinces of Manitoba and

Saskatchewan have the lowest percentage of residents of Italian descent of those provinces which received large-scale migration in the late 19th and 20th centuries. Alberta and British Columbia have larger numbers of Italian settlers, but – with the exception of pockets of fruit cultivation in the Okanagan Valley and of a few ranches and planned colonies, more mythopoeically important to Italian Canadian writers and multiculturalism-mongers than extensive, in Alberta – Italians never came to farm in Canada West.

Before World War II, 81% of Canada's Italians lived in urban centres, and while 31% of Canadians were part of the agricultural sector, only 7% of Italian immigrants farmed, mostly as truck farmers and in orchards on the outskirts of the cities. Between 1912 and 1914, typical years of mass migration to Canada, 66,000 immigrants, professing an intention to farm, entered the country. Among them were only 850 Italians. In those same two years, 20,000 of the 96,000 immigrants who entered the country as labourers were Italians, almost all of them with farming experience. About 35,000 Italians migrated to the industrial heartlands of Quebec and Ontario in those years while fewer than 150 declared their intention to go to Saskatchewan, the scene of the most feverish homesteading activities. English, Galician, German, French, Polish, Jewish, Russian, Scandinavian, Dutch, Belgian, Icelandic, even Romanian settlers outnumbered Italians on the prairies at a time when higher numbers of Italians were leaving their homeland than any other European people.

In the end, Italians played a greater role on this "last best American frontier" than such statistics suggest. An archipelago of mining, railway, and construction camps, along with many temporary or unincorporated "Little Italies" arose across the West. Especially strong Calabrese, Friulian and other Venetian migration chains and traditions developed to people the fringes, foothills and outskirts – "il bosc" of the prairies,[8] but their significance has generally eluded those who are writing the Canadian epic in much the same way as their meaning was lost on the Italian officials who crossed Canada in the early 1900s dreaming a dream of large scale Italian agricultural bloc settlement. It is typical of the distance between national political discourse in Italy and village or *paese* discourse that while the organic intelligentsia lamented the failed opportunity of founding farm *colonie* in Canada West, *piazza* conversation in Grimaldi in Calabria or in parishes around Treviso reflected the sharing of detailed mental maps of migration chains, work opportunities, and topographical features of that same target region, albeit the images were less of fertile fields and more of rock to be blasted, track to be laid, and timber to be cut. As in most national cultures, the printed texts of intellectuals was privileged in the hierarchy of discourse over the spoken and semiotic texts of the common people. The latter, of course, contained elements of intertextualizing, for example, the incorporation of some remarks from a parish priest, themselves derived from a serial in *Civiltà Cattolica*, might enter peasant lore as an argument for or against migrating to a certain target.[9] Sadly, there is no evidence of intertextualizing working upward, and, except in so far as Italian intellectuals travelled to the Canadian West or listened to the voices drawn out by the various *inchieste* carried on among returnees in the South, their knowledge of the prairies came from Canadian texts and the other texts in their own political discourse. Several points follow from this one. First, to this day, the best way to reconstruct an accurate sense of the Italian presence on the prairies, to create an atlas of Italian settlements, temporary and permanent, would be to listen to the voices of Italian Canadians and *ritornati*. A corollary would be to approach the Italian political discourse with as much caution as one does the Canadian propaganda of recruitment then and modern Canadian historiography on the subject now.

This paper is in a sense, purposely oblique. (I have written elsewhere about *paese* discourse and Italian prairie settlement.)[10] Its subject is the national discourse in Italy about the Canadian Prairies not the reality of Italian reconnoitring and settlement of the Canadian West. It also deals with the level of discourse in Italy most remote from the decision-making of the actual migrants, although, of course, to the extent that the debates of the organic intelligentsia affected public policy on emigration in Italy, they affected the tactics of the migrants as well. My approach is oblique, or perhaps just obtuse, in other ways. First, it does not require a close reading of the Canadian officials and organic intelligentsia involved in making immigration policy to realize that they did not wish large scale Italian settlement and that lurking behind phrases such as the "right class of settlers" and "assimilability" was a racialist hierarchy, later made overt when the Dominion government issued formal lists of preferred and non-preferred settlers according to nation of origin. Italians – although both a rhetorical and real exception was made for North Italians – joined other Mediterranean, Asian, and coloured peoples on the lists of the non-preferred or excluded. Even "le vere padrone del paese," as one acute observer described the Canadian Pacific and Grand Trunk railroad interests,[11] saw Italians as useful seasonal and transient track labour, as sojourners, but not as potentially permanent settlers, not as heads of stable families to be encouraged to settle the lands opened up by the very transcontinental railways which those same Italian navvies built. Of course the fundamental nature of migration push and pull as the flow of labour to capital meant that Canada West generally got the sojourning Italian males it sought and not the Italian farm families it did not welcome.[12] This was especially so since no one in Italy who could afford to buy land and live a year in anticipation of crops was likely to migrate, and no one in Canada was offering Italians free land and advance until the first harvest.

This is the second sense in which the paper is obtuse. It begs the question as to whether the migration projects and strategies of the mass of those forced to look outside of Italy for work in the 1900s included farm work in a remote, cold and lonely land. It also sidesteps a secondary, but interesting issue, raised by Joseph Lopreato and others,[13] as to whether the peasant of southern Italy was equipped technically and psychologically for large scale dry-farming in a harsh climate and remote from nucleated agrotowns. Italian peasants do not live on the farms which they work. "They are urban farmers" Lopreato wrote, "like industrial workers, they traditionally have worked in one place and resided in another." Ironically, it may be that the only Italian agriculturalists prepared for prairie grain farming were the very ones – prosperous and experienced farmers from Lombardy and Venetia – that the Canadian authorities might welcome and that many of the Italian organic intelligentsia, more concerned with national reputation than social solutions, advocated as ideal emigrants to represent the nation and reverse the bad image of Italians in Canada which they blamed on the *elementi bassi e meridionali* that migrated to American cities. Although the problem is an interesting one, it lacks historicity in the Canadian context because no opportunity was given to poor southern peasants to acquire land on the prairies. Certainly the better Italian officials and observers understood the sojourning tactics and polyseasonal migration projects of most Italian immigrants, their search for cash and effort to maximize savings or remittances, well enough to realize that they were not tempted to go into agriculture. As Girolamo Moroni wrote in 1914, "the reason why our emigrants have not come in great numbers to the prairie provinces is because the area has no industries and live chiefly from farming; our emigrant, once abroad, is unwilling to work as a farmhand preferring work as a day labourer in which occupation, he is better paid – above all they fear passing the six long months of winter, isolated completely on a farm, surrounded by snow."[14] One Italian official in Montreal noted also that migrants preferred dangerous and dirty construction or factory work to the "sottoposto al continuo sindicato di una padrona" that came with life as farmhands or domestics.[15]

The time frame of the failed convergence between available Canadian arable land and excess farm population in Italy coincided, as I have suggested, with the most intense years of discourse about emigration in Italy. If the Italian peasant and the Canadian landscape never came together, the texts, dreams and preoccupations of the organic intelligentsia in both countries intermingled, and in that sense, the institutions on both sides of the ocean which sought to *impadronarsi* or impose discipline in the form of a population policy did come together. Between 1901 and 1925, a congruence and interpenetration of texts existed between those of Canadian officials, especially in ministries of interior and agriculture, and propagandists on the one side and those of the Italian organic intelligentsia on the other. For example, J.S. Woodsworth's influential *Strangers Within Our Gates*, or *Coming Canadians* received a detailed and thoughtful twenty page review in the *Bollettino del'Emigrazione* in the same year it was published.[16] In 1914, Dr. Erasmo Ehrenfreund, Italian vice-consul in Montreal produced over 400 pages on Canada.[17] In a tradition begun in the 1870s by Gianelli, the first Italian consul in Montreal, Ehrenfreund, drew his material from official Canadian publications which he quoted and paraphrased extensively.

The central institution on the Italian side was the *Commissariato dell'Emigrazione*, created by parliamentary legislation in 1901, to regulate and protect Italian migrants abroad. By the time the Fascists disbanded the *Commissariat* and replaced it with the *Fascio all'estero* in 1926, the Canadian government had moved toward restrictionist immigration policies and all hope for a compatible flow of Italian agricultural labour to Canadian land was gone. However, from its inception until the failed Manitoba settlement schemes of Italia Garibaldi, the liberator's granddaughter in 1923, the *Commissariat* and those around it sought for the linkage that might lead to large scale bloc settlement on the prairies. As early as 1902, Egisto Rossi, a new commissioner on his way to help immigrants in New York was told to detour to Canada to look into the conditions of Italian immigrants there and the possibilities for organized migration schemes.[18] Rossi was dispatched to a Canada which did not have a good reputation within the "polemica sull'emigrazione." A series of exposé articles in *Corriere della Sera* the year before describing the exploitation of migrant's drawn to Canada as seasonal labourers and even suggesting that some were being hoodwinked and diverted into serving as workers with the British forces in the Boer War had made the name of Canada synonymous with the dangers of unregulated labour migration. That such a view of Canada had entered the political discourse in Italy was obvious when two years later, the foreign minister, Pantano, remarked in the Italian parliament that "the name of this immense British Dominion, Canada, is connected in our memory to the sad expedition of immigrants organized in 1900."[19] Pantano's remark is a good example of how texts are deciphered through earlier texts within a discourse. He was reminding his audience to view Canadian opportunities and government promises through the filter of account of notorious episodes of padronism, false advertising by travel companies, and racialist or capitalist insouciance by Canadian authorities toward the treatment of sojourning foreign labour. Whatever positive prospects for Italian settlement in Canada, Egisto Rossi, or Adolfo Rossi after him, reported in the *Bollettini* of the *Commissariat*, they would be read by readers who had among their first images of Canada those conjured up in 1900 by the consul in Montreal, Giuseppe Solimbergo, who had described the "irresponsible luring of our peasant by Canadian authorities" and "the insouciance with which Canadian government desires to people the desert plains of the Dominion."[20]

In less than a decade, the debate on Canada as a target of emigration had taken its own small place – Canada, after all, continued to receive a minuscule proportion of annual Italian emigration in comparison to the United States, Argentina, Brazil and western Europe – in "La polemica sull'emigrazione."[21] More thoughtful observers realized that the discussion of Canada as a migration target had truly joined the polemical aspects of the discourse since texts on the matter were more often partisan assertions than efforts at true description. After all, if the question of whether the Prairies were too cold for south Italian peasants had become a political rather than a climatic one, all other aspects of the target's suitability were fair game.

Eugenio Bonardelli, writing in *Italica Gens* in 1912, saw this clearly. "About Canada finally a great deal of good and great deal of bad has been said. I have before me books by partisans and by detractors and the echoes of this debate have even reached into the heart of the *Consiglio dell'Emigrazione*."[22]

Although Bonardelli felt torn by the conflict of opinion about Canada, he should have recognized a coherence to the discourse which went beyond intertextualization. Italian and Canadian officials, despite divergences of culture and purpose, came from similar social strata and held many ideas in common. At the turn of the century, Italy through emigration and Canada through immigration were groping toward a population policy, a way of reconciling free market forces such as labour flow with the social order. An example from Bonardelli's own thinking points up this convergence of objectives. He believed that the purpose of the Homestead Act was "the creation of sparse population over all the vast territory" in order to avoid "all the moral and biological maladies that characterize *le populazioni agglomerate* (crowded urban conditions)." Bonardelli then went on to quote Napoleone Colajanni's *Manuale di Demografia* about "the great inconvenience that result in various states from the agglomeration of the rural populations in large centers."[23] At first glance, the texts that inform Bonardelli's view of homesteading may seem remote from the considerations that went in to the Canadian decision, spearheaded by Minister of the Interior, Clifford Sifton, to people the prairies. However, at a more fundamental anti-urban and socially conservative level, the distance diminishes and becomes a matter more of idiom than objective.

To an extraordinary degree, intelligentsia and officials in both countries saw the free flow of labour to capital, of migrants to opportunity, as a force to be harnessed, to be controlled and manipulated for the national purpose. Both states hoped to solve questions of nation-building, of the integration of recalcitrant regions, of labour supply by trying to redistribute population. Italy's preoccupation with the "problem of the South" and the related, almost pathological, search for colonies, international prestige and informal empire was matched by Canada's commitment to holding the West against American "manifest destiny" by peopling the prairies with farmers, human livestock loyal to the British crown or at least ethnocentric enough to be impervious to the American republic.

There were more precise parallels than that. Anglo-Canadian

views of how to neutralize Metis and Indian resentment after their defeat in the Real Rebellion matched Sabaudian needs to deal with the "southern question" as an economic one, to ignore the civil war engendered by the Bourbon defeat by labelling it brigandage. Although penny dreadful novels about cowboys and Indians abounded in Italy at the time, the discourse about Canada barely mentioned the presence of Indians or Metis on the prairies. And after Egisto Rossi in 1902, no Italian official or intellectual suggested that Italian farmers settle in francophone pockets in the West,[24] although a certain number of French Canadian Church leaders continued to suggest the possibility and a North Italian colony at Lorette, among the French along Manitoba's Red River, achieved some success. Although no Italian intellectual seems to have been aware of it, Real himself had, in an 1885 diary entry, proposed the creation of a "New Italy" on the prairies, a bloc settlement which would be a loyal ally to his Meti nation in its struggle against the English.[25] No other Canadian public figure after him spoke so warmly about the possibility of Italian colonies in the West. A careful Italian reader of the context of Real's sympathetic text would have noted that the Canadian government declared him mad and then hanged him.

Men in both countries saw their population policy in global perspective. Canadian authorities thought in terms of the racialist hierarchy already mentioned; Italian writers thought in terms of a hierarchy of targets and destinations. Each held a dream of an optimum population solution. The Canadians wished for British and American farmers. The Italians, if they were loyal to the ideas of the "padri liberali", dreamed of a solution to the southern question, and end to the economic necessity of migrating for the poor, and perhaps the birth of an informal empire in the Rio Plate region of the sort Luigi Einaudi described in his novel *Un Principe Mercante*.[26] If they were instead the "figli nazionalisti," they dreamed of turning Italy's fecundity into an instrument for colonial expansion. For the organic intelligentsia of both countries then, the question of Italian mass migration to the Canadian prairies existed as a vexing one about an unsatisfactory and expedient solution to a problem. Most Italian advocates of the Canadian possibility most often explained themselves in the context of the necessities imposed by the fact of continuing uncontrolled emigration and the existence of less attractive alternatives from *fazendas* in Brazil to slums in New York.

Italian and Canadian "organic intelligentsia" whether they

defined themselves in the one case as *Destra* or *Sinistra*, in the other as Conservative or Liberal, agreed on several other aspects of population policy. On both sides there was a strong anti-urban bias, or at least a preference for the images of happy yeoman and *contadini* over those of an emerging proletariat or slumdwellers. Cities, especially industrial cities, were, despite the overwhelming evidence to the contrary, not in their eyes a natural or healthy target for migrants.[27] Canada wanted agriculturalists and felt threatened by the increasing non-Anglosaxon-ness of her cities. On their side, Italian officials also rejected the city as target, despite or because of the obvious growth of urban Little Italies. Bonardelli's *méprison* of the Homestead Act has already been noted, and Father Pisani, while writing sympathetically about Italians in Canadian cities in his several articles and book insisted that only agricultural migration was truly healthy.[28] In his 1914 survey of Canadian conditions for the Commissariat of Emigration, Girolamo Moroni warned that

> our emigration must not forget that Canada is not an industrial country but an agricultural land par excellence and its rich future will depend on increasing its crop yield. Therefore our emigrants must be wise, and instead of putting their money into speculation to acquire lots of land near cities or future cities, they should invest in agricultural land.[29]

Moroni displayed the incomprehension of peasant migration projects and sojourning strategies, typical of those involved in the national discourse, when he added that if they had put their money into farmland rather than postal cheques for remittances to the Italian *paese* or down payments on urban property in Canada, they would "at that moment be on their own property, in their farmhouses, not suffering the indignity of having to seek work." Maroni would not have understood Walter Benjamin's aphorism that "outskirts are the state of emergency of a city, the terrain on which incessantly rages the great decisive battle between town and country."[30] Few of those who spend their time lamenting the exploitation of Italian *braccianti* in urban ghettoes or regretting the failure to create agriculture bloc settlement replete with *Italianità*, have noted the degree to which, the truckfarming and marginal land investment strategies of south Italian immigrants have led the battle of the outskirts and how much the immigrants have been enriched by their speculation and initiative as North American cities have expanded. If Moroni and other Italian intellectuals had looked more closely at the situation, they would have recognized a pattern stretching from the vineyards of the Niagara peninsula through the market farms run by immigrants from Termini Imerese around Winnipeg to the apple valleys of British Columbia, a pattern in which Italian migrants became agricultural settlers when the conditions were right for it.

A second point of convergence between the Canadian and Italian texts might be seen as a corollary of the first if it did not have even more antique origins. Neither intelligentsia favoured south Italian migration to Canada. From the very first tentatives of an immigration policy independent of Whitehall – and long before racialist definitions of north and south Italians became idiomatic in American debates about immigration – Canadian representatives had made it clear that they wanted only north Italian immigrants. An 1875 report for the Minister of Agriculture from Canada's agent general for immigration, an English MP named Jenkins, apologized for failure to procure Swiss recruits and proposed enrolment centers at Susa and Turin.

> I should mention that my information goes to show that the north of Italy is at this moment one of the best fields to which to look for emigrants in Europe. The people are hale and sturdy. They emigrate in large numbers to various parts of Europe, where they are employed chiefly as outdoor labourers and navvies. Those that I saw in the streets at Berne were large and powerful men. They're not debilitated by a hot climate... The Australian colonies are trying hard to get some of these valuable emigrants, and I strongly advise that an effort should be made to reach them.[31]

When Cavalieri recorded the Governor General's remark about the need for a larger population, he also quoted Jenkins' remarks without dissenting.[32] Thus an intertextualization and mingling of Italian and Canadian discourse as early as the 1870s established shared guidelines for the preselection of Italian emigrants to Canada. It might at first appear strange that the Italian organic intelligentsia came to favour northern rather than southern emigration. After all, emigration had been justified first and foremost as a safety valve to ease the pressures produced by southern poverty and overpopulation. Their view becomes intelligible only if one understands how much they suffered from *atimia* (ethnic lack of self-esteem) and to what extent the discourse on emigration had become entangled with issues of national dignity and great power status in their minds. The very ambiguity of their use of the word *colonia*, as Gianfausto Rosoli[33] had pointed out, and the names of the journals

which sustained the discourse "Rivista coloniale", "Emigrazione e
Colonie" – betrayed the nationalist context of their thought.
Prosperous colonies of northerners, maintaining their *Italianità* and
their commitment to a *madrepatria* would stand for the greater glory
of Italy in the world, erasing the imagery of emigration as a national
haemorrhage, as Corradini's "anti-imperialismo della servitu,"[34] as
illiterate labourers in crowded Brazilian *fazendas* or New York slums.
Thus the real   immigrants were made to suffer the double
opprobrium of being superfluous at home and embarrassing once
abroad.

There was one further point of agreement between Canadian
and Italian texts. Although each polity wished to regulate the
preselection of migrants, the targets, the socio-economic insertion of
immigrants, neither wished to pay the bills such an organized effort
at imposing *la disciplina* – a word much used in the Italian discourse
– would incur. If land was unattainable on the Canadian prairies
without $2,000 in savings – for even with a free homestead grant a
family needed enough for transport, to survive a first year without
crops, to buy livestock and build shelter – both Canadian and Italian
officials could only envisage those funds coming from one of three
sources:

- a rich patron or latifundist,
- a co-operative colonization scheme, or
- a venture company or system of government guarantee of
  bank loans.

Little Canadian governmental or private help was available to Italian
immigrants as non-preferred immigrants. Although the Italian texts
showed an awareness that the Canadian government had helped
some groups such as the Mennonites and that others such as the
Galicians had organized successful cooperative institutions, the
Italian discourse dwelt on the presence of a few, real or mythical,
Italian nobles or great landowners in Alberta and British Columbia
who professed to have plans to recruit *contadini* in Italy to create
colonies. Showing a remarkable mix of the two discourses,[35]
Ehrenfreund used examples from the decline of the *fazenda* system
in Brazil after 1900 into miniculture and *mezzadria*, a report on
Eritrean planned settlements by Luigi Mercatelli, and remarks from
the Canadian High Commissioner, Strathcona, denouncing both the
Salvation Army's and Rider Haggard's "imperial colony schemes"
to discredit the idea of co-operative attempts at bloc settlement.
"Men individually or in groups that know they can count on outside

aid and don't have to rely on themselves will not work to their full capacity," wrote Mercatelli. Rarely, even in the annals of Italian public service, was so much scholarship employed to miss the point.

The bankruptcy of the Italian discourse and the final signal of the failure of convergence came in 1923 and 1924 with Italia Garibaldi's "propaganda and study trip" in Canada.[36] On her way to look into the possibility of organizing large scale Italian migration to Alberta, she organized, according to her own accounts sent to Mussolini, the *fasci all'estero* in Montreal, Toronto, and Winnipeg. By the time of her trip the Garibaldi name had been associated with a number of colonial schemes and business ventures. In 1899 Ricciotti Garibaldi, Giuseppe's son, had approached the Argentine government about buying up large sections of Patagonia for a potential colony. A company using the Garibaldi name, organized by Italia and her brothers, had been registered as a legal trademark in the state of Delaware; it had offices on Broadway, in Paris, and in Rome as well as a reputation for shady business if critics in the Commissariate are to be believed. So with the Duce's blessings and with the advantage of a monopoly on the most evocative of Italian surnames, Italia Garibaldi fell into direct negotiations with the government of Manitoba, or perhaps just some politicians operating on their own, about the purchase of 22 villages, at that time being deserted by their Mennonite inhabitants who were leaving for Mexico rather than allow their children to be anglicized and secularized in public schools. Almost all the conditions seen as optimum in the discourse were present – a government that would welcome settlers from northern Italy, a group of bankers interested in providing guaranteed loans to the settlers, sympathy and perhaps even support from the Italian government, a well-connected entrepreneur or leader in the person of Italia Garibaldi, a series of nucleated villages, reminiscent more of Italy than the open prairies. Detailed plans for each village's population, including plans for a pharmacy and priest for every two or three villages, as well as meetings with the Premier of Manitoba and prominent bankers and promises from Mussolini notwithstanding, no Italian immigrant ever arrived in the Mennonite villages. The plan collapsed without a whimper.

Notes

1. Pisani "L'Agricoltura Nel Canada Centrale," *Rivista Internazionale di Scienza Sociale e disciplini*, Ausilian Vol. XLIX Anno XUI 1909, Fasci CXCIU, Feb., p. 223.

2. F. Manzotti, *La Polemica sull'Emigrazione nell'Italia unita* (Milan, 1969).

3. E. Cavalieri, "Il Dominio del Canada. Appunti di viaggio in *Nuova Antologia* 16 Feb. 1879, pp. 700-747; 16 March 1879, pp. 314-353 and 16 April 1879, pp. 665-692.

4. G. Jaja, "Per il Commercio e l'Emigrazione nelle colonie inglesi" in *Rivista Coloniale* (1907), p. 35.

5. I. Calvino, *The Uses of Literature* (New York, 1987), p. 60.

6. On Canadian government policy, see M. Timlin. "Canada's Immigration Policy, 1896-1910" in *Canadian Journal of Economics and Political Science*, 26:4 (1963), pp. 517-532 and R.C. Brown and R. Cook. *Canada 1896-1921. A Nation Transformed* (Toronto, 1974) and G. Friesen. *The Canadian Prairies* (Lincoln, 1984).

7. Pisani. Ibid., Vol. XLIX, Anno XUI, 1909, Fasci CXCU, Marzo, p. 329.

8. On Calabresi in the West, see J. Potestio. "Itinerant Grimaldesi: Paesani on the Railroads of North America" and also J. Potestio. ed. *The Memoirs of Giovanni Veltri* (Toronto, 1987); on Friulani see priest's travel memoirs. Prosopographic study of Italian families and chains in the West is possible through volumes like *Crowsnest and Its People*. (Crowsnest Pass Historical Society, 1979) and the sort of work G. Scardellato has undertaken on the vital statistics of Trail, etc.

9. I have been preparing a critical edition of the Jesuit novel by F.S. Rondina, *L'Emigrante Italiano* which appeared in serialized form in the "Civiltà Cattolica" in 1892 to honour the 400th anniversary of Columbus' voyage. My interest in discourse theory derives from an inability to explain the impact of this level of discourse on the *paese*-based migrant. It is a matter of text without readers being useless to both the intellectual and social history of emigration.

10. R.F. Harney, "Imagining America: Prospective Immigrants Confront the Migration Tradition" in A Century of European Migrations, 1830-1900, Comparative Perspectives (November 1986), never published.

11. E. Bonardelli, "Il Domino del Canada e la nostra emigrazione" in *Italica Gens*. III:10-11 (October 1912), pp. 297.

12. R.F. Harney, *Dalle Frontiera alle Little Italies. Gli Italiani in Canada, 1800-1945* (Rome, 1984) esp. chapters 2, 4 and 5. See also M. Piore. *Birds of Passage*, (Cambridge, 1979) for the context of seasonal labour migration and D. Avery. Dangerous Foreigners. *European Immigrant Workers and Labour Radicalism in Canada, 1896-1932* (Toronto, 1979) for the independent immigration policies of the *vere padrone* in drawing labourers from southern and eastern Europe.

13. J. Lopreato, *Italian Americans*, p. 41.

14. G. Moroni, "La Regione della provincie centrale del Canada" in *Bollettino dell'Emigrazione* #2 (1915), pp. 43-44.

15. E. Ehrenfreund, "La Disciplina dell'immigrazione secondo la legislazione degli Stati Uniti e nei rapport come Italia, Studiata dal gia R. Addetto per l'emigrazione al Canada Capt. Erasmo A. Ehrenfreund, medico della R. Marina e vice console onorario" in Montreal. *Bollettino dell'Emigrazione* (1914) #7-8, p. 31.

16. The review of Woodsworth is "Gli stranieri nel Canada giudicati da un Canadese" *Bollettino dell'Emigrazione* #19 (1909). pp. 56-75.

17. Ehrenfreund's study ran more than 400 pages appearing in the 1914 *Bollettini* #7 and #8, pp. 3-314 and 3-161. See A. Gianelli. "Sulle presente condizioni del Canada" in *Bollettino consolare* VIII:II July, 1872, pp. 87-120 for the first specimen of the practice of "depouille"-ing Canadian official publications and calling it a report.

18. E. Rossi, "Delle Condizioni del Canada rispetto all'immigrazione italiana" *Bollettino dell'Emigrazione* 4 (1903), pp. 3-28. A convenient list of all Commissariat publications about Canada can be found in F. Sturino. *Italian Canadian Studies: A Select Bibliography*. (Toronto, 1987).

19. The *Corriere della Sera* of Milan sent a reporter with migrants to Canada in 1900. His revelations as well as those of the consul in Montreal, Solimbergo, caused dismay in Italy. The articles appeared in the Spring of 1901 (typically of the interpenetration of texts, they were immediately translated and made available to officials of the Canada Ministry of the Interior). Two headlines will suffice to show their nature: March 18, 1901 "Emigrazione sospetta" and May 22, 1901 "Al Canada Lo sbarcoi degli emigrati. Nuove delusioni."

20. G. Solimbergo, "Il Canada sotto l'aspetto economico e politico" in *Bollettino di MAE* (1901), p. 169.

21. G. Rosoli, (ed), *Un Secolo di Emigrazione italiana, 1876-1976.* (Rome, 1978).

22. Bonardelli, "Il Dominio del Canada", p. 296.

23. Bonardelli, "Il Dominio del Canada", p. 304.

24. E. Rossi, "Delle Condizioni", p. 16. Rossi met F.C. Blair of the immigration service and Dr. Brisson of *la Societe de colonisation francaise* to discuss settlement among French Canadians.

25. The Diaries of Louis Real, 21 August 1885, p. 128, inspire with enthusiasm "the Irish, Italians, Bavarians, and Poles" for the new foundation of a New Ire, of a New Italy, of a New Bavarian, of a New Pole in the North West to the east of the Rocky Mountains.

26. L. Einaudi, *Un Principe Mercante. Studi sulla espansione coloniale italiana.* (Turin 1900).

27. Canadian conditions fell between the ideals of agricultural settlement in Latin America and the worst excesses of temporary and seasonal exploitation in Western Europe and the United States. As a result, the discourse hovered between texts about the possibility of farming and emphasis on the exploitation of labourers as well as their own seasonal strategies. See for example, B. Attolico. "Sui campi di lavoro della nuova ferrovia transcontinentale canadese" in *Bollettino dell'Emigrazione* #1 (1913), pp. 3-26 and D. Viola, Ispezione ai campi di lavoro di La Tuque" in *Bollettino dell'Emigrazione* #13 (19110), pp. 24-31. Seasonal labour continued to be viewed in the discourse as not the norm but a pathology, dangerous both to the migrant and the Italian image.

28. Pisani, Ibid. p. 341.

29. G. Moroni, "La provincia dell'Ontario" in *Bollettino dell'Emigrazione* (1915) #6, pp. 60-62.

30. W. Benjamin, *Reflections. Essays, Aphorisms, Autobiographical Writing,* (New York, 1986).

31. W. Jenkins, *Annual Report of the Dominion Department of Agriculture 1876?*

32.   E. Cavalieri, pp. 344-346.

33.   G. Rosoli, "La Colonizzazione italiana delle Americhe tra mito e realta, (1880-1914)" *Studi Emigrazione* X:29 (October 1972).

34.   E. Corradini, "Il Nazionalismo italiano" in *Il Carroccio*, p. 14.

35.   El Ehrenfreund. "La Disciplina" #7, pp. 34-36.

36.   *Viaggio di propaganda e studio nel Canada della signorina Italia Garibaldi*, 1923-1926. Busta in the MAE. Again the Canadian immigration records show the intertextualization and include a letter about a Mr. Dupont who was "interested in the movement of a party of Italian farmers from the Piedmont district to Southern Manitoba" in collaboration with Garibaldi.

Appendices

On Being Italian Canadian: 1910-1930

*T*raditional historiography arranges chronology objectively but fails to explain process from within documents. In an historian's effort to record the experiences of an ethnic group he or she must remember that the ethnic group is not quite a polity. It is more like a part-culture. So, there is a need for an intensive, holistic study of small communities, a need for a one-time vision of process rather than a chronology. Intellectual history is not a history of thought, but that of people thinking. Ethnocultural history is not the history of acculturation or of ethnicism but of people in these partial polities thinking and being themselves along the continuum from where they and their parents are (and unthinkingly practising and adapting aspects of *la via vecchia* to their individual and collective North American reality). This chapter then, tries to understand being Italian Canadian, if regionalisms here and there did not render that idea silly. It seeks to elaborate what folkways, shared *mentalités* and objective conditions make a North American ethnic group, neither Italo-American, Italian, Italo-Argentine, but Italian Canadian.

It is a sketch of retrospective ethnography, trying to understand the texture of the ethnoculture, the things that mattered within it, the patterns of life within it, daily life especially. It seeks the patterns that were different from that of the larger society, and the way in which the patterns of that ethnoculture sustained people but also brought them if not into conflict, but put them in disjuncture with the larger society. This approach might give us a better understanding of the definition of ethnicity and its persistence, both as nostalgia and as function.

The methods that we are going to use are those of the social anthropologist and folklorist. The way in which we understand the group has to be across a profile of age and sex. We must realize that ethnicity is not adult males alone, although that may have been the case for a very long time. Males outnumbered females in the early years within the Italian Canadian immigrant experience; but, in fact, to sketch a more accurate portrait of Italian Canadians we must see that ethnic experience carries different meanings and different values for women, children, and adolescence.

The nature of this kind of work depends on observation,

intuition and detailed knowledge of the *ambiente*. This means that I will have to concentrate on Toronto, because in this instance it is clear that the immigrants' place is not from one nation to another nation but a matter of his household and his hometown, of his neighbourhood and his settlement areas. So while I make reference to things at variance in western Canada and Montreal or the United States, in general, this is a study of Toronto in the heyday of the ethnic community as an *ambiente* and neighbourhood, that is from right before the First World War until the Depression.[1]

We have in an earlier section tried to develop the details of the daily life and the impact of social, economic, cultural and familial factors of the days of male sojourning, of the boarding house and of the camps in the north. This chapter will deal with a number of themes in daily life, folklore and activities and habits of mind surrounding it. The headings for this chapter are as follows: Family and the Home; Childhood and the life of the streets and school; Leisure and Ethnicity (everything from the annual picnic to the question of the sports played); Work and lure of the work place and the relationship of the neighbourhood to the work place; Religion and Beliefs (from religious practice and problems with the Irish clergy, the *doganale*, anti-clericalism, various superstitions and the Protestants and their place in the community's cosmos, to the place of the sacramental in the daily life); Space, Seasons and Nature.

In this last subheading, I will try to place the Italians in their ecology, particularly in how the uses of that ecology differs from that of their neighbours and how a kind of holistic approach to the family economy, to the role of seasons and to the uses of free space are both at once jarring to the host society and useful in Canada, including things like the *furbo campestre*; the idea of a psychic village in the world or wherever the *compaesani* are gathered as part of a single world; the idea of city maps, i.e., knowing certain parts of the city in ethnic terms and not other parts; the idea of property both in the Vergan sense,[2] as for the Jews in the Ward, and as the sense of distinction of agricultural or small agro-town people of property as domicile and property as family uses including businesses, is lost on the newcomers, more on some groups than on others, the serendipity of this approach; and the tendency to buy up the margins of what are obviously growing industrial cities, or to probe and penetrate for bottom lands and other things and the use of vacant lots for tomatoes, etc., and how this impacts on the buying up of the northwest fringes of Toronto particularly; and the simplicity of the idea of property as enabling Italians, particularly developers, Friulans and others, to think of themselves as not so much prescient as simply common sensical or the Anglos don't seem to understand the value of land); and The Others, an attempt to see inside Italian views of the other ethnic groups around them instead of a simple two-dimension relationship between the Italians and the so-called host society, or the Anglo-Celtic or WASP society, what the Italians thought specifically, or if one talks of a collectivity of a variety of other groups encountered for the first time – naming the English in their strange ways to the Irish clergy and nuns, etc.; and finally the Cultural Product that comes from the splits within the community, the role of dialect and semi-literacy and the so-called language of -*iesse* and -*oraitte*, so that future social or ethnolinguists will be able to make maps of which group came to dominate an area, from what sending region of the old country in terms of the parts of the dominant town here, particularly how boundaries and paesanism as a continuum on the one hand and a barrier on the other, and the use of Friulan and Sicilian separate patterns to confirm this, and how one can decelerate into localism using paesanism or using dialect as a third language with a third purpose.

We need also in this chapter to talk about the emblems of ethnicity too. Columbus versus Caboto, a Verdi hall, Dante societies and Garibaldi usages. To understand the texture and nuances of processual ethnicity we also need to talk about the rites of passage, about baptisms, engagements, weddings, wakes, funerals, etc.. We need to understand religious practice particularly the devotional and announcements of village saint cult days, and also the number of people involved in fighting the evil eye or in being clairvoyants or in being *chiromante* and the so-called law of reading the cards, reading the hands on how to aid problems in business and love, satisfaction guaranteed, cards slipped under doors. These practices and the outdoor public nature of religious practice outside the religious place, i.e., processions, etc., are a little jarring to North America.

Material in my "Italians in Canada"[3] article about being Italian immigrant, being Italian Canadian or being acculturated, and that this is not just strictly a generational question, but a question of volition as any ethnic process or formation is. The statistics in 1940, as opposed to enclave statistics, and the high percentage of men to females, etc., does suggest that while we continue to talk about Italian Canadian settlement system and culture, in terms of the actual genetic impact if one likes, of the emigration, there is a great confusion that is going on constantly and is always in the interests of the ethnic network. Those who need the ethnic group, either for honest reasons or cohesion or for their own political/cultural uses, to underemphasize this impact and flow into the larger society and to treat it as a danger which it is from their perspective, occupational or geographic, involve loyalty slippage of some kind.

This chapter will study the ways in which the emblems used for an Italian identity speak to the whole problem we have with the disuses of the word "ethnicity." But beyond the continuum, which I talk about, of *paese* to Italian nation, or indeed the continuum from *paese* to Italian nation through Italian Canadian...

So that the emblematics in the names of clubs and the names of bread products, whether a place is going to call itself the Abruzzi Bakery or the Italian Bread Company or the Home Bread Company or the Italian Portuguese Style Bread, says a great amount about individual and settlement wide identities of the actual *paese*. These emblematics, I think, need pursuing because it is the only way in which one will understand the context of fascism and response to fascism, of flight from any ethnic identity, and of the creation of an Italian in North America. It is easy enough to see it coming out in its nationalist form, of bringing together the community by the First World War – first in the face of prejudice in North America and then in the face of shared patriotism, i.e., that the Italian immigrant becomes Italian in North America.

But we should see how that is reflected in the names and emblems and titles of clubs and one assumes goes further beyond into chances in associational life and the social life of immigrants, so that family and region in fact break down or don't break into these categories.

We must watch out for these things like John Zucchi's discovery that even though the early mutual aids might have preferred national slogans, symbols and emblems such as calling themselves Umberto Primo rather than Abruzzi, as opposed to those down to the level of the St. Agnes (?) Mutual Aid Society. The membership reality might reflect a much more regional or *paesan* basis. Only through density or the emergence of a sub-intelligentsia in a certain group would there be an assertion of a local rally or loyalty, or that simply the continuum would work; that for some things one would be from Pescara and for other things one would be from Abruzzi or even an Italian in Canada. But to talk of Italian emblems – the standard of the time, I think it is Cinel (?) originally and John (Zucchi) picked it up, that you never trust a man who starts his speech *Noi Italiani*, or worse yet, that you always trust a man who starts his speech *noi Italiani*.

The basic way to do this would be to study comparatively with one group... give i.e. the career of Furlans or Terminesi (??) in select locales in a number of countries etc., would we get to psychic maps. Is their now or then an Italian Canadian?

Food and subpaese and two levels of acculturation... not trivializing paesanism and women and society

The "neopolitanization" of Italian food and popular imagery – localisms – boarding houses and restaurants..
muset and brovada to the varieties of soppressata and salami,and salumifacere and cheeses – variety of dialect names for food – breads and the uses of sublabels such as Calabrese, Sicilian, etc...

Notes

1.   It should be noted that in his notes it is clear that he intended to extend this chapter to the emblematics, material cultural and nuances of the post war community too.

2.   This refers to Giovanni Verga's discussion of property in his short stories about Sicily. See Giovanni Verga. *Little Novels of Sicily* (New York, 1953).

3.   "Italians in Canada." In *The Culture of Italy, Medieval to Modern*. Edited by S.B. Chandler and J.A. Molinaro (Toronto, 1979).

The Myth of the Americas:
Migration and Village Discourse

This paper is about the sending towns of Italy and how targets and projects of migration were and are perceived by those who may or may not be prospective migrants. Its chief purpose is to put the United States in perspective as one of the many targets and to try to use the literary critic's metaphor of a discourse to say some things about the circumambient culture of migrants and about the migration tradition. It represents my attempt to make whole my two careers as historian of Italy and of migration by discovering the intersection of two planes in Italian life – on one of which, the national, the chief motifs of political debate (public discourse) in the 19th and early 20th century were emigration, empire and social reform and the other – obscured for me by the state of the art of immigration and ethnic studies – the local discourse of the artisans and peasants as actors making decisions to migrate and decisions about targets and duration of projects.

Gramsci describes every agro-town of the South as being a salient of the *blocco urbano* that must mean that there are speakers in the discourse in those towns, priest, pharmacist, *carabinieri*, communal secretaries, *pagliette*, whose texts represent the polemical fragmentation of the so-called national debate (*la polemica sull'emigrazione*). I want to be able to see or hear those texts and to understand how they were read or heard and then encoded into new texts by prospective immigrants. I should add as an aside here that my recent time in three sending towns in Calabria and Australia, along with more than twenty years an expatriate, colour my paper which is, in a way, an attack on residues of thinking characterised by the idea of American "exceptionalism" at least to the extent that I believe that Italian migrants are seen as proto-Americans more often than as Italians. Reaching the discourse of the migrating culture is made extraordinarily difficult by some historiographical and ideological traditions in Italy and the United States.

In *Christ Stopped at Eboli* (1947), his memoir of confinement in a south Italian town during the Fascist era, Carlo Levi, describing the place of America and of emigration in the Italian peasant cosmos, wished to show how America served as a "version, magic and real at the same time, of an earthly paradise" firing the prospective migrant's imagination. As Levi saw it, America was for the peasants "a dream refuge from their woes." To reinforce his view, Levi ridiculed the peasant's blinkered and narrowed vision, demonstrated for him, by the inability of the returned *americani* of Gagliano to articulate any but the sketchiest description of America and its ways and values, or conversely, by the detail with which they could describe the immigrant quarters and workplaces they had inhabited.

When it was published in 1947, Levi's description of the peasantry found easy acceptance in both Italy and the United States. That America would be paramount "among the hundreds of myths cherished by the peasants" and that the myth of America would "embody fable and fact concrete existence and romance, necessity and imagination" seemed obvious to many from the Italian organic intelligentsia of the Left, emerging in the postwar, usually of northern and urban background themselves, to the ethnocentric American conquerors of the South. Although their plans for the peasantry differed they shared the south Italian upper classes' pseudo-anthropological view of *contadini* as childlike and primitive.

Levi published an article in *Life* (1947), bluntly entitled "Italy's Myth of America" that gave his ideas even wider circulation. Although he had described the peasant's vision of the American migration target as "magic and real at the same time" Levi tended to turn signs of practical knowledge and purpose into signs of magic and myth at work. Thus he viewed the pinning of Washington (dollars) to a Madonna during a Gagliano festival as superstition rather than as a clear semiotic text, a message about the relationship of status and wealth to being *a ritornati* or a recipient of remittances and therefore a family member in good standing with a kinsman abroad, itself, a relationship which was a form of capital.[1] No matter how great Levi's literary skills or his commitment to ameliorating life in rural southern Italy, he must be seen in the context of this paper, as contributing to an intellectual tradition, almost as old as the migration tradition itself, which dismisses or undervalues the role of knowledge (lore), rational decision-making, and choice of migration targets and projects involved in Mediterranean population movements. The obscuring of the human activity and of the local discourse which is its context has many forms; it deals with symptoms, contexts, aspects but for me lacks the power to explain the decision to migrate because it never penetrates what Jacobo Timmerman calls "the affective world of the other" that is the political culture of the prospective migrants.

I do not want to spend a paper on ideas I am trying to discredit so let me characterize the historiography elliptically and a bit unfairly because some versions do possess some explanatory power. First, there are similes and metaphors of illness, especially *febbre* and *malattia contagiosa*, throughout the nineteenth century texts. Frenzy or delirium are used as reasons not to need to analyze the decision to migrate. Second, there are assertions about the elemental and natural order. Migration is like a mountain torrent, like lemmings, like birds of the air (birds of passage) or like Mosso on evidence from natural science that species which migrate are more intelligent[2] or the Calabrian official report of 1984 on the hundreds of thousands of *calabresi si sono dovuti forzatamente insediare nei vari paesi*[3]. One might ask if it is elemental that they ended up, according to the report in France, Germany, Switzerland, the United Kingdom, the United States, Argentina, Brazil, Canada, Venezuela, Uruguay, Australia, North Africa, and New Zealand; this diversity of locations suggests some targeting, timing and thinking. It was difficult for officials to give up the elemental, Cinel quotes a Sicilian prefect thus. "I realized that the most powerful arguments in favour of leaving had been the stories they heard from returnees and the fact that they had no alternatives left. It is either starvation or emigration."[4]

These early analogies to illness and animal instincts, insufficient as explanations, give way to another pair after 1880, *miseria* and *agenti*. Since few were willing to see *miseria* as a socially-produced rather than a natural situation these two explanations can be seen as speaking to a natural condition and an induced evil respectively. *Miseria*, the most powerful non-explanation of them all, *disperazione* in Lopreato, chronic melancholy in Banfield, overpopulation, *nullatenza*, and exploitation are real, but they are a context of perception and perspectives not an absolute. *Miseria* is not what Sen. Nobili-Vitelleschi described in 1902, "without emigration, the land would suffocate in its own plethora and everyone would have to end up eating one another" but it is rather something more akin to John Baxevanis' concept as a changing sense of the gap between levels of existence and levels of expectation, measured against a map of opportunities.[5]

It is worth noting when and how *miseria* became such a popular explanation since with the exception of Rudy Bell's *Fate and Honour. Family and Village*[6], it has been accepted by most American students of migrating *paesi*. The term *miseria* was used in a questionnaire circulated by the Minister of Agriculture, Industry and Commerce beginning in 1881 which asked prefects of Italy why people emigrated. The prefects were given two choices only, *miseria* or a cause the central government found more easily handled and less self-incriminating, *agenti*. Most prefects honestly and honourably chose the former. Typically, the government began a series of legislative acts against *agenti*, but not the whole *borghesia mediatrice* or the commerce of migration, and did nothing about *miseria*.

Miseria and the *agenti* of the commerce of migration give way or are now joined by chain and serial migration theory (Tilly and McDonald)[7] which uses assumptions about familialism to explain how people assumed to be naive and parochial negotiate so well the world. I should hasten to add that I am not trying to invalidate chain migration theory as a study of modalities and target choice. It is used magnificently by John Gjerde and Frank Sturino, John Zucchi and Donna Gabaccia[8], but I will not grant it explanatory power in the decision to migrate only a place of honour in the local discourse. A moments reflection shows us how such an anthropological mechanism diverts us from looking for a richer discourse and structure of choice.

There has been in the last dozen years a remarkable improvement in scholarship about Italian migration from the American side – Briggs' *Italian Passage*, Barton's *Peasants and Strangers*, Bell whom I have mentioned, Dino Cinel's *From Italy to San Francisco* and Donna Gabaccia's *From Sicily to Elizabeth Street* and William Douglass' remarkable book *Emigration from a South Italian Town*.[9] All of these have made the immigrants actors in their own history, questioned *miseria* as an ultimate cause in various ways, but all, but Douglass and Cinel, have been proofs of Trevelyan's plaint that "social history is history with the politics removed" and are, I believe examples of American "exceptionalism." Briggs with perverse Crevecouerianism, Barton with assimilation, Gabaccia looking for a radical labour tradition give proto-American politics and the agenda of American social/labour history on top of European social history and remind me of Tocqueville on the nobility and *noblesse oblige* that by a last gesture of selfishness made serving classes into family. None deal with the whole migration tradition and the changing map of opportunities. Whatever its faults then this literature has dealt a death blow to *miseria* as an absolute and made the migrant an actor in history[10]. It has failed though to show the meaning of a multiplicity of migration targets and strategies.

Cinel speaks of returnees not as nostalgic or failed but "rather they were individuals actively pursuing goals they had set before departing." Bell speaks of the choices for the individual: stay in the village, move to the nearest city, etc. They were the choices of strategies of survival or calculations of gain. William Douglass' study of Agnone, even though the author is an anthropologist and an outsider, it is remarkable, in the way it succeeds at least in suggesting the multiplicity of targets, the complications of the choice and the presence of echoes at least of the *il dibattimento nazionale*.

There are two ironies or paradoxes I am impelled by here. First, in Italy the public documents which could have been confronted as human sources in order to do what Lawrence Levine describes as our obligation "to make articulate again, people who in their own time were articulate, thinking human beings,"[11] are many and rich. The *Inchieste parlamente sulle condizioni nelle provincie meridionale* are full of direct testimony, starting with Jacini[12] in the 1880s and going to the Comissariat reports of the 1910s – Rossi bumps into Nitti in a Potenza hotel – except for Cavallaro on *Molise Inchieste*,[13] no one has done it.

The second paradox, or perhaps residual racialism came clear to me in Uppsala in 1987, that is that so much has been done on Northwestern Europeans who showed so little variants of targets and patterns of return or multiple migrations as compared to the Italians. With Miller the febrile Irish lose their fever forever, with Gjerde simple images of Scandinavian crofters driven by conditions from one farm in Europe to another in the Midwest vanish before a complex exercise in the new social history, started by Thistlethwaite and Erickson,[14] but I feel an uncomfortable relationship here to the images of the welcome, literate, north European immigration and conversely the lack of such study for the *analfabetismo*, fecklessness, sojourning urban pathology of the new immigration, especially Mediterraneans who had so many more choices to make of target, timing, return rates, and faced partisan politics.

There is a deprivation in Italian or Mediterranean migration studies. Twenty-five years ago in a *festschrift* for Blegen, Ingrid Semmingsen[15] asked rather innocently where are the Italian American letters, today Emilio Franzina "'Merica, 'Merica" (1979) (*lettere venete*) and S. Baily and F. Ramella[16] (Biellese letters) are here with us, there is no more and they are *settentrionali* to South America and confirming of a problem. With Tedebrand, Runeby, Reinert[17], there is a wealth of material on the Scandinavian press image of

America. We have only Filipuzzi's study (1976) of the Venetian press and *la polemica*.[18]

To understand who migrates and why, and where they go and why and when and how do conditions and knowledge affect their decisions, I believe I need to read and hear the discourse in the agro-town or *spazio d'informazione*, to identify (in a Gramscian way) *blocco urbano*, the speakers in the discourse who directly or indirectly produce texts which bring the national debate into the prospective migrant's world. I need to find ways to understand how the *contadini*/artisans *salariati* performs as readers of these and other texts precoding them for themselves into new texts; finally I want to be able to see how this encoding produces the migration tradition and a changing atlas of opportunity.

The space in which discourse takes place – *villagio pettagolo*, Sturino et al on information areas – constant local migration, work, pilgrimages, commercial and government intrusions – two quotes about this space and discourse strike me as so similar: *Voce Cattolica* in Trento (1877), "In the piazza, in the alehouses, and in the fields, they talk of nothing else except of emigration, of Brazil, and of 'Merica." The anthropologist, Clifford Geertz wrote "at base, thinking is a public activity. Its natural habitat is the house yard, the market place and the town square."[19] Discourse in the agro-town is not Banfieldian but it is segmented because of class and gender. One can get a sense of this discourse from Norman Douglas' *Old Calabria* (1928), "Well as a rule I begin by calling for advice at the chemist's shop, where a fixed number of the older and wiser citizens congregate for a little talk. The cafes and barbers and wine-shops are also meeting places of men; but those who gather there are not of the right type – they are the young or empty-headed or merely thirsty."[20] (now party headquarters too) * see Verga *Malavoglia* – the discourse Garibaldi telegraph.[21] When Rosa's husband is recruited in the cafe by labour agents, she doesn't even know he is gone because she is in a different world of discourse/space – in front of churches, in fields. P. Arlacchi differentiates between *sistema del latifondia* and *sistema contadina*[22]... Dillingham consul's report (Vol.4:228) that there was an American in every town. From America over 400 *reintrate per* 1000 third class passengers leaving Italy. "*I ragazzi parlano sempre di andare.*" The centrality of talk and *analfabetismo*. Patricia Spack's *Gossip*[23] – "surmise in the guise of certainty" and Sydel Silverman's *Three Bells of Civilization. The Life of an Italian Hill Town* (1975) *chiacchera* are useful here.[24]... "the best talk requires a minimum of 5 or 6 men, for there must be at least 2 or 3 participants to take turns speaking while the others form an audience" – skills in discourse and argument.

It should be clear then that by a discourse in the town, I mean to create something akin to Raymond Williams' argument in *Marxism and Literature* (London, 1977) for a continuum of texts in relation to one another continually encoded into new texts by those who hear or see them, which I hope will show how the national debate, local situation, individual condition and migrant lore come together as a subaltern discourse. I have arbitrarily divided the continuum into printed texts (including creative texts (?), newspapers, etc. public documents, schoolbooks and what Italians call *literatura commovente* (such as Edmondo De Amicis' *Cuore* [Milan,1886]) written texts (letters), texts in the air (sung) (A.V. Savona and M.L. Straniero. *Canti dell'emigrazione* [Milano, 1976] – direct and indirect texts – Molise "If I could kill the train that took my son to New Jersey" or the songsheet "*I cinque poveri italiani linciati a Tallulah* in America) and warning against German cities, – oral – discuss *analfabetismo* and gossip and recoding of texts, and semiotic "signs taken as wonders[25]" what we used to call mute testimony.

Each of these set of texts according to who reads them has migration information ranging from the fictive to the practical. These texts offer information about how to get a passport, why Eritrea is or isn't better than Buenos Aires. They are encoded again by reading and talking, "talk story" people and gossip into a discourse which gives back wholeness to the migrant's world. Intrusions such as the cash economy, steamships, returnees, urban texts, "the printed word as violence and the threat of apocalypse" – taxes, *leva*, medical regulations, school, wonder stories, alongside lore of targets, projects, durations, chains about work not family, mute testimony, "signs as wonders," agents, commercial messages are made whole and through the simulacrum of the discourse, of gossip, (*chiaccheria*), becomes the town's, are the processual migration tradition.

I then try to reconstruct a sample discourse,.. by describing speakers,... by a series of typical printed texts,... by showing the complicated relationship among texts and readers and trust – an example of this is Douglass' letters in Agnone newspapers[26] – illiteracy, class distrust, and constantly new oral encoding provide "the several intermediate environments between man and opinion and the world" –

- speakers of the *blocco urbano* – the fractured elites and its organic intelligentsia – *signori* (migration as anarchy) communal secretary and *marescialla* (safety valve – newspapers and *Nuova Antologia*), chemist – sovversiva lett., priest-Civ Cattolica-Scalabriani, teacher (*Cuore*),

- lore and distrust – a mayor in Calabria told Rossi (1907,p. 28) of uselessness of new committees of emigration because emigration is an old tradition of twenty or thirty years. There are no families whose head has not already emigrated to America or which doesn't have a friend already there; and finally, *"per i lunghi abusi subiti in passato*, there is a complete distrust for all those that serve the government or local authorities",

- examples, Gjerde quotes a man about Lutheran pastor is a priest as trusted? from the pulpit "trying to cure fever," Cordasco's *Corriere della Canada* in 60 villages, Canadian government with "an immense number of addresses" and "generally pedlars, hawkers, and others who are moving through the country and in that way disseminate quickly but efficiently quantities of literature" – how good were the prospective migrants in encoding such texts wisely" – Cronin, *Sting of Change: Sicily and Australia* (Chicago, 1970) "who can believe what other people say? When my brothers went out and said the same thing, then I believed it." A Polish quote, "Let nobody listen to anybody but only to his relatives whom he has in the golden America." P. Arlacchi notes that a Calabrian migrant can call resources of the *contadini – la famiglia, la parentela, il vicinato, l'amicizia.*[27]

The evidence suggests that the prospective migrants, making rational choices about their targets, projects, and durations understood much about the national debate and the world, i.e. need study of resistance to African and internal colony he schemes – and their resistance to some internal targets – Maiorato today and the hierarchy of choices – Melbourne, Santos, Chicago, Stoccardo – as debate about the continued quality of informing.

An aside – resisting the creative and looking to the oral and semiotic was not just familial or closed peasant mentality, lore tested out as providing more useful and can even say truer texts, for despite Levi the myth lay more with the creative/print texts... Kafka, when he wrote *Amerika*, responded to a friend's question, "I know the autobiography of Ben Franklin and I always admired Woodrow Wilson and I like Americans because they are healthy and optimistic" – Polish noble and Huron princess – Giacosa, Verdi, Puccini, Mussolini, Cuore, L'Emigrant – none of them knew to say Howston rather than Houston St. in New York, or the best bordellos in La Boca or how to get work on the CP. The atlas of changing opportunity and the small universe of credible knowledge came from inside out.

Speak a bit to the idea of signs taken as wonders as a part of the continuum of texts which make up the discourse or cultural medium by which migrants make choices – this mute testimony which becomes text by being the subject of gossip can be anything from a calendar from a Brooklyn ethnic bakery, postcard photographs of well-dressed kin in America, glossies from the commerce of migration, a kangaroo skin, or Empress Taitu's lips on a lithograph or the remittances and big clean houses of ritornati (Calabria now and the Little Canadas) one text of this kind became almost literary convention – the semiotic importance of the successful return migrant – a true sign taken as a wonder – in Panunzio's *Soul of the Immigrant* (New York, 1921) a stickpin, a white colour and a look of the *signore* about a returnee, for Adamic in *Laughing in the Jungle: The Autobiography of an Immigrant in America* (New York, 1932), a man with loud necktie, diamond stickpin (horseshoe) standing drinks and talking of West Virginia, for Rose Pesotta[28] it is Israel Telpner, the storekeeper's son back from New York with gold teeth. "*Gli americani vanno ben vestiti, L'America e grande,*" Rossi was told about the failure of three brothers from Rende, who return from Penna to buy up land – *il grande eccitamente* – Norman Douglas (New York, 1928) pp. 127-128.

The return to the readers of the text, the actors, for I am not suggesting that their objective conditions or perceived situations are irrelevant; they are the prism through which the readers approach the discourse and encode anew. Two examples are useful here: the testimony of Anthony Salerno being deported (1903 – Catanzaro origin) and Rosa's husband, Santino.[29] After a fight with his mother-in-law, Santino picked up by agents from iron mines in Missouri at the cafe went off to America and didn't even come home for clothes. Salerno's testimony in New York is from Catanzaro. Salerno took 7 or 8 months to go to see the agent who had come to town even though there was "quite a little talk about the agent" and "they were saying that many people were sailing to America"... more to this point – traders, targets, choices, age and *leva*, mental states and position in family affect the reader of the discourse.

F.S. Nitti (1910) *Inchieste*, "Contadini don't travel toward the unknown; many have already been in America 3 or 4 times, *si va, si torna, si riparte*".[30] I believe they knew the way because of the discourse and their activities and accounts provided new texts to it constantly.

Maiorato, San Giorgio, Grimaldi today – Bonavita story, *vice sindacto, carabinieri,* school kids, and funeral – migration – not emigration and *rimparti, reintrati,* and even less an idea of immigration and becoming American characterizes the full discourse and atmosphere of those towns today – their atlas of targets is alive in the town... the new movement "imagined community", Marxist anthropologists mondialization and *apaesemento* may not be the truth but a useful corrective to the making of American people or simple vector concepts like emigrant and *ritornati, reintrati, rimparti* and migration again elsewhere – The Mayor of Albano understanding that the local is the only universal... brings us back to my own work on sojourning and responsibilities...

Darwin's last work, "The Formation of Vegetable Mould, Through the Actions of Worms with Observations of their Habits" (1881)[31]... changed the earth's surface by 3 inches of loam every year. They disregarded national boundaries and found their labour market on any piece of ground they could. They deserved to be studied and known as totally as possible in their own terms as do migrants. Darwin saw it as a way of testing all his major hypotheses.

Notes

1. Carlo Levi, *Christ Stopped at Eboli* (New York, 1947),pp. Carlo Levi, *Words are stones. Impressions of Sicily,* (New York, 1958). See the first chapter about the visit of the Italian American mayor, Impellitteri to his family's ancestral *paese*, pp. 29-96. Carlo Levi, "Italy's Myth of America" in *Life* (July 7, 1947) 23:84.

2. Angelo Mosso. *"Gli Emigranti."* In *Nuova Antologia* V.202 (1905), pp. 193-208. "It is clear that all things being equal – more intelligence exists in those creatures who emigrate than in animals that live sedentarily in one place... Malgardo il rischio dei viaggi e l'intemperie del clima, il viaggiare non è danno, anzi un vantaggio, perchè le specie che non emigrano sono general mente meno popolose: onde possiamo conchiundere che negli animali l'irrequietezza del viaggiare colle sue peripezie sono un segno di maggiore vitalita e di maggiore fortuna nella lotta per la vita."

3. Luigi Tarsitano, (Consigliere della Regione Calabria) "Relazione, L'emigrazione calabrese negli anni '80 in una situazione contrassegnata dalla crisi economica dei paesi europei." In *L'Emigrazione Calabrese in Europa Nel Contesto Della Situazione Meridonale*, Laruffa (ed.) 1984. p. 71.

4. Dino Cinel, *From Italy to San Francisco. The Immigrant Experience*. (Stanford, 1982). p. 41.

5. J. Lopreato. *Peasants No More. Social Class and Social Change in an Underdeveloped Society* (San Francisco, 1967). E. Banfield. *The Moral Basis of a Backward Society* (New York, 1958). Sen. F. Nobili-Vitelleschi. "Espansione coloniale de emigrazione" *Nuova Antologia* (May 1902) 183:107. John Baxevanis. "The Decision to Migrate." In *Economy and Population Movement in the Pelopennesos of Greece*. (Athens, 1972). pp. 60-72.

6. Rudolph Bell. *Fate and Honour, Family and Village: Demographic and Cultural Change in Rural Italy since 1880*. (Chicago, 1979).

7. John S. MacDonald. "Italy's Rural Social Structure and Migration." *Occidente* 12, no.5 (September 1956):437-456. MacDonald, Agricultural Organization, Migration, and Labour Militancy in Rural Italy," *Economic History Review*, 2nd Series, 16 (1963), pp. 61-75. Charles Tilly, *An Urban World* (Boston, 1974).

8. Jon Gjerde. *From Peasants to Farmers. The Migration from Balestrand, Norway, to the Upper Middle West* (Cambridge, 1985). Franc Sturino, *Forging the Chain. Italian Migration to North America, 1880-1930* (Toronto, 1990). John Zucchi, *Italians in Toronto. Development of a National Identity 1875-1935*, (Montreal, 1988). Donna Gabaccia, *From Sicily to Elizabeth Street: Housing and Social Change Among Italian Immigrants, 1880-1930* (Albany, 1984).

9. Josef Barton, *Peasants and Strangers. Italians, Rumanians, and Slovaks in an American City*, 1890-1950, (Cambridge, 1975). John W. Briggs, *An Italian Passage. Immigrants to Three American Cities*, 1890-1930, (New Haven, 1978). William Douglass, *Emigration from a South Italian Town. An Anthropological History*, (New Brunswick, 1985).

10. Robert F. Foerster, *The Italian Emigration of Our Times* (Cambridge, 1919).

11. Lawrence Levine, *Black Culture and Black Consciousness. Afro-American Folkthought from Slavery to Freedom*, (New York, 1977), p.ix.

12. S. Jacini. *Atti della Giunta per la inchiesta agraria e sulla condizioni della classe agricola*. 15 volumes between 1881-1886.

13. R. Cavallaro "Inedite dall'Inchiesta parlamentare del 1909: Appunto per una storia sociale molisana." in *Il Comune Molisano Anno* 4, No. 1 (1974).

14. Kerby Miller, *Emigrants and Exiles*, (New York, 1985). Frank Thistlewaite, "Migration form Europe Overseas in the Nineteenth and Twentieth Centuries," in Herbert Miller *Population Movements in Modern European History*, (New York, 1964) pp. 73-92. C. Erickson. *American Industry and the European Immigrant, 1860-1885.* (Cambridge, Harvard, 1957).

15. I. Semmingson, "Emigration and the Image of America in Europe." In H.S. Commager (ed.) *Immigrants and American History. Essays in Honour of T.C. Blegen* (Minnesota, 1961).

16. E. Franzina, *Merica! Merica! Emigrazione e colonizzazione nelle lettere dei contadini veneti in America Latina, 1876-1902* (Milan: Feltrinelli, 1979). S. Baily and F. Ramella (eds.), *One Family, Two Worlds: An Italian Family Correspondence across the Atlantic*, 1901-1911 (New Brunswick, New Jersey, 1988).

17. Lars-Goran Tedebrand, "The Image of America among Swedish Labour Migrants." In C. Harzig and D. Hoerder (eds.) *The Press of Labour Migrants in Europe and North America*, 1880s to 1930s (Bremen, 1985). Nils Runeby, "The New World and the Old." *American Studies in Scandinavia* No.5 (Winter 1970) pp. 5-23. O Reinhart, "The Perplexed Promise. The Image of the U.S. in Two Popular Norwegian Magazines, 1835-1865." In S. Shard (ed.) *Americana Norvegica*. Vol. 2 (Penna, 1968).

18. A. Filipuzzi. *Il Dibattito sull'Emigrazione. Polemiche nationali e stampa Veneta, 1861-1914* (Florence, 1976).

19. Clifford Geertz, *The Interpretation of Cultures* (New York, 1973).

20. Norman Douglas, *Old Calabria* (New York, 1921). p.140.

21. Giovanni Verga's "Liberty" In *Little Novels of Sicily* (New York, 1953).

22. P. Arlacchi. "Perché su emigrava dalla Società contadina e non dal Latifondo." In P. Borzomati (ed.) *L'Emigrazione calabrese dall'Unità ad oggi* (Rome, 1982).

23. Patricia Mayer Spack, *Gossip* (Chicago, 1985).p.8. "Gossip occurs at the ... intersection of the social and the individual [familial]* serving social purpose, defining social opinion, embodying social power (the power of opinion) but issuing from individual mouths and tracing psychic agendas as well."
   * R. F. Harney's word addition.

24. Silverman, (New York, 1975) p. 37, "*Chiacchiera*, gossip or idle talk,... It takes place in the piazzas, the bars, the clubhouses, at the bocce grounds, in the spectator stands at football fields, interspersed with work and business in stores and workshops, and wherever several men may be gathered ([in Canada] the Anglo-Celts marvelling in the 1950s that Italians made animated conversation with one another even after they had been together on a long work day).

25. Franco Moretti, *Signs Taken for Wonders. Essays in the Sociology of Literary Form* (London, 1983).

26. Shalom Aleicham, "Dreyfus in Kasrilevke," in I. Howe and E. Greenberg (eds.) *Tales from the Yiddish* (New York, 1954).

27. P. Arlacchi. "Circuiti economici e rapporto sociale della Calabria tradizionale: la piana di Gioia Tauro," in *Sviluppo* No. 10 (1976).

28. Rose Pesotta, *Bread Upon The Waters* (ed.) John Nicholas Beffel (New York, 1944).

29. M.H. Ets, *Rosa: The Life of an Italian Immigrant* (Minnesota, 1970), p. 157.

30. Nitti. *Inchiesta sulle condizioni dei contadini in Basilicata e Calabria (1910)* Vol. 1, p. 154 (Bari, 1968).

31. C. Darwin, "The Formation of Vegetable Mould, Through the Actions of Worms with Observations of their Habits," (1881). Cited in Stephen Jay Gould *Hen's Teeth and Horse's Toes. Further Reflections in Natural History* (New York, 1984). pp. 120-133.

"From the Shores of Hunger": Italian Immigrants in Canada

Introduction: The Forging of an Italian Canadian Ethnie

1. Caboto and Other Italian Canadian Parentela

2. Italophobia: An English-speaking Malady

3. If One Were to Write a History of Toronto Italia

4. Undoing the Risorgimento: Emigrants from Italy and the Politics of Regionalism

5. Commerce of Migration (additions planned including material from completed article entitled "The Myth of the Americas: Migration and Village Discourse")

6. Men Without Women (additions planned)

7. Italy and the Canadian Prairies (additions planned as well as amalgamations with parts of earlier long article entitled "Italians on other People's frontiers")

8. The Rise of Little Italies

9. Depression, Fascism and World War II

10. "Primitive Rebels" and Petty Capitalists: Italian Labour Migrants in Canada, 1885-1924

11. The New Migration: The Encounter Between "Italo-Canadians" and the Newcomers

12. On Being Italian Canadian: Lore and Culture

13. Statistical Appendix and comment on the census as a poll

14. Bibliography

* (Intended Table of Contents)